# I'M SO GL  D
# ME T

## A Second ~~Compilation Of~~

## Answers

### by
### Robert Cubitt

# Other work by the same author:
# Books by the same author:

Fiction

The Deputy Prime Minister

The Inconvenience Store

The Charity Thieves

**Warriors Series**

The Warriors: The Girl I Left Behind Me

The Warriors: Mirror Man

**The Magi Series**

The Magi

Genghis Kant (The Magi Book 2)

New Earth (The Magi Book 3)

Cloning Around (The Magi Book 4)

Timeslip (The Magi Book 5)

The Return Of Su Mali (The Magi Book 6)

Robinson Kohli (The Magi Book 7)

Parallel Lines (The Magi Book 8)

**Carter's Commandos Series**

Operation Absalom (Carter's Commandos Book 1)

Operation Tightrope (Carter's Commandos Book 2)

Operation Dagger (Carter's Commandos Book 3)

Operation Carthage (Carter's Commandos Book 4)

Operation Leonardo (Carter's Commandos (Book 5)

Operation Terminus (Carter's Commandos Book 6)

Operation Pegasus (Carter's Commandos Book 7)

Operation Banyan (Carter's Commandos Book 8)

To be released in 2023 – Operation Banshee (Carter's Commandos Book 9)

**Non-Fiction**

A Commando's Story
I Want That Job
I'm So Glad You Asked Me That: A Book Of Answers
I'm So Glad You Asked Me That The Third
I'm So Glad You Asked Me That Goes Fourth

# INTRODUCTION TO THE BOOK

This is not a book that is designed to be read like a novel. However, readers may find that it takes about the same amount of time to read an answer as it does to travel between two stops on the London Underground, so it makes an ideal companion for the commuter as it doesn't require the reader to re-familiarise themselves with the plot every time they look up to identify which station or bus stop they have arrived at. It's also quite good for a quick read during a coffee break, while waiting to see the doctor or dentist, while making the kids their tea, while waiting for a bus, well, you get the idea.

Since 1993 the Daily Mail has run a column called Answers to Correspondents' Questions. It wasn't the first time the title had been used, as Alfred and Harold Harmsworth had first used it as a title for a weekly magazine published in the Victorian age. The questions are many and varied in nature, just as they were in the days of the Harmsworth brothers, sometimes stemming from a desire to find out about some aspect of family history, sometimes just a matter of curiosity.

Almost from the beginning, in 1993, I have contributed to the answers to the questions that are published each weekday. Many of my answers have been published, but just as many have not. Sometimes the editor would edit my answers before publication, and sometimes they were used to augment the answers of others in order to make them more complete, while answers from other contributors were edited into mine to supplement them. These were common sense editorial decisions, of course, but it did mean that some of the material I worked so hard to compile wasn't used, wasn't complete or wasn't even recognisable as being mine.

Regular readers of the Daily Mail will probably recognise my name, but as more of my contributions were published the editor took the decision to publish some of my answers under pseudonyms.

So some of my work was printed under the name Dillon (my wife's maiden name) or Sutherland (my mother's maiden name). For a period my wife's first name, Bernadette was used, also with the various last names. However, all the work printed here resulted from my own research.

This may be seen as something of a vanity project and I plead guilty as charged, but I wanted to bring all my contributions together under a single cover. The answering of these questions became something of a hobby, if not an obsession, and I am proud of what I produced. In 2013 I compiled my answers up to that point into a book called "I'm So Glad You Asked Me That". However, the urge to carry on answering the questions was not diminished and since then I have written many, many more. These newer answers are the ones you will find in this edition.

I must offer my thanks to the good people who run Wikipedia and those who contribute to their articles. This website is often maligned but I have found that it is usually my first port of call in answering a question and it is often the most complete source. Its reliability has been proven many times by cross referencing to other sources.

My second thank you goes to all the people who have written in to the Daily Mail with their questions over the last 23 years. Without you there would be nothing for a geek like me to answer. I live in dread of the day when you all buy computers and discover the joys of surfing the internet and are able to research your own answers.

Friends have often asked me what inspired me to answer a particular question. Sometimes it was a half remembered fact from childhood, or something I learnt along the way in later life. I am an avid reader and spent a lot of my life studying for my higher qualifications and when you do that you pick up a lot of extraneous information. Professional training over three different careers has also left its mark on my memory. Certainly there was usually enough to form the basis of my answer, which was then supported and expanded upon by research on the internet. In many cases I was just interested enough in the question to want to find out the answer for myself.

I started my RAF career as an electronics fitter, specialising in communications, so I am naturally attracted to questions relating to that topic and there are several answers on that subject in this volume. I then went on to become an officer in the Supply Branch of the RAF, so Logistics is also an interest. Following a change of career I then went to work for Royal Mail so questions related to postal services are bound to attract my attention.

I am particularly interested in the military and aviation history, as will be seen from the numbers of answers related to these topics, so any questions in those areas were bound to draw me in. This stems from my own 23 years of service with the RAF which followed on from my father's 22 years in the army. My wife's Irish ancestry has inspired me to research answers to questions related to her country of birth, which often get ignored by other regular correspondents. With an insatiable curiosity, a computer, a broadband connection and a little time it's possible to answer most questions.

I am also asked if there are questions that I won't try to answer. The answer to that is yes. I usually stay clear of science and mathematics based questions as there are people far better qualified than I am to answer. The same applies to music (pop or classical) and the arts, though I will sometimes have a bash at them if I have some clue as to the answer. While I love sports I'm not a sports geek, so I will only try and answer a sports question if there is a tie in to another area of interest, such as my fondness for golf and rugby.

I'm not a train spotter and don't possess an anorak so I don't answer questions about trains and I'm not too great on questions about cars either. Other than that I'm happy to fire up the computer, type a few words into the Google search bar (other search engines are available) and see what comes up.

Have I ever been beaten and not found an answer? Yes, several times. Sometimes there just isn't much information available on a particular subject and my own knowledge isn't adequate enough to formulate a meaningful answer. Just like a fisherman, I am often taunted by "the one that got away". I'm happy to say, though, that those occasions are rare.

The dates shown for each answer reproduced in this book was the date on which I wrote the answer, which is not the same date as that on which it was published by the Daily Mail – if it was published at all. Answers are usually published about two weeks after the question is printed.

Keen observers will note that I sometimes answer several questions within a few days of each other, sometimes even two on the same day, while at other times there are lengthy gaps between answers. This is purely arbitrary and is dependent on the questions that are being sent in to the Daily Mail.

When I originally wrote my answers I didn't include any personal opinions with regard to any of the things I discovered. It didn't seem to be appropriate to do so and it may have resulted in my answer not being published if my opinion was contentious. However, in this book I'm not fettered by such considerations. Interspersed with the answers I have added a few opinions, anecdotes, musings and asides to break things up. If any of my opinions don't meet with your approval then I'm unapologetic. I'm as entitled to my opinions as you are to yours. Article 10 of the European Convention on Human Rights applies, so please don't e-mail me to tell me I'm wrong, unless I'm wrong about a point of fact rather than opinion.

Now for a short health warning. Every effort was made to ensure that the answers to the questions were as accurate as possible at the time they were written. However, like all researchers, I'm at the mercy of both time and my sources. Wherever possible material was cross referred to other sources to ensure accuracy, but in some cases I was only able to find one source and so was unable to be as academically rigorous as I might have liked. So, if you intend using the contents of this book to settle pub disputes, to settle bets, or as the basis for school or college assignments then I accept no liability if it later turns out that my answer was either incorrect or is now out of date. There is no substitute for doing one's own research. Where possible I have provided updated information in my "Author's notes" if I am aware of any changes since the original answer was published.

If you wish to submit your own questions as a challenge for me to answer then please e-mail them to this address: robert.cubitt@robertcubitt.com. I can't promise I'll come up with an answer, but will guarantee to reply to you and to do some initial research.

If you are a reader of the Daily Mail I hope you will enjoy future answers to correspondents' questions, because I haven't stopped submitting them yet. Finally I hope that you find this book interesting and/or amusing. If you did then putting a review of it on your favourite review site will help to boost sales, which in turn will benefit Help For Heroes, so please feel free to do so. Negative reviews are not required.

**An earlier answer said Henry Kaiser designed the Liberty ship. Is this True?**

The design of the Liberty ship was based on a British concept, which the Americans took and adapted in order to reduce costs and speed up production.

In 1936 the American Merchant Marine Act was passed to allow the construction of 50 cargo vessels which would be suitable to for use by the U.S. Navy in wartime. The requirement was doubled in 1939 and again in 1940, to give 200 planned vessels.

In 1940 Britain ordered 60 Ocean class freighters to be built in American yards, in order to replace war losses and to boost the merchant fleet. The design had been created by Gibbs & Cox to meet Lloyds standards for construction. The ships were of 6,174 gross tonnage, 476 ft long and 52 ft at their beam and were powered by coal fired steam engines. The U.S contract was let to Todd California Shipbuilding. The original design had been built in Sunderland by J. L. Thompson and Sons.

The design was modified by the United States Maritime Commission to make them quicker and cheaper to build. Amongst the changes was a shift from riveting to welding of the ships' hull plates and the replacement of the coal fired boilers with oil fired. This became the design which met the standard required of the Merchant Marine Act, and by default the design for the Liberty ship.

When the U.S. Government let the contract for the Liberty ships it went to a conglomerate of different shipyards, but the overall project was placed in the charge of Henry J Kaiser (9 May 1882 – 24 Aug 1967), an American industrialist and owner of the Kaiser Shipyard.

Through the efforts of the Kaiser Shipyard the construction time for a cargo ships was reduced to just 45 days. For the Liberty ships this was reduced to just 10 days using the sort of assembly line techniques developed by Henry Ford. A world record was achieved when the 10,500 ton SS Robert E Peary was built in just 71 hours and 40 minutes.

The first Liberty ship to be built, the SS Patrick Henry, was launched in September 1941 and was the first of 2,710 ships in that class. Three have been preserved and one, the SS John W Brown, is still in operation as a travelling museum.

\* \* \*

## 22nd August 2013

**In the BBC dramatization of The Cousins' War (The White Queen), scarcely an episode went by without another call to 'raise an army'. What inducement had the common soldier to march to bloody battle for leaders who often changed loyalties?**

The Normans had a system of feudal service which was still in use at the time of the Wars of the Roses, at least in name. Lords were granted land by the Crown in exchange for which they had to provide soldiers when called upon to do so. As the soldiers were drawn from the serfs, little better than slaves, they had no say in the matter. However, both the Crown and senior aristocrats also maintained armies to ensure security and enforce the law.

The hierarchical nature of the aristocracy made it possible for any tenant to know how many soldiers he had to provide when called upon, by type of soldier: archers, men at arms, horsemen etc as it was written into the deeds of his land. If it was possible to raise an army for the Crown then it was also possible to do the same on one's own account, which is why there were occasional rebellions. The Second Barons' War (1263-64), led by Simon de Montford, is an example.

The Black Death (1348-49) had largely wiped out feudalism as a practice. With a shortage of labour to work the land the idea of keeping serfs tied to a single landlord was untenable, especially if the landlord and his family had died in the outbreak, so workers were able to hire themselves out to the highest bidder. However, old concepts die hard and the requirement for the aristocracy to provide an army at need still existed, at least in theory. The big change, however, was that the soldiers would now be paid to fight rather than compelled. This was actually nothing new, as the records for the Hundred Years War (1337 – 1453) show that the English Kings paid professional armies to go to France. However, it hadn't been so common in domestic warfare.

The richer landowners, Dukes and Earls, paid the less wealthy to raise soldiers for them, and each negotiated their own rates of pay. The Earl of Warwick, Richard Neville, who was a major figure in the Wars of the Roses was the richest nobleman in England and therefore could afford to raise large armies at need. He wasn't "The King Maker" just because he was an astute politician, but also because he had the deepest pockets. In return King Edward IV lavished land, wealth and privilege on him. As was seen in the TV series, and as history tells us, when Warwick changed sides he took his armies with him as the soldiers followed the money as much as they followed Neville.

Family alliances were important. If you married into a family it was assumed that you would side with them in a conflict and bring your own armies, or those of your relatives, to support them if called upon to do so. This was Lord Stanley's dilemma before the Battle of Bosworth (22$^{nd}$ August 1485). He owed his position and loyalty to Richard III, but was married to the mother of Henry Tudor.

On one level the Wars of the Roses were a family argument, albeit one fought on a national scale. For the nobles at least there was the chance of advancement. A grateful victor would grant land and status to his supporters and some of that would be passed down to the common soldiers. High office could be won, with vacancies created by the outcome of the battle itself or by deaths on one's own side. On the other hand the penalties for backing the losing side were severe. There were no trials for those on the wrong side, only execution or exile. There was undoubtedly a degree of risk in choosing to join any army, but the potential reward made it worthwhile.

Other than the promise of payment there was also the attraction of loot. It is no surprise that bodies found after a battle were often naked. A suit of armour, weapons, a horse and whatever valuables the deceased had on his person could set a man up for life. If a town were captured from the enemy it was taken for granted that the possessions of the population would be up for grabs. There were even agreements written into contracts regarding the way loot would be shared out between the lords and the soldiers.

Finally, if a large enough army couldn't be raised from the population, there was also the ability to use mercenaries. With warfare being endemic throughout Europe there were always bands of unemployed soldiers who would be happy to hire themselves out to whoever paid the most. There were even specialist mercenaries. During the Hundred Years War the city of Genoa was well known for hiring out crossbowmen to the French army. Mercenaries would often work for low pay in exchange for the promise of large amounts of loot. Henry Tudor's army at Bosworth had a high percentage of foreign mercenaries in its ranks.

\* \* \*

### 27th August 2013

As a child in the mid-Fifties, while staying in a beach bungalow on Hayling Island (near the old Nab Club) I recall a rotating lighthouse beam visible from our bedroom window. Is this childhood nostalgia or was there a lighthouse out to sea off the coast of Hayling Island.

It is interesting that the beach bungalow was near the Nab Club, because the lighthouse that was visible is the Nab Tower.

The tower wasn't originally built as a lighthouse, but as one of eight fortifications to provide an anti-submarine screen during World War I. The towers were designed by a Mr G Menzies. The towers were to be linked together by steel nets to prevent submarines passing between them and would be armed with 4 inch guns. The net would be strung across the English Channel and would effectively close the Channel to enemy shipping. Up to 80 towers would eventually have been required.

By the end of the war only one tower had been completed at an estimated cost of £1 million; A huge sum in its day. It was built in Shoreham harbour.

In 1920 the tower was towed out to the Nab rock, an obstacle in the Eastern Solent between Hayling Island and the Isle of Wight. The hollow concrete base was filled with water to submerge it and the base settled on the sea bed to form the tower of a new lighthouse. Unfortunately it didn't quite remain vertical and has a visible three degree tilt.

The lighthouse was originally manned, but has been unmanned since 1983. It provides a rotating beam flashing once every 10 seconds and is visible for a range of 10 nautical miles. Its fog horn gives two blasts every 30 seconds.

During World War II the tower also served as an anti-aircraft artillery post responsible for bringing down several German aircraft. In 1999 the tower was struck by a freighter, the Dole-America, and required major repairs which weren't completed until 2001. Since 1995 the light has been operated by solar power.

In 1951 the tower provided the major location for the Hammer film The Dark Light.

Currently the light of the tower is extinguished as the tower goes through a major renovation which will see its height reduced from 89 ft to around 80ft, but the range will increase to 12 nautical miles by the fitting of a more powerful light. Work is expected to be completed by October 2013.

\* \* \*

**Is the Artists Rifles, a volunteer regiment of the Army, comprised of artists?**

Although not specifically comprised of artists now, the regiment was originally made up of volunteers from the arts.

In 1859, during a threat of invasion by the French by Napoleon III, there was a fervour for volunteering and several volunteer regiments were formed. The Artists formed in 1860. It was founded by Lord Peel. The idea was supposed to have been proposed by Edward Sterling, an art student and ward of Thomas Carlyle. The founders of the regiment were drawn from a wide range of the arts, including writing and music as well as the visual and performing arts. The first officers were appointed following an election held between the members. The personnel of the regiment funded their own clothing and accoutrements and paid a membership fee.

The official title awarded to the regiment was the 38th Middlesex (Artists) Rifle Volunteers. This was changed to the 20th in 1881 and in 1908 to the 28th Battalion London Regiment (Artists' Rifles). In 1937 they became the Artists Rifles, the apostrophe being dropped along with the other parts of the title.

The regiment saw service during the Boer War and World War I, where they won 14 battle honours, but during World War II became a training unit for officers. They were effectively disbanded as a regiment during this time, but reformed in 1947 as 21 Regiment Special Air Service (Artists Rifles).

During World War I 15,022 men trained and served with the Artists. 2,003 lost their lives, 3,250 were wounded, 53 posted missing and 286 taken prisoner. The regiment won 8 VCs, 822 Military Crosses with 63 bars and 6 second bars.

Since 1947 the Artists Rifles have specialised as being a volunteer special forces unit. They are unique in that the present 22 Regiment SAS was formed from them, the only time that a regular army unit has been formed from a part-time volunteer unit. Entry is no longer limited to people from the arts, but applicants would have to undergo the physically and mentally challenging special forces selection process. The HQ and A Squadron are based in London, B Squadron split between Basingstoke and Cambridge and C Squadron between Newport and Exeter.

\* \* \*

## 16th September 2013

### Why are the London Docks so empty?

The 1960s and 70s produced what might be called a "perfect storm" of change that led to many ports going into terminal decline. In Britain it included Bristol, Glasgow, Leith and many smaller ports but, most significantly, London. Elsewhere in the world it included the docks of the Lower East Side of Manhattan Island, Hamburg, Antwerp and many others. As cheap international air travel developed, the need for passenger carrying ships disappeared virtually overnight, but it was changes in freight handling methods that were the most significant.

The traditional method of carrying freight was as loose items such as bales, barrels or packing cases stacked up in the holds of ships. This made for very slow handling as a single crane could only handle a small number of items of cargo at a time, even using cargo nets to pick up multiple items. The freight also had to be protected from the weather by storing it in a warehouse until customs formalities were completed and the cargo could be loaded or collected. The whole process was very labour intensive and expensive.

On land, especially in the USA, there was an increasing use of containers to transport freight. They were reusable, weather proof and they could be loaded on the ground and then lifted onto the back of a lorry using a crane or large forklift truck. In terms of handling they required a much lower level of manpower. Importantly, the freight didn't have to be manhandled again before being loaded onto a ship. Shipping companies wanted to make savings in the cost of freight handling and moved towards the use of containers as the primary freight handling system. They introduced new ships, and they also wanted bigger ships that could carry larger loads at a lower cost.

Up river docks like London, especially between St Katherine Dock and the Royal Docks, were at a disadvantage during the transition from loose loading to containerisation. They were geared up to deal with the old type of ships, which were still in use, but weren't able to expand to handle the new type of ship, especially the bigger ones which wouldn't fit through the locks. With housing and industry encroaching right up to the dock walls there was no space to expand to accommodate container handling and the loose handling of freight side by side. This competition for space also prohibited the building of new access roads to take the larger container carrying lorries. The solution was to build new ports.

One of the other disadvantages of the London Docks was that they sat on a river with a very large tidal range. At low tide ships couldn't enter and leave the docks, which were connected to the River Thames by locks. They had to wait for the tide to rise. This led to queues of ships waiting in the Thames estuary for their turn to enter the docks. The river was also very narrow in places, making it difficult for larger ships to manoeuvre. A ship that isn't working is losing money, so ship owners wanted to use ports that didn't suffer from these problems. London became less and less attractive as a port.

Throughout the world new container ports were built to accommodate the new operational model. In Britain, Tilbury was expanded and a brand new container port was built at Felixstowe. Thanks to the decline in passenger traffic Southampton had the space to convert to container handling. Liverpool declined in use for some years, but then recovered. Another new port was built at Avonmouth near Bristol. In Europe there were new ports built at Rotterdam and Bremerhaven in Germany, to take two examples. In the USA container ports were built in New Jersey to replace the old port of New York.

Some shipping still continued to use the London docks, with bulk paper still being handled at Convoy's Wharf in Deptford as late as 2000. The Port of London Authority still controls 70 independently owned terminals and port facilities stretching from the Thames barrier as far as the Isle of Sheppey.

The cost of the closure of London's docks was high. It is estimated that 150,000 jobs were lost in the docks and related industries in the 1960s and 70s, inflicting massive damage on the economy of East and South East London. Today the docks area has been regenerated to provide business premises, housing and an airport, but the docks basins themselves are now used only by leisure sailors.

* * *

### 17th September 2013

**What do the letters and numbers on the side of fishing boats mean, eg YH, LT and CK?**

Under international maritime law all commercial ships must have a port of registration, where its documentation is held. Many small countries, such as Panama, The Bahamas and Cyprus, generate an income by acting as ports of registration for shipping. This is not the same as the vessel's "home port" which is usually the port where the shipping company's offices are, or from which it operates. In order to identify where a ship is registered the name of a country or the name of a city is displayed on the stern of the vessel, usually below the ship's name. It will also be displayed on lifeboats and life preservers. An enduring image in film is a ship's name and port of registration on a floating life preserver, eg "Titanic, Liverpool".

Fishing boats, as commercial vessels, are subject to similar laws. It is their equivalent of a car's registration number. The letters and numbers seen on these vessels are an abbreviation of the vessel's home port and the registration number of the boat. The examples given in the question all fall under the control of the Marine and Fisheries Agency. YH is Great Yarmouth, LT is Lowestoft and CK is Colchester. Scotland has its own registration letters, as does Northern Ireland. Similar systems exist across the EU. Recently, in Dubrovnik, I saw fishing vessels using the letters DK.

Similar registration schemes also exist for yachts and other leisure craft and are operated by an approved agency, such as the Royal Yachting Association. For sailing boats the registration letters and numbers are displayed on the vessel's sails.

* * *

17th September 2013

**In a book about film stars, Trevor Howard claims to 'have been awarded the Military Cross in World War II, almost drowned in the invasion of Sicily and seen action in Norway'. For what did he win the Military Cross?**

Trevor Wallace Howard-Smith was born on 29th September 1913. There is no record of an award of a Military Cross to anyone of that name, or under his acting name of Trevor Howard.

Trevor Howard attended RADA and first appeared on stage in a paid roll in 1934 in "Revolt in a Reformatory". He was originally rejected for service by both the RAF and Army, but a shortage of manpower resulted in him being "called up" to serve in the Royal Corps of Signals in 1940. He was discharged in October 1943 for allegedly having "a psychopathic personality". The invasion of Sicily took place between 9th July and 10th August 1943, so it is feasible that Howard could have taken part. However, some biographies refer to him as having not undertaken any active service and to him being posted around various locations in Britain between enlistment and discharge.

If Howard had enlisted under "hostilities only" terms, which were the norm for both conscripts and volunteers during World War II, he wouldn't have been discharged from the Army until late 1945 at the earliest, except on medical or psychiatric grounds.

A biography published by Terence Pettigrew in 2001 alleged that Howard had "embroidered" his war record, a claim that was initially denied by his widow. However, when confronted by official documents she softened her denial to simply state that he had had an honourable military career.

Stories about Howard having been awarded a Military Cross first began to circulate in 1945, as his film career started to take off. It's alleged that he was visited by police and warned against making such a claim as it was a criminal offence under the Army Act (Daily Telegraph 24th June 2001). An earlier article in the Daily Mail (22nd August 1998) also cast doubts on Howard's war record.

There is something of an irony to this story, as Howard was well known for playing military officers of an heroic type. Trevor

Howard died on 7th January 1988 and his military records won't be de-classified until 50 years after his death.

* * *

## 30th September 2013
**What is the origin of the term "jankers" meaning a spell in military prison?**

The Oxford English dictionary describes the term "jankers" as military slang of unknown origin. From citings in various sources it appears to originate from around the time of the Boer War or slightly later, but was in regular use by the time of the First World War. There are some suggestions that the J in jankers has been substituted for another letter of the alphabet to create a word that rhymes.

Jankers does not refer to military prison or detention. In the Army it is used to denote the official punishment of Confined to Barracks (CB) and in the RAF to Confined to Camp (CC). Today the official term is "Restrictions". This is a punishment meted out at summary level by a junior officer for minor infringements of military discipline such as being late for work, being untidy or for a minor failing in duty, such as forgetting to secure a window at the end of the working day.

The purpose of jankers was to restrict the ability of the individual to enjoy their off duty time by preventing them from leaving camp or enjoying the facilities on camp. As an RAF apprentice in the late 1960s on a spell of jankers I wasn't allowed to use the NAAFI club, even to buy non-alcoholic refreshments, the TV lounge, the camp cinema or any of the hobby or sports clubs. I had to remain in uniform or overalls at all times to mark me out as being on duty.

To ensure that I wasn't able to enjoy any leisure activities I had to parade for inspection at the Guardroom three times a day, at 07.00, 18.00 (6p.m.) and 22.00 (10p.m.). I had to be in my best uniform and spotlessly clean and tidy. Not to be so would result in being put on another charge (or fizzer to use army slang) and earning another spell on jankers. I also had to undertake two hours of "fatigues" or work of a manual nature during the evening such as litter picking, washing dishes in the junior ranks mess, cleaning the barrack block toilets etc.

If the period of jankers ran over a weekend there would be additional parades and periods of fatigues. Typical spells on jankers ran from 3 to 7 days, but a more senior officer could award up to 14 days. My spell on jankers was considered to be "soft" by the older hands and I dare say that older soldiers may remember jankers as being a somewhat more onerous punishment. Married personnel were required to move into barracks for the entire period of their punishment.

Jankers was considered to be part of the normal disciplinary processes of the armed forces rather than an indication of a bad character. Short or infrequent spells on jankers wouldn't prevent someone being promoted, for example. Officers don't do jankers but may expect to undertake extra spells of Orderly Officer for minor infringements of discipline.

**Author's note:** I love these sorts of questions. They bring back memories of my youth.

\* \* \*

## 1ˢᵗ October 2013

**Was the Ukrainian famine of 1932 to 1933 deliberately effected by the Soviet government?**

In November 2003, twenty five member nations of the UN, including Russia, signed a statement that effectively declared that the Ukrainian famine of 1932/33 was an act of genocide and held Joseph Stalin accountable for it. Between 4 and 5 million Ukrainians died as a result of Stalin's policies. In the Ukraine this period is known as Holmodor, which in a literal translation means 'death by hunger'.

This was not the first famine to affect the Ukraine following the Russian revolution. From 1921 to 1923 a similar famine had resulted following the collectivisation of the Russian farming system. The cause was the forced export of grain to the rest of Russia, but later some of the exported grain was also sold to the west. A large part of the exported grain went to the Red Army which was still engaged in a civil war with the White Russians. A fraction of the amount taken would have prevented the famine occurring. The main area affected was the Southern part of the Ukraine. Between 1.5 and 2 million Ukrainians are thought to have died as a direct result of these policies.

The 1932/33 famine had different causes and a far greater impact over a shorter time scale.

Stalin had a distrust of the Ukrainians and considered them the greatest internal threat to the Soviet Union. The traditional belief of the peasant farmers was that what they grew was theirs, and any surpluses provided the opportunity to expand their ownership of the land. This ran contrary to Soviet beliefs and the policy of collectivised farming. Lenin and Stalin both felt that the powerhouse of communism was industry and the only purpose of agriculture was to feed the industrial workers.

In 1927 Stalin blamed food shortages on the peasant farmers, who he believed to be hoarding food. He created the term 'kulak' to describe this type of peasant farmer and ordered their destruction as a class, however it was unclear exactly who he meant. Hundreds of thousands of farmers were killed or deported to gulags (labour camps in Siberia and Russian Asia).

The Ukraine in particular suffered. It was a major producer of grain, along with the Caucasus and upper Volga regions. In 1930 there were several revolts which were ruthlessly crushed by the NKVD (forerunner of the KGB). By 1931 famine was rife in the regions as the lack of farmers, crop failures and crop seizures resulted in more food shortages. As the biggest grower of food the Ukraine had most of its harvest exported to feed more favoured areas, exacerbating the shortages in the Ukraine itself. As well as the 4 to 5 million Ukrainians there were also millions of deaths in Kazakhstan, the North Caucasus and Upper Volga. Up to five million households were also affected by the deportations, imprisonment and executions.

Stalin died unrepentant and was said to have confided to Winston Churchill that it had been a "terrible struggle" but had been "absolutely necessary".

On 27th April 2010 the Parliamentary Assembly of the Council of Europe passed a draft resolution that the famine was caused by the "cruel and deliberate actions and policies of the Soviet regime".

Since 2007 there has been an official remembrance of Holmodor in the Ukraine each year on the fourth Sunday in November. Memorial services have been held elsewhere and there are several monuments in the Ukraine, three in Canada and one in the USA.

\* \* \*

## 11th October 2013
### Is "choate" a real word?

Choate is an American legal term. In literal terms it means complete or perfect. In use it would be used to describe an undefeatable right that is totally valid and can't be lessened or altered by later claims. It may, for example, be used to describe absolute ownership of a piece of land.

The term derives from a much older word, inchoate, which means something incomplete, or imperfectly formed or developed.

The dropping of the "in" part is intended to turn choate into the antonym of inchoate, but this has been argued against in the United States Supreme Court where a lawyer was admonished for its use in that way.

Inchoate derives from the Latin Inchoatus, which is the past participle of inchoare, to begin. It may have been in use as far back as the 16<sup>th</sup> century.

\* \* \*

### 16<sup>th</sup> October 2013

**My father was in the British Expeditionary Force and was at Dunkirk, El Alamein and the D Day Landings. How were he and his comrades fed?**

There were two ways of feeding soldiers in the field. Each battalion had cooks from the Army Catering Corps attached to them and they would establish a field kitchen using petrol fuelled cookers on which they cooked a wide range of meals. Ingredients were mainly provided in the form of large catering size tins of meat and vegetables, but the Battalion Quartermaster had a cash imprest that could be used to buy fresh fruit, vegetables, eggs etc if they were available. The cooks also had the ability to make their own bread. Hot meals could be sent up to the front line in large "dixies" if conditions allowed, or soldiers could be recalled to the rear area to eat in shifts.

If soldiers were in a combat situation they were each issued with a 24 hour ration pack known as the Composite Ration, or compo for short. This contained a range of dried and powdered ingredients such as oatmeal, biscuits, soup, sweets and tea. The tea leaves came pre-mixed with sugar and dried milk. There was also a tin of cooked meat, such as chicken, ham or corned beef. The pack came complete with its own little tin opener and a few sheets of toilet paper. The whole ensemble was packed into a cardboard box about the size of a mess tin (approx. 7 inches by 5). Inside was a sheet giving cooking instructions and menu suggestions.

To heat water the soldier was issued with a "Tommy cooker", a small stove heated by setting fire to a solidified alcohol block, similar to a fire lighter. Water was heated in a mess tin and then dried ingredients were added to make up the meal or beverage. Typically soldiers would eat in pairs, with one cooking the food and making tea while the other stood guard.

The ration pack has its origins in the trenches of World War I when soldiers were issued with tins of food to keep in their packs and eat if they were cut off from their unit. Because the food came in tins they became known as Iron Rations.

To keep the soldiers fed Battalion HQ sent ration packs forward each day along with the ammunition and other battlefield consumables. A major part of battlefield logistics was, and still is, the transportation of rations.

British soldiers envied their American allies who had a more elaborate ration pack known as the C Ration. It was derived from the British compo ration but more thought had gone into it. The C ration contained three tins of meat products and three of basic commodities. The meat products were basically a meal in themselves, such as a stew, while the basic commodities included coffee, cereals, sugar etc. All the food could be eaten cold if it wasn't possible to light a stove.

German soldiers were issued with what was called Halbieserne Portion, literally a half Iron Ration, which was basically made up of a tin of cooked meat and a chunk of bread or hard biscuit. The bread and meat were paired in a paper sack and a soldier was issued with two of these to make up a full day's ration.

The British armed forces still eat compo rations in the field, but modern menus provide a better variety and quality of food.

Nowadays their official title is the Operational Ration Pack, or ORP and it makes up about 5,000 calories (kcal) of nutrition per day. At the MoD's logistics depot near Bicester there are two warehouses full of ORPs at any time. Transporting them to locations such as Afghanistan is a major logistical challenge. Present day ORPs also come in halal and other special dietary variations, which allows them to be used to feed prisoners as well as soldiers.

**Author's note:** It wasn't until after I had submitted this answer that I recalled several anecdotes that could have been included, relating to my own consumption of compo rations whilst serving in the RAF. One of these was the notorious "3 day effect". Essentially compo rations didn't contain a lot of fibre and had the effect of bunging up the digestive system for a couple of days, but when the 3$^{rd}$ day arrived nature was bound to take its course. It was often said that if the Russians could work out when "Day 3" was they could win World War III without firing a shot.

* * *

## 28$^{th}$ October 2013
### What, in relation to the Internet, is Godwin's Law?

Michael Wayne "Mike" Godwin was born on 26$^{th}$ October 1956 and grew up in Houston, Texas. He is trained as a lawyer and also works as an author. Godwin became an early practitioner of internet law, which is where he formulated Godwin's Law or, to give it its correct titles, either Godwin's Law of Nazi Analogies or Godwin's Rule of Nazi Analogies.

Godwin's Law is based on the observation of online discussion groups. He proposed that "As an online discussion grows longer, the probability of a comparison involving Nazis or Hitler approaches."

A corollary to the law is that once this point is reached the discussion may be considered exhausted and whoever first mentioned the Nazis automatically loses the argument. Newspapers and other formal discussion groups often use Godwin's Law as the justification for closing a discussion topic.

Godwin believes that the tendency to introduce Hitler and the Nazis into a discussion trivialises the Holocaust, as many of the comparisons are themselves trivial.

The discussion need not have any obvious political or religious overtones for Godwin's Law to come into effect. Indeed the more arbitrary the mention of the Nazis is, the more hyperbole used, then the more Godwin's Law is seen to apply. It's often called "Playing the Hitler Card". Deliberate use of Godwin's Law to terminate a discussion prematurely is seen as foul play.

Godwin's Law doesn't apply when the inclusion of Hitler or the Nazis is justified and in context, such as discussions about totalitarian regimes, eugenics, racial superiority, the Holocaust etc.

In 2012 Godwin's Law was included in the third edition of the Oxford English Dictionary.

Author's note: Despite numerous internet articles about Godwin's law, the behaviour in internet chatrooms remains pretty much unchanged. There is always someone who is so self-righteous that they can't resist accusing others of behaving like Hitler or condoning Hitler like behaviour, despite the most reasonable arguments having been made. They rarely see the irony of their argument, which is more Hitler like than anything anyone else has said. Technically speaking, this note also falls foul of Godwin's Law.

\* \* \*

1<sup>st</sup> **November 2013**

**The Sten gun was used in World War II by British and Commonwealth forces. Who designed it and why was it popular?**

The name Sten is an acronym of the last initials of its designers, Major Reginald P Shepherd OBE and Harold Turpin, with the EN for Enfield making up the full name. Up until 1940 the British had been purchasing the American Thompson sub machine gun, but with US factories still operating at peacetime levels supply was restricted. Faced with replacing thousands of weapons lost at Dunkirk the British went into the development of a sub machinegun of their own.

Major Shepherd was Inspector of Armaments at the Ministry of Supply's Ordnance Division at the Royal Arsenal, Woolwich and Turner was the chief draftsman at the Design Division of the Royal Small Arms Factory, Enfield, producers of the Lee Enfield rifle, standard weapon of the British Army. Turner had also worked at the Birmingham Small Arms factory and so was very experienced in weapons design.

The principle feature of the Sten was that it was made of stamped metal parts which required the minimum of welding. This made it cheap and quick to produce parts in small workshops, with final assembly being done at the Enfield factory. Some marks had only 47 components and it could be produced for the equivalent of about £2.30. For these reasons it was very popular with the military High Command.

The basic action was to cock the weapon thereby compressing a spring. The bolt was held in the rear position until the trigger was pulled. The bolt flew forward under the pressure of the spring, forcing a round from the magazine into the breach. Inertia then caused the firing pin to strike the rear of the round, firing it. Waste gas and the bullet's own recoil sent the bolt to the rear again, ejecting the spent cartridge case, and the action would continue until the trigger was released or until the magazine was empty. It was similar in operation to the German MP40 (Schmeisser) and Russian PPSH41 designs. The magazine held 32 rounds of 9mm ammunition, though typically only 30 were loaded to prevent jamming. The weapon could fire at a rate of about 500 rounds per minute.

Because the weapon required very little lubrication it was very effective in environments where lubricating oil would attract dust and sand and cause weapons to jam.

Although generally reliable the weapon's magazine design, based on that of the German MP40, did cause malfunctions if it became dirty or if the lips of the magazine became deformed. The MP40 itself suffered from those flaws.

The effective range of the weapon was about 100m. Its light weight, only 7 lbs, and high rate of fire were probably what made it popular for close quarters combat, compared to the much slower firing and clumsy bolt action rifle. Many thousands were air-dropped to resistance fighters in Europe. The weapon wasn't universally popular, however, and attracted the nick names "stench gun" and "plumbers nightmare."

The weapon remained in service until the mid 1950s when it was replaced by the Sterling sub machine gun, which remains in use today. As many as 4 million Stens of various marks were produced, including those produced abroad under licence.

\* \* \*

5th November 2013

**During the Queen's visit to Dublin, in 2011, she laid a wreath at a statue called Children Of Lir. Who were they?**

The Statue of the Children of Lir stands in the Garden of Remembrance in the Rotunda Garden in Parnell Square, Dublin. It commemorates all those who fell in the cause of Irish Freedom, specifically in rebellions and wars between 1798 and 1921. The use of the imagery of the Children of Lir is intended to symbolise the rebirth and resurrection of Ireland.

In Irish mythology the story of the Children of Lir tells of an Irish King, Bodb (pronounced Bove) Derg, who sends one of his daughters, Aoibh (pronounced Eve), to marry his rival Lir as an act of appeasement. Aoibh produces four children: one daughter, twin boys and a third son. Sadly Aoibh dies and is deeply mourned by Lir. To please his rival, Bodb Derg sends his second daughter, Aoife (pronounced Eefa), to marry Lir. She becomes jealous of the love between her step children and their father so Aoife uses magic to turn the children into swans. Lir then casts a spell to turn Aoife into an air demon for all eternity.

As swans the children had to spend 300 years in each of three different parts of Ireland. The legend says that to be freed the children would have to hear the sound of a bell tolling for a new god and would be freed by a holy man. During this 900 year period St Patrick converted pagan Ireland to Christianity and a monk, MacCaomhog (Mochua), cares for the swans in Inis Gluaire (an island off the coast of Co Mayo, Western Ireland). There is a record of a saint by the name of Mochua who lived for a while in Balla, Co Mayo, around 600 AD. At this time the West of Ireland was still largely pagan. The official record of this saint doesn't connect him to the legend, perhaps because of its pagan beliefs in witchcraft.

There are at least three alternate endings to the story, each brought about by different means, but all three involve the tolling of a bell at a monastery or church. The most commonly told ending has the children restored to human form and baptised into the church before dying. Whether the inclusion of Christianity in the legend is part of its original form or a later addition isn't clear.

The story of the Children of Lir is an inspiration for many folk songs and ballads and for a classical piece by Patrick Cassidy, as well as featuring in stories and plays. The site of Lir's castle is commonly believed to be Tullynally Castle, home of the Earl of Longford. Tullynally is an Anglicisation of *Tullach na n-eala* or Hill Of The Swan.

\* \* \*

## 5th November 2013

**Who first "sold the pass"? Did he/she flog off an entrance ticket or betray a route?**

This phrase almost certainly had its origins in sport, but by some coincidence may have been derived from an older retailing term.

To "sell a pass" in football the player uses his eyes and body language to make it appear that he's just about to pass the ball. If the defender "buys it", ie moves to intercept the pass or to tackle the intended recipient, it leaves the attacking player unobstructed and free to continue in possession of the ball. The attacking player has therefore "sold the pass".

In rugby this technique is known as a "dummy pass" and consequently the player who succeeds in playing the trick has "sold the dummy". The dummy may be a reference to the pass or to the player who fell for the trick.

This is where the derivation of the phrase may go back further, to the retail trade. Retailers often displayed perishable goods in their shop windows, such as wedding cakes. In order to reduce wastage the display item would be a replica, or dummy, made from wood and/ or plaster. To "sell the dummy" was to sell the replica item, whether deliberately or accidentally is unclear. Pubs and wine bars still use this technique to display champagne or wine brands, using a plastic replica or an empty but re-corked bottle in place of the real thing.

\* \* \*

## 7th November 2013

**What is the history of the phonetic alphabet, ie A = Alpha, B = Bravo, C = Charlie etc?**

With the introduction of the telephone, and later two-way radio, it became necessary to have a clear way of spelling out words that overcame static and interference. Too many letters sound similar, such as B and V, F and S, and so messages could become quite confusing.

Not surprisingly most countries adopted their own phonetic spelling system that suited their own language best. However, even between English speaking nations there was, at first, no agreed system of letters. Even within nations there were variations. The Royal Navy used Apples, Butter, Charlie etc from 1914 to 1918. From 1924 to 1942 the RAF system was used, starting Ace, Beer, Charlie, but from 1942 to 1956 the United States system of Able, Baker, Charlie was adopted. From 1956 onwards the present day system was adopted by all the armed forces of the North Atlantic Treaty Organisation (NATO).

The first internationally accepted alphabet was adopted by the International Telecommunications Union (ITU) in 1927. Some letters didn't suit variations in pronunciation, such as the Germanic W being pronounced as V, so in 1932 the ITU made some changes based on lessons learnt. This was the general language used right up until World War II, despite the variations described above, and was based on place names. It started *Amsterdam, Baltimore, Casablanca.* Airports and airlines, who use two-way radio for a lot of communications, were early adopters of the new alphabet and it continued in use up until 1965 in some countries.

In 1947 the International Air Travel Authority (IATA) proposed a new phonetic alphabet, similar to the one in use today. It sounded right in English, French and Spanish. After testing in numerous other languages changes were made to the letters C (Coca), M (Metro), N (Nectar), U (Union) and X (Extra) to create the system that we use today (Charlie, Mike, November, Uniform and X-Ray), which was finally implemented in 1956. As well as specifying which word to use for each letter, a standard pronunciation was also described, placing the emphasis on particular syllables. Eg U = *You* nee form, V = *Vic* tah

As well as there being a standard system of pronunciation for letters there is also a standard for numbers, which includes *fower* for four, *fife* for five and *niner* for nine.

The adoption of this system by the military and police forces across the world makes it familiar to all of us through exposure on the television.

Some countries still use their own variations, at least amongst themselves. Denmark is one, which has a number of non standard letters in it, such as æ and ø which change the meanings of words. German is another language that uses special letters, as their language contains a lot of umlauts eg ö, which also change the meaning of words. Some countries also use a shorthand version based on male first names, Alan, Bobby, Charlie etc.

In Indonesia L for Lima is replaced with London, as Lima means 5 in Indonesian, which can confuse messages containing both letters and numbers, and in the USA airports with a large number of flights by Delta Airlines will often replace D for Delta with Dixie, Data or David.

\* \* \*

## 14th November 2013

**What is the story of the Dagenham greyhound track betting coup, which resulted in bookmakers across the country refusing to pay out?**

This betting coup, which might have been perfectly legal if it had been executed differently, worked by using the same odds making systems that the bookmakers themselves use. That is working out which dogs are unlikely to win and which are, then adjusting the odds accordingly to encourage betting on the outsiders and shortening the odds on the more likely winners to discourage betting on them.

John Turner was a junk dealer from Romford, Essex, who got together with some off-track bookmakers to put up the money for the scheme. He persuaded 20 East London betting shops to bank roll him to the tune of about £250. He then employed 125 friends and friends of friends as agents to place bets for him. 80 of the agents would work at the Dagenham track and the remainder at off-track betting shops. The 80 on track agents were required to monopolise the tote betting shop windows, thereby restricting the ability for other punters to place bets which might adversely affect the odds from Turner's point of view.

Turner chose the 4.05 race at Dagenham dog track on 30th June 1964 to put his plan into operation. He identified two dogs that had little chance of winning and got some of his agents to back those. This shortened the odds on those two dogs and lengthened the odds on the remaining four. Turner focused on a particular wager that required a forecast of the correct combination of 1st and 2nd placed dogs. This gave a possible combination of 12 bets to cover the four selected animals.

With the on-track agents monopolising the tote windows Turner used his off track betters to place bets on the 12 combinations when the odds lengthened in their favour.

The resulting win of Buckwheat at 2/1 with Handsome Lass second at 9/2 paid out at enormous odds. A single 2 shilling ticket paid out £987, 11 shillings and 9 pence and Turner's agents had 300 of these tickets paying in excess of £29,000, about £280,000 at today's value. The bookies, however, didn't take this loss lying down. They promptly sued the Stadium operators for failing to operate the tote correctly, thus leaving them liable for the pay-out. They also sued Turner and three colleagues for attempting to fix tote odds by unfair means.

In a court case that ran for two years, Turner argued that his bets were fair, as all of the four dogs that he had backed could have failed to be placed first or second. Therefore, he argued, his claim was legal. The judgement was that while the bet was legal the manipulation of the odds wasn't, as the requirement of the Betting Act was that odds should be derived from the opinions of *all* gamblers present, through their placing of bets, and therefore should not be manipulated by monopolising the tote windows. The judgement was that all stake money should be refunded, but any ex gratia payment of winnings by the bookmakers was their affair. The judge also found that the tote had acted in accordance with its own rules and therefore wasn't at fault. The bookmakers had to pay costs to the stadium owners.

Turner tried to claim his winnings. Most bookmakers paid out reduced amounts of around £50 per winning ticket, but only to people they were sure weren't part of Turner's syndicate. It's likely that Turner would have been unable to claim against most of his bets.

\* \* \*

## 20<sup>th</sup> November 2013

### Why did people in late 17<sup>th</sup> century London get so worked up about Adrian Beverland?

Adrian Beverland was a Dutch philosopher born in Middleburgh, Zealand, around 1653. He attended the University of Leiden and also, in 1672, Oxford University.

Beverland was regarded as something of a genius but made himself unpopular by writing works that undermined accepted church doctrine. His most notable early work was a treatise that implied that original sin was merely a result of man's attraction to woman and vice versa, not the temptation of Adam by Eve at the instigation of Satan. For this Beverland was summoned back to Leiden, struck off the register of its students and imprisoned until he paid a fine.

Beverland moved to Utrecht, but was warned to mend his dissolute ways or be imprisoned again. After writing a satire of the Magistrates of the town called "Vox claaiantis in deserto," he was forced to move to England. Here he worked for Dr Isaac Vossius, himself a Dutch scholar and collector of manuscripts. Despite Beverland's low income he became a collector of artefacts, including rare sea shells, manuscripts and "immoral" prints.

Beverland seems to have repented of his earlier life, and in a prefix to his work "De Fornicatione Cavenda, published in 1698, he publicly acknowledges his earlier sins. He later invites people who purchased his earlier work to return their copies to him so that he might burn them.

However, as a result of the satires he had written about a number of prominent people Beverland fell into poverty after the death of his patron, Vossius. It was these satires that got some people worked up. He wandered the country for a while convinced he was being pursued by assassins and appears to have died around 1712, which is when he was last heard of.

His fame has been immortalised in a number of paintings, including one by Godfrey Kneller which hangs in the Bodleian Library in Oxford.

\* \* \*

21st November 2013

**When the pioneers of electricity named the polarities (+ and -), did they get them the wrong way round?**

The study of electricity predates the study of atoms, probably because electricity was an observable force whereas atoms are invisible to the naked eye. The earliest studies of electricity are reckoned to go back as far as 600BC when effects of static were recorded. In more modern terms early European studies can be traced to around 1600 when the scientist William Gilbert was examining electricity and magnetism, predating Newton's study of another observable force: gravity.

It was from the study of chemistry, rather than physics, that the electric cell emerged through the work of Frenchman Georges Leclanché in 1866. He labelled the terminals of his electrical cell the cathode (+) as the source of electricity and the anode (-) as the recipient of it, though at this time the terms were purely conceptual.

The production of electricity in a cell like Leclanché's was the result of a chemical reaction between two plates of differing metals and a chemical electrolyte which strips electrons from one plate and transfers them to the other, creating a 'store' of energy. At this time Leclanché couldn't have known which plate was which, as he had no device to measure their electrical charges, hence the conceptual nature of the terminology.

However, electrons can't float about willy-nilly and are attracted into the orbit of the atoms that are present. When a wire is attached to the plate which is deficient in electrons it tries to attract electrons from the wire to replace the missing ones. This demand for electrons is fed along the wire. If the wire is then attached to a source of surplus electrons, the positive plate, then a current will flow between the two until a balance of elections is achieved between the two terminals.

What we regard as a battery going 'flat' is in fact it achieving its natural balance of electrons on its component plates. Imagine a full water tank connected by a pipe to an empty tank; the water will flow from the full tank to the empty one until a balance is achieved between the two tanks, at which point the water will stop flowing.

The discovery of the components of an atom, which chemistry uses but didn't fully understand, didn't come about until the late 19$^{th}$ and early 20$^{th}$ centuries, through the work of scientists such as Rutherford. This suggests that it was the physicists, rather than the chemists, who named their charges incorrectly.

The word 'incorrect' is, however, inappropriate in these terms. If one substitutes the word 'more' for positive and 'less' for negative then both disciplines mean the same thing.

In electricity the +, or positive, symbol is used to represent an atom that has a surplus of electrons in its make-up. The -, or negative, symbol is used to indicate a deficit of electrons in the atom. The nucleus, or core, of the atom is deemed irrelevant.

In the study of atoms, however, the symbols are reversed. In nature an atom is neutral, having the same number of protons in its core as it does electrons in orbit around it. An atom with a positive charge is one that has more protons than it does electrons. Negative means the reverse. It's the make-up of the nucleus of the atom that is important and the electrons are irrelevant. So in these terms positive means more and negative means less, just as it does in electricity.

Nowadays the use of the + and – symbol are more for our benefit so that we can insert batteries into equipment the right way round for them to provide power to the device, as some equipment is sensitive to the direction of flow of electrical current. This only applies to direct current. In alternating current circuits the terms used are 'live' and 'neutral'.

\* \* \*

22$^{nd}$ **November 2013**

**Why did the Allies paint white stripes on their aircraft on D Day?**

The use of alternating black and white stripes was an aid to recognition aimed at preventing aircraft from being shot down by their own side. The markings consisted of two black stripes and three white, painted on both wings and around the fuselage. They were painted on all Allied aircraft except for the heavy bombers of the 8th Air Force and RAF Bomber Command. It was considered that these aircraft were distinctive enough as the Germans had no equivalents.

With so many nationalities involved in the invasion, operating so many different aircraft types, the D Day planners realised that aircraft recognition might be something of a problem. Not just for anti-aircraft gunners on the ground or at sea, but also for fighter pilots. The combination of smoke, cloud, camouflage and fear made it easy for mistakes to be made and it wouldn't have been the first time that an over enthusiastic AA gunner or fighter pilot had made such a mistake.

All allied aircraft wore camouflage. On the upper surfaces they were dark coloured to make them harder to spot from above and the under surfaces were light coloured (usually shades of blue/grey) to make them harder to see from below. If the camouflage was working properly then it might conceal the shape of the aircraft, making it more difficult to identify aircraft types in the heat of battle.

As a consequence of Allied bombing and fighter operations it was known that the Allies would enjoy air superiority over the battlefield. This made concealment less of a necessity than it might otherwise have been. The planners therefore decided to mark all aircraft to identify them as being friendly.

The idea had been tried during previous air operations, the first of which was Operation Starkey in 1943, a fake air/sea invasion carried out to confuse the enemy. Other pioneers of the system had been the Hawker Typhoon and Hawker Tempest aircraft, both of which had a similar profile to the Focke-Wulf 190 which the Luftwaffe were operating in Northern France.

The stripes were reintroduced in the 1950s for both the Korean War and the Suez crisis when the RAF and Fleet Air Arm used them.

* * *

26<sup>th</sup> November 2013

**Which was the bloodiest engagement of the Napoleonic War?**

Fought between 1792 and 1815 the Napoleonic Wars accounted for the death or wounding of some 6¼ million French and their allies, including deaths in French territories overseas and in naval engagements. The majority of these weren't military casualties; they were the result of starvation or disease. On the side of the allies there were approximately 2 million killed, of which the largest populations were from Spain (585,000) and Austria (376,000). Britain is estimated to have lost 311,000 dead or missing. The total military casualties amongst all the warring nations is estimated at 2½ million.

The largest single loss wasn't as a result of a single battle, but on the French retreat from Moscow. Napoleon began his invasion of Russia on 24<sup>th</sup> June 1812. He took an army of about half a million and a sizeable contingent of civilians, including suppliers to the army and camp followers. At first things went well, with Napoleon winning a number of small victories and the Russians falling back in front of him. However, the Russian forces were operating a 'scorched earth' policy, removing all food from the path of the invaders and destroying what couldn't be taken.

Seventy miles West of Moscow, at the small town of Borodino, the French finally faced the Russians in a major battle on 17<sup>th</sup> September 1812. It was fought between 130,000 French troops and 120,000 Russians. Although fairly evenly matched the battle hardened French overcame the Russians, which allowed them to enter Moscow unopposed a week later. In that battle the French suffered around 30,000 killed and missing and the Russians about 45,000, the second highest battle casualty rate of the wars.

Napoleon's victory was a hollow one. The Russians had evacuated Moscow taking all the food with them. Instead of the expected capitulation, the Russians fought on. Napoleon tried again to defeat the Russians in the field but failed to bring about a decisive victory. Faced with the onset of the severe Russian Winter, Napoleon was forced to retreat in order to shorten the supply lines to his bases at Smolensk and Vilnius.

The Russians harried the French all the way back. The army suffered disease and malnutrition. The horses died from lack of fodder or were killed for food meaning that cannon had to be abandoned, the cavalry walked instead of riding and re-supply became impossible. The pursuing Russian armies inflicted severe casualties on the French in a number of engagements. There were reports of cannibalism, especially amongst the civilians. Napoleon abandoned his army in order to hurry back to Paris to counter an attempted coup by General Claude de Malet, though some say he ran for his life. The French suffered losses of about 210,000 of the military force with uncounted numbers of civilian deaths, though some accounts give a higher number of military casualties with as few as 22,000 soldiers making it back to Vilnius.

The biggest single casualty toll for a single battle was at the Battle of Leipzig fought from 16th to 19th of October 1813.

In 1813 Napoleon mounted a fresh invasion of the German states, however he failed to capture Berlin. He was forced to retreat to the west bank of the Elbe river and based his army of about 185,000 around Leipzig. On 16th October he repelled two attacks from Allied forces numbering 78,000 and 54,000. The allies were made up from the Austrian, Prussian, Russian and Swedish armies.

On 17th October the allies attacked with 300,000 men towards the perimeter of Leipzig and eventually forced the French to retreat into the suburbs. At 2 a.m. on 19th October Napoleon began to withdraw his army over a single bridge across the Elster River. At about 1 p.m. a frightened Corporal in charge of the demolition of the bridge exploded the charges prematurely, trapping the 30,000 rear-guard inside the city along with the French wounded and stragglers, all of whom were captured the next day. The French lost 38,000 killed or wounded during the fighting before the bridge was blown. The allies lost a total of 55,000 men killed or wounded.

**Author's note:** For anyone who likes history and adventure, try Bernard Cornwall's "Sharpe" books, if you haven't already read them.

\* \* \*

26th **November 2013**
**In one of Walter Scott's letters, he mentions the mysterious 'Dwarfie Stone'. What was this?**

The Dwarfie Stane (or stone) is a 5,000 year old monument lying in a valley between Quoys and Rackwick on the Island of Hoy in the Orkneys'.

The Stone is a huge block of sandstone about 8.5m long, varying in width from 3.5 to 4.5 m and in height from 1 to 2m. It is hollowed out to form what is thought to be a tomb, though archaeologists are not in total agreement with regard to the purpose of the stone. It is thought to have been carved somewhere between the Neolithic and Early Bronze Age, about 3,000 BC, making it about the same age as Stonehenge. At some point an attempt was made to enter the stone by cutting a hole in the roof, though it isn't clear why or when this was done. It was first noted, however, in the 16th century. The hole has now been filled with concrete.

It has been suggested that the stone fell, or was cut, from the steep cliffs above where it sits, known as the Dwarfie Hammers. However, this is also disputed as it is considered that the fall would have smashed the rock into pieces. There is a similar stone about 200 yds further along the valley, known as the Patrick Stane, which suggests that both stones may have been deposited by retreating glaciers at the end of the Ice Age.

An opening about 3ft square is cut into the west face of the stone and leads to an inner chamber. Outside this entrance is the original blocking stone. Two surfaces resembling bed spaces are contained within, giving rise to the theory about the stone having been a tomb. However, the spaces are too short for anyone of normal stature (even for the Neolithic period) giving rise to the legend that the occupants may have been dwarves and giving the stone its name.

Visitors to the stone are known to have been in the habit of leaving offerings, which suggests that at some time the stone may also have been the home of monks or hermits.

The existence of the stone was well known, having been visited by several archaeologists and antiquarians. Scott himself may have visited the site before writing his book The Pirate, published in 1822, in which the stone is mentioned. He certainly visited the Shetland Islands in 1814. Scott credits the stone as the residence of Trollid the dwarf, famous in Norse sagas. There is graffiti inscribed on the stone, some in Persian left by Major William Mounsey, but this all dates from the 18th and 19th centuries.

* * *

## 27th November 2013

**Why does my Father refer to a sandwich as a Dagwood?**

The American comic strip Blondie, originally drawn by Chic Young, has run in American newspapers since 8th September 1930.

It follows the adventures of the somewhat scatter brained eponymous character. In the strip Blondie met Dagwood Bumstead and married him on 17th February 1933. The British equivalent of Blondie and Dagwood would be the Gambols, though there are distinct differences between the two strips in terms of style and content.

One of Dagwood's favourite foods is the multi-layer sandwich. The ingredients can vary but typically the sandwich contains a variety of meats, cheeses and condiments. No reference is ever made to salad or vegetables. There is a considerable amount of peril involved in eating a "Dagwood" as its width to height ratio makes it extremely unstable. Food can also be expected to be ejected laterally from between the two slices of bread. According to Chic Young's son, Dean, the sandwich made its first appearance in 1936.

There have been a number of Dagwood themed restaurants specialising in the sandwich and Dagwood has also had his own range of sandwich meats and cheeses sold in supermarkets and grocery stores. In my youth I certainly heard of multi-layer sandwiches being referred to as Dagwoods. The comic strip probably first came to the notice of the British public through contact with American servicemen during World War II. The American forces had their own newspaper, the Stars and Stripes, in which the comic strip was syndicated.

From 1938 until 1950 Columbia Pictures made 28 Blondie films and there was a radio series that ran from 1939 to 1950, switching between the NBC, CBS and ABC networks. There was a TV series on NBC in 1957 and another on CBS in 1968/69. Animated 'specials' were produced in 1987 and 1989 and are available on DVD.

Despite the death of Chic Young in 1973 the Blondie comic strips are still produced and the statistics are impressive. Blondie appears in 2,300 newspapers worldwide and is translated into 35 languages in 55 countries. The current creators of the strip are Dean Young assisted by John Marshall and Frank Cummings. Two other artists, Jim Raymond and Stan Drake, worked with both Chic and Dean until their deaths in 1989 and 1997 respectively. Despite the longevity of the comic strip Blondie and Dagwood are forever in their early thirties.

\* \* \*

## 2nd December 2013

**Some authors have claimed that a number of 'witnesses' to the Kennedy assassination died in 'mysterious circumstances. Is there any truth in this?**

Along with a number of other historical events the assassination of John F Kennedy has spawned a number of conspiracy theories regarding both the perpetrators of the event and its method. The 'shooter on the grassy knoll' is one of these theories as is the suggestion that the act was commissioned by the CIA or the Mafia. Believers cite a range of 'evidence' to support these conspiracy theories, amongst which is the idea that a number of witnesses died in mysterious circumstances, presumably to silence them forever.

This idea emanates mainly from a book entitled Crossfire, written by Jim Marrs and published in 1989. In the book he lists the names of 103 'witnesses' who died between 1963 and 1976. A Sunday Times reporter stated that the statistical likelihood of a number of deaths occurring by 1967 as one hundred thousand trillion to one. However, when questioned about that claim by the House Committee on Assassinations the reporter admitted that it had been a 'careless journalistic mistake'.

The majority of the people named by Marrs died of natural causes. However, a sizeable minority did die in suspicious circumstances, but in general they were not considered to have any significant connection to Kennedy's death. Some deaths of CIA agents were linked to covert operations authorised by Kennedy and were therefore rolled into the conspiracy theory.

Amongst those named, three names stand out. The first is Karyn Kupcinet who supposedly tried to make a telephone call warning that the President was about to be assassinated. She was most likely killed by her boyfriend on or around $30^{th}$ November 1963. Grant Stockdale, a close friend of the President, died when he fell from the Du Pont building in Miami on $2^{nd}$ December 1963. He was known to be suffering from depression and the death of his friend may have triggered his suicide, or he may have been pushed.

Gary Underhill was a voluble proponent of the idea that the CIA had assassinated Kennedy and was found dead of a gunshot wound on $8^{th}$ May 1964. However, it was the author of the book Destiny Betrayed, James deEugenio, who suggested Underhill had been murdered. The official verdict was suicide.

There were several other deaths in suspicious circumstances, including that of two journalists and an attorney who had visited Jack Ruby in his cell. Bill Hunter was the victim of an accidental shooting by a police officer in April 1964. Having decided to write a book on the assassination Jim Koethe was killed in his apartment by an intruder in September 1964. The attorney Jack Howard died of a heart attack in March 1965 but this was conflated with the deaths of the two journalists.

The list of suspicious deaths and murders goes on, however there is no conclusive evidence to link any of those to the Kennedy assassination, or to attribute the deaths to anything other than being in the wrong place at the wrong time. Several murderers of these 'witnesses' were apprehended and convicted, which would suggest that any conspiracy was poorly organised or very clumsy. The suspicions, however, started to escalate when several CIA agents, due to give evidence to the House Select Committee on Assassinations, died in 1975 and 1976. However at least two of those deaths were from natural causes and a third was recorded as suicide.

It can't be conclusively ruled out that any of the suspicious deaths and murders weren't the result of a conspiracy. However, any 'proof' that is cited is purely circumstantial.

In 1978 The House Committee on Assassinations overturned the Warren Commission investigation into the assassination of Kennedy by concluding that there was a 'high probability' of a conspiracy between two gunmen involved in the killing, one of whom was Lee Harvey Oswald. The other has never been identified. No organisation was named as being behind the killing. In terms of suspects there is a long list that includes the CIA, the Mafia, Lyndon B Johnson, Fidel Castro, J Edgar Hoover and the loosely defined 'military industrial complex'.

**Author's note:** Why Kennedy's assassination should still be attracting so much attention astonishes me. I'm sure Lee Harvey Oswald didn't come up with the plan all by himself – he could hardly read and write let alone plan something like that, but whoever was behind him is almost certainly dead by now and therefore beyond the reach of the law.

\* \* \*

## 28<sup>th</sup> December 2013

**My Late father was in the RAF during World War II, when an ordinary airman was referred to as an 'ERK'. What was the origin of this expression, and is it still in use in today's RAF?**

The origins of the term "erk" are unknown, but may be a corruption of the abbreviation AC, meaning Aircraftsman. It was originally applied only to Aircraftsman, the lowest rank of airman, but could mean any airman below non-commissioned rank, of which there were another three grades: Leading Aircraftsman (LAC), Senior Aircraftsman (SAC) and Junior Technician (JT). The term was specifically used with regard to male personnel, not females.

The term first appeared in the 1920's, which would be expected if it was a purely RAF in origin as the RAF didn't come into being until 1$^{st}$ April 1918. Prior to this, Army ranks were used by the Royal Flying Corps and Navy ranks by the Royal Naval Air Service. There is a suggestion that the term originated in the Royal Navy, but this is unconfirmed and isn't supported by any etymology.

While the expression was in use throughout the Second World War it started to die out after that, possibly with the ending of National Service when it became unusual to see airmen of the most junior rank outside of training units. Before that Aircraftsmen were often employed on 'general duties', referring to any unskilled work such as guarding.

With the ending of National Service the employment of unskilled airmen became uneconomical. After that the rank of AC was held only by recruits undergoing training, following which they would be promoted to LAC to indicate they held a defined level of knowledge or skill, but not experience. When I joined the RAF in 1968 the term was heard only rarely, and by the time I retired in 1991 I don't recall it being in use at all.

**Author's note:** The rank of Junior Technician no longer exists. It has been replaced by Senior Aircraftsman (Technician) or SAC(T).

\* \* \*

## 10$^{th}$ January 2014

**Was there an 18$^{th}$ Century politician who suggested that the Irish could solve their famine by eating their children?**

Jonathon Swift, author of Gulliver's Travels and many other works, wrote a satirical essay entitled A Modest Proposal for Preventing the Children of Poor People From Being a Burthen to Their Parents or Country, and for Making Them Beneficial to the Publick, more usually abbreviated to A Modest Proposal. One of the 'suggestions' was that the poor sell their children to the rich as a source of food. The pamphlet was published in 1729 and was aimed at mocking attitudes towards Ireland's poor and government policy towards Ireland in general.

Jonathon Swift was born on 30th November 1667 in Dublin. He was ordained as a protestant minister and friends secured him the post of Dean of St Patrick's Cathedral, Dublin after his writing caused a rift with Queen Anne and he was effectively barred from any sort of church appointment in England. As well as being the author of Gulliver's Travels, itself seen as satire of the politics of the day, Swift was well known for writing essays and pamphlets on a wide range of topics, often causing offence to great figures and especially politicians, as he made them the butt of his satires.

In A Modest Proposal Swift parodied the social engineering styles of people such as William Petty and followers of Frances Bacon. He even goes into methods for the preparation of children for cooking. Swift was particularly harsh on people who regarded the poor as a commodity that could be dealt with through overly simplistic, one-size-fits-all solutions. He illustrates his work with the sort of statistical nonsense that was widely used by public figures of the day to support their arguments before statistics became a more rigorous and reliable discipline. As a work it is widely regarded as the greatest example of the use of sustained irony in the written word.

In modern culture A Modest Proposal has been cited in a number of books, plays and song lyrics including the 1991 Kurt Cobain line "sell the kids for food" in the song In Bloom.

Jonathon Swift died on 19<sup>th</sup> October 1745 after suffering several years of mental illness. His legacy of £12,000 was used to found a hospital for the mentally ill in Dublin, which still exists as a psychiatric hospital.

It is something of an irony in itself that during the Irish Potato Famine of 1845 to 1852 it is thought that cannibalism did occur among the poor as they fought to avoid a death by starvation. The death toll may have been over 775,000, and the combined effects of death and emigration was to reduce the Irish population by 1.5 million. There had been a famine in Ireland of similar magnitude in 1740-41 while Swift was still alive, though that was caused by extreme cold weather and affected a significant amount of Europe.

\* \* \*

**10<sup>th</sup> January 2014**

**In the Forties, the US Navy experimented with electromagnets attached to warships to avoid radar detection. One ship, the USS Eldridge, is claimed to have disappeared and reappeared hundreds of miles away. What are the facts surrounding this?**

The USS Eldridge was a Cannon Class destroyer escort vessel of the United States Navy, launched in July 1943. Between January 1944 and May 1945 the ship escorted convoys on nine return crossings of the Atlantic, delivering men and materials to Casablanca, Bizerte and Oran. Following victory in Europe the ship was transferred to the Pacific theatre, arriving in Okinawa a week before VJ Day. She was transferred to the reserve on 17<sup>th</sup> June 1946 before being sold to the Greek Navy in 1951.

The incident referred to was supposed to have taken place on 28<sup>th</sup> October 1943. It was alleged to have been called the Philadelphia Experiment and the ship was supposed to be fitted with a 'cloaking device' which would render it invisible to the naked eye. The United States Navy denies that such an experiment ever took place and no records have ever been published. The operation has also been referred to as Project Rainbow. The story is regarded as a hoax.

The Philadelphia Experiment itself was supposed to have been an exploration of the unified field theory expressed by Albert Einstein. Using this theory it was hypothesised that it was possible to bend light around an object, preventing either reflection or refraction and thus rendering the object invisible to the naked eye. The same hypothesis would apply to other electromagnetic waves such radar signals.

Witness reports relating to the experiment, including reports of severe effects on crew members, have never been substantiated and no witnesses or documents have ever been produced that suggest the experiment ever took place. The story also stated that the ship was teleported (my choice of word) from Philadelphia to Norfolk, Virginia, a distance of about 250 miles, and back again and was seen at Norfolk by members of the crew of the USS Andrew Fureseth. In 1943 Norfolk Naval Yard would have been packed with warships so witnesses from other ships might have been expected but have never been mentioned.

A Youtube film clip supposedly showing the Eldridge disappearing from view is an obvious fake as the location is neither the Philadelphia nor the Norfolk naval yards and the ship isn't a Cannon Class destroyer. Finally the maker of the film interpreted invisibility as the ability to see *through* an object, which is not what the hypothesis of the supposed experiment would predict. It would be more likely to result in the observer seeing a ship shaped 'hole' in their field of vision and the sea behind the ship would still not be visible.

The source of the story appears to be an amateur scientist and automobile parts salesman by the name of Morris K Jessup. Jessup was researching into theoretical ways that alien spacecraft might be propelled. In 1955 he published a book on the theme of UFOs and he published other books later. In 1955 Jessup was in correspondence with a man who first called himself Carlos Allende and then Carl M Allen. Allende/Allen claimed to be an eye witness aboard the Andrew Fureseth and also to be able to provide the names of other crewmen witnesses aboard his own ship and the Eldridge, but when asked to provide more information Allende/Allen was unable to do so. All he ever provided were two very poorly sourced local newspaper articles.

An anonymous person sent a copy of Jessup's book, *The Case For The UFO,* to the Office of Naval Research (ONR) in the Spring of 1957, with annotations in the margins relating to the Philadelphia Experiment and the USS Eldridge. The ONR invited Jessup to comment on the annotations and he identified the handwriting as belonging to Allende/Allen, but made no further claims with regard to the notes. A research company called the Varo Corporation printed about 100 copies of the annotated version of Jessup's book for dissemination within the Navy as a topic for discussion, which may have been the source of the Philadelphia Experiment hoax.

The factual origins of the stories may result from misunderstandings about experiments in degaussing carried out at the Philadelphia Naval Yard which were aimed at making ships 'invisible' to magnetic mines. Degaussing is the process of removing residual magnetic fields from large metal objects, such as ships, and was first developed by the Royal Navy during World War II as part of their mine counter measures.

Today the story of the Eldridge lives on as a conspiracy theory alongside the Roswell Incident and stories of the Bermuda Triangle.

\* \* \*

13<sup>th</sup> January 2014

**Who was the 'floosy in the Jacuzzi'?**

The Floosy in the Jacuzzi is the nickname given by Dubliners to the statue correctly called Anna Livia. It was created by sculptor Éamonn O'Doherty as part of the celebrations of Dublin's millennium in 1988. It's said to be a personification of the River Liffey, which flows through Dublin. Anna Livia Plurabelle is the name of a character in James Joyce's Finnegans Wake, whose name is generally interpreted as *the river woman*. The statue originally depicted a woman reclining in a cascade of water.

The statue was first positioned in O'Connell Street near to the General Post Office, site of the declaration of the Easter Rising of 1916 and formerly the site of Nelson's Pillar. However, it was decided that Anna Livia should be moved to make way for a new monument so in 2006 she was installed in the Croppies' Memorial Park just over a mile from the City Centre. The park is close to Heuston Station and directly in front of the Ashling Hotel. However, it's easy to miss as the park is quite small and seemingly insignificant. In her new position Anna Livia reclines in the centre of an ornamental pond.

My husband and I stayed in the Ashling Hotel in May 2013 and were frustrated at not being able to find the statue, as the Dubliners we asked about her didn't seem to know where she had gone after she was removed from O'Connell Street. We were therefore surprised to find she had been under our noses all the time.

The Croppy Boys, for whom the park is named, were members of the Society of United Irishmen who adopted a cropped hairstyle, copied from the French revolutionaries, and who mounted a short lived rebellion in 1798. Their cropped hairstyles made the rebels very easy to identify. The remains of those who died in the rebellion are interred in a field known as Croppies' Acre which stands in front of

Collins Barracks, now a museum, a few minutes' walk along the river bank from the park.

In O'Connell Street (formerly Sackville Street) in place of Anna Livia there now stands The Spire of Dublin, a 397 ft tall tubular metal spike. It isn't universally loved but it is impressive. It cost 4 million Euros to build and was officially dedicated in 2011. Nelson's Pillar was installed in 1809 and was blown up by the IRA in March 1966 without causing any injuries. The pillar in Dublin pre-dated the more famous column in London by 34 years. Following its demise the remains of the pillar were known as 'the stump' until they were removed to make way for Anna Livia.

Dubliners are well known for giving their statuary irreverent nicknames, which are often in the form of a rhyme. On a bench near the Ha'penny Bridge sit two women out shopping, now nicknamed 'the hags with the bags', while the image of Molly Malone, at the East end of Grafton Street, is known as 'the tart with the cart', 'the trollop with the scallop', the 'flirt in a skirt' or 'the dolly with the trolley'.

In the run up to the global millennium celebrations a digital clock was placed in the River Liffey to provide a countdown to midnight on 31$^{st}$ December 1999. This became known as 'the time in the slime'. Neither of the nicknames for the Spire of are suitable for a family newspaper and the same applies to the statues of both James Joyce and Oscar Wilde. On a corner of St Stephen's Green stands a statue which shows Theodore Wolfe Tone, a 19$^{th}$ century Irish politician, backed by a semi-circle of concrete pillars, so it isn't surprising that the installation has become known as Tone Henge. Finally a modern representation of Thin Lizzey guitarist Phil Lynott is more affectionately known as 'the Ace with the Base'.

So what nicknames might we give to some of our own statues?

**Author's note:** As this book is not a family newspaper I can now reveal the nicknames omitted above. The Spire is known as either "The Stiffy at the Liffey" or "The Erection at the Intersection".

James Joyce's statue us nicknamed "The prick with the stick" while Oscar Wild is "The queer with the leer". As can be seen from the use of the term "my husband and I", this was one of the letters submitted under my wife's name. At the time I was working for the Ministry of Defence in their logistics depot at Bicester, Oxfordshire. Unauthorised correspondence with the media is frowned upon by the MoD, so I took to the simple expedient of having my wife "write" the letters.

\* \* \*

## 15th January 2014

**Three British Generals who played significant roles in the D Day landings were Crocker (Gold Beach), Bucknall (Sword Beach) and Graham (Juno Beach). What happened to them?**

On D Day the overall command of the British, Canadian and Free French forces was assigned to General Bernard Law Montgomery who had previously commanded the 8th Army in Africa and Italy. He was designated Commander in Chief 21st Army Group. The Group was made up of the First Canadian Army and the British 2nd Army. Combat divisions of these two armies made up the units which would assault Sword, Juno and Gold Beaches, along with the Commando Special Service Brigades and two Royal Marine Commandoes.

In command of both Juno and Sword beaches was Lieutenant General John Treddinick Crocker, commander of I Corps. The assault on Juno was carried out by the 3rd Canadian Infantry Division under the command of Major General R F L Keller, while Sword beach was assaulted by the British 3rd Infantry Division under the command of Major General Tom Rennie.

General Crocker was born on 2rd January 1896 to Mary Treddinick and Isaac Crocker, he was educated at home because of ill health. He enlisted as a Private in the Artist Rifles at the outbreak of World War I and trained as an officer before being posted to France where he won the DSO and MC. Between the wars he trained as a solicitor before returning to soldiering with the Middlesex Regiment and later the Royal Tank Corps. By the start of World War II he was a Brigadier and continued to advance through the ranks while serving in France with the BEF and later in Tunisia. In 1943 he was appointed to command I Corps in preparation for D Day.

Following D Day, and the failure to capture Caen on the first day as planned, Crocker's I Corps was placed under the command of General Crerar of the First Canadian Army and conducted the unglamorous but essential work of mopping up enemy units along the French and Belgian coasts. By the end of the war in Europe I Corps hadn't even entered Germany. General Crocker continued his military career until he retired in 1953. He died on 9th March 1963.

Gold Beach was commanded by Major General D A H Graham of the 50th Infantry Division, which was one element of XXX Corps, commanded by Lieutenant General Bucknall. General Graham was born on 16th March 1893. He was already in the Army at the outbreak of World War I, serving with the Cameronian Rifles. His career, and life, might have ended in 1914 when he was wounded and had to be rescued under fire by Pvt Henry May, an action that won May the VC. Graham continued to serve in the army between the wars rising to the rank of Lieutenant Colonel. He served in Africa and Italy before progressing to Major General and taking command of 50th (Northumberland) Division in January 1944. Following D Day he was involved, as part of XXX Corps, in Operation Market-Garden, the failed assault on the Arnhem Bridge, before he went to Norway to assist in its liberation.

General Graham retired from the army in February 1947. He became Colonel of the Regiment of Cameronians (Scottish Rifles) and Lord Lieutenant of the County of Ross and Cromarty from 1956 until 1960. He died on 28<sup>th</sup> September 1971.

The rest of XXX Corps didn't take part in the assault itself, going ashore after the beach was secure, so its commander Lieutenant General Gerard Corfield Bucknall didn't command the troops who landed first that day. However, he was Graham's commanding officer and assumed command of the beach once the rest of the corps had landed. Born in 1894 he was educated at West Downs School. He was commissioned into the Middlesex Regiment in 1914 and served with some distinction throughout World War I. Between the wars he served with the Egyptian Army, which wasn't officially part of the British Army, before attending Staff College. During the Second World War Bucknall rose steadily through the ranks until Montgomery appointed him to command XXX Corps in January 1944. It wasn't a popular appointment amongst the General Staff, who didn't feel he was up to the task. They were right and he was replaced in August 1944 by Lieutenant General Horrocks. Bucknall was posted to take command of the Northern Ireland District where he remained until his retirement in 1948. He was Lord Lieutenant of the County of Middlesex from 1963 to 1965 when the post was abolished. General Bucknall died in 1980.

* * *

**21<sup>st</sup> January 2014**

**How do Bangalore Torpedoes work and how did they get their name?**

The Bangalore Torpedo is essentially a very large pipe bomb; a metal tube packed with explosives and detonated by a fuse. In modern versions the detonator will be fired electrically, but the originals were fired by a match fuse, the traditional fizzing piece of string seen in countless films. A number of lengths of pipe can be joined together to create an explosion along a significant length of ground. Each pipe is 1.5 m (4.9 ft) long and is threaded at both ends to allow tubes to be connected together. A smooth 'nose cone' can be attached to the leading tube to prevent it snagging on the ground. Non-explosive extender pipes can also be attached to the end of the explosive pipes to increase the reach of the weapon without the soldier laying it having to expose himself unduly to enemy fire.

Combat engineers use the weapon to clear barbed wire on the battlefield, inserting the tubes into the coils of wire which break apart under their own spring tension when the pipe explodes, creating gaps through which soldiers can advance. Typically a path 15 yards long and 1 yard wide can be created with a single explosion. It can also be used to clear paths through minefields. The explosions create sympathetic detonations in mines close by, once again clearing a path which the engineers then mark to prevent soldiers from wandering off of the safe route.

The device was named after the place where it was invented, Bangalore in India. In 1912 Captain McClintock of the British Indian Army, serving with the Madras Sappers and Miners, created it as a means of destroying booby traps left over from the Boer and Russo-Japanese wars which his unit had been tasked to clear.

The Bangalore Torpedo was used extensively in both World Wars and there is plenty of film of it being used to clear the wire on the D Day invasion beaches in the American sector. By D Day it was obsolescent in the British Army, having been replaced by the rocket launched Conger missile fired from an armoured engineer vehicle, which was also capable of damaging concrete bunkers. A modernised version of the Bangalore Torpedo remains in use today, having been reintroduced into the Royal Engineer's equipment table, and is manufactured by Mondial Defence Systems of Poole, Dorset.

\* \* \*

**27<sup>th</sup> January 2014**

**Is the 'I before e except after c' rule largely useless?**

Further to the earlier answer it is something of a wonder that this is regarded as a rule at all, as the number of words that don't conform to it is 21 times more than those that do. In total 923 words in the OED that contain either ie or ei don't conform to the rule. Many of the words that don't conform, such as concierge and beige, are of foreign origin and have been adopted into the English language, but even that isn't a universal truth.

Of the 923 non-conforming words some aren't in everyday use, being specific to specialist areas such as science, however, enough are in use to make the rule confusing at best. It is true that the many words making an ee sound follow the rule, but as the rule is broken so often it can't really be thought of as a rule but more of a guide.

One must take into account of the age of the children being taught to spell and the sorts of words that they are likely to use. Young children are far more likely to use the words field and ceiling, which conform, than they are the word financier which doesn't, so it is useful to provide them with a simple mnemonic to help them to remember the spelling. However, as the child gets older and starts to use more complex language the rule becomes less reliable and it might be helpful for teachers to 'de-train' older students from the rule and definitely to make sure it isn't applied at GCSE level or higher.

If in doubt use a dictionary rather than relying on an invalid rule.

**Author's note**: As can be seen, I didn't respond to the original question, but sent a letter in response to the answer that was published, which claimed that the I before e rule was valid, even though it quite clearly isn't. My follow-up wasn't published.

\* \* \*

**28<sup>th</sup> January 2014**

**What's the story of about the thousands of padlocks attached to the wire fence on the Hohenzollernbrucke railway bridge over the Rhine in Cologne?**

This relatively modern phenomena is known as the love lock and is a symbol of unbreakable love. It could be seen as a modern version of lovers carving their names into the bark of a tree. In most cases the lovers write, scratch or even engrave their names or initials onto a padlock, lock it to a bridge, fence, railing or gate and then throw away the keys so that the padlock can never be unlocked. Why a particular site is chosen for the padlocks is unclear, but accessibility and popularity amongst lovers must be a factor. While the Hohenzollern Bridge may be a well-known example it is by no means the only one and certainly isn't the oldest. The practice started in Europe but has now spread worldwide.

The first known example of love locks is in Serbia where it is thought that the first padlocks appeared on Most Ljubavi (love bridge) before the First World War. The story is that a local schoolmistress fell in love with a Serbian army officer who went off to Greece to fight in the Second Balkan War (1913), where he met and fell in love with a local woman on the island of Corfu. The schoolmistress died of a broken heart. Since then young women from her village, Vrnjačka Banja, started leaving padlocks on the bridge to symbolize and protect their unbreakable love.

In the rest of Europe the practice seems to date to around 2000. However, the 1992 book *Three Metres Above the Sky*, by Italian author Frederico Moccia, is attributed with initiating the practice at the Ponte Milvio in Rome. The book was later turned into a film which may have helped to spread the idea.

Officialdom doesn't seem to love lovers and at a number of sites there have been attempts to remove the padlocks. The railway company Deutche Bahn, owners of the Hohenzollern Bridge, threatened to do so but were forced to leave them when public opposition became too great. In 2012 at Dublin's Ha'penny Bridge council workers started to remove padlocks from the protected structure but in May 2013, when I visited, they were still very much in evidence. Similar attempts have been made in Paris, Florence and Bamberg. In most cases padlocks immediately started to reappear as soon as they were removed. In Algiers padlocks started to appear at a bridge previously nicknamed the suicide bridge, but youths removed them when an Imam condemned them as being un-Islamic.

In Britain the practice seems to have arrived more recently with reports showing padlocks appearing on the Millennium Bridge in London from 2011. An article in the Daily Telegraph showed an increase along the Embankment and on Tower Bridge prior to St Valentine's Day 2013, though officialdom has again tried to nip the practice in the bud by removing some of them. There have also been reports of love locks appearing in Manchester.

Love locks have also made their appearance on the other side of the Atlantic Ocean, with New York's Brooklyn Bridge being the most prominent site. In the TV series Homeland, Brody takes his daughter to see the fence on which he and his wife attached their love lock, though given his daughter's age this is probably taking poetic licence as the practice wouldn't have reached the USA at the time the Brody's were courting.

**Author's note:** When we were visiting Dublin in May 2013 I offered to attach a padlock to the Ha'penny Bridge but my wife declined the offer. And she calls me unromantic!

\* \* \*

## 31st January 2014

### Did the Japanese use paratroopers in World War II?

The history of parachute operations is a comparatively short one in military terms. The Russians are credited with the first viable paratrooper units. From the mid-1930s onwards the Russians trained hundreds of thousands of soldiers in the paratroop role but there is little evidence of them ever carrying out airborne operations. The first recorded airborne invasion was carried out by German paratroops (Fallshirmjäger) when they dropped into Denmark on 9th April 1940. They were used again in Holland and also to invade Crete.

In Britain the first paratroops weren't trained until 1941 when No 2 Commando , founded in June 1940, was converted to become firstly the 1st Special Air Service Battalion (no relation to the modern SAS) and then the 1st Battalion the Parachute Regiment. Their first assault took place on 10th February 1942 when 37 men and two Italian interpreters parachuted into Italy to blow up an aqueduct.

The Japanese Army started parachute training in the late 1930s but their units didn't receive much backing until there was a review of German parachute operations in 1941. The airborne troops were given the title of Teinshin Shudan (Raiding Group) and were expanded in size to a divisional level force of around 5,500 personnel. Because of the high attrition rate of paratroops they were used sparingly and the Japanese mainly employed theirs on the ground as elite light infantry.

Their first parachute operation was the Battle of Palembang in the Dutch East Indies on 13th February 1942, when the 1st Parachute Raiding Regiment dropped onto the Palembang airfield in Sumatra. The 2nd Parachute Raiding Regiment seized the nearby town and its vital oil refinery. Paratroops were again deployed during the Burma Campaign. Following the success of these operations the 1st Glider Tank Troop was formed in July 1943.

A force of 750 men of the 2nd Raiding Brigade were flown to the American occupied island of Leyte on 6th December 1944, but most of their aircraft were shot down en-route. Those that weren't dropped about 300 men who destroyed some planes on the ground and inflicted casualties before being annihilated. It was the last parachute raid mounted by the Japanese in World War II and the Teinshin Shudan then remained in the Philippines until the end of the war.

The Imperial Japanese Navy also trained three battalions of paratroops, commencing on 20th September 1941, who were known as the Special Naval Landing Force. Their first operation was at the Battle of Menado (11th to 13th January 1942) and they also took part in the invasion of in West Timor (19th February 1942). However, as with their army counterparts, they were mainly used as light infantry, in their case in an amphibious role, and spent most of the later stages of the war in Japan.

The terrain through which the Japanese Army had to operate prevented the greater use of paratroops. They were lightly armed and equipped and had to be re-supplied by air until they could be relieved by ground forces. It requires a considerable force of transport planes to both deliver the troops and keep them supplied, of which the Japanese didn't have enough. With so much of the Japanese military effort taking place in jungle conditions or on scattered islands, the ability to re-supply from the air was restricted and relief within a set time frame couldn't be guaranteed.

The British learned this lesson the hard way when the majority of the 1st Airborne Division was lost in the battle for Arnhem in

September 1944, when the advancing ground troops of XXX Corps took 9 days to reach the bridge instead of the planned 3 days. With 1$^{st}$ Airborne's landing grounds overrun by the Germans it became impossible to re-supply or to reinforce the paratroops to any significant degree. Only a 2,000 of the 10,000 that were dropped made it back to the British lines having first swam the River Rheine in the dark.

\* \* \*

### 4$^{th}$ February 2014

**At what battle in World War I did a general officer ask: "Where are the Sherwood Foresters?", which was supposedly answered by a subordinate who pointed to the rows of bodies in No-Man's Land of the decimated battalion.**

The Sherwood Foresters Regiment was formed after the Childers Reforms in 1881 out of the 45$^{th}$ (Nottinghamshire) Regiment and the 95$^{th}$ (Derbyshire) Regiment, both of which had histories going back over 140 years prior to that. At the outbreak of World War I they numbered 8 battalions, of which two were regular army, and had a depot in Derby. The 2$^{nd}$ Battalion formed part of the British Expeditionary Force which landed in France in September 1914. The 1$^{st}$ Battalion had been serving in India and were brought back to arrive in France in November 1914. The regiment was rapidly expanded and at its peak made up 33 Battalions. In all 140,000 men, mainly from Nottinghamshire and Derbyshire, served with the regiment, of which 11,409 did not return home.

It would take too long to detail all the battles of World War I that the regiment served in. It would probably be easier to list those in which they didn't take part. Their first action was on 20$^{th}$ September

1914 and they remained in contact with the enemy until the final day of the war.

The quote referred to was from a conversation between Major General Sir Henry Rawlinson and Brigadier Reginald Oxley, which took place during the Second Battle of Artois which was fought between 9th May and 18th June 1915. The 139th (Forester) Brigade, a Territorial brigade, was participating in the battle and the conversation allegedly took the following form:

Rawlinson: "This is most unsatisfactory. Where are the Sherwood Foresters? Where are the East Lancashires out on the right?"

Oxley: "They are lying out in No-Man's Land, sir, and most of them will never stand again."

It isn't clear if General Rawlinson was actually present on the battlefield or if he was in a command post and asking for situation report.

The participation of the British 1st Army in this battle was in support to the French Tenth Army under the command of General Joffre. The contested territory lay between the towns of Lens in the north and Arras in the south and included the notorious Vimy Ridge, which was one of the primary objectives of the French assault.

On 9th May the British attacked the Aubers Ridge but made no significant gains at a high cost of 11,000 casualties. It is officially regarded as a British defeat. From 15th to 25th May the British undertook the Battle of Festubert, which was on the right flank of the Aubers Ridge battlefield. The British were able to make only minor advances against a well dug in enemy, suffering over 16,000 casualties in the process. Overall the Second Battle of Artois failed to make any significant territorial gains or to achieve any sort of breakthrough. Having captured Vimy Ridge in an early assault by a Moroccan Division the French were unable to retain possession of it.

In 1970 the Sherwood Foresters Regiment merged with the Worcestershire Regiment to become the Worcestershire and Sherwood Forester Regiment and since 2007 has been the 2$^{nd}$ Battalion the Mercian Regiment. Their current base is in Palace Barracks, Belfast. The historical collections of the Sherwood Foresters Regiment are split between Nottingham Castle and the Derby City Museum.

**Author's note:** On a visit to the First World War battlefields in August 2018 I saw the memorial placed to mark the attack of the Moroccan Division on Vimy Ridge. It is tiny in comparison to the nearby Canadian memorial. The Canadians eventually captured Vimy Ridge on 12$^{th}$ April 1917.

\* \* \*

**5$^{th}$ February 2014**

**I was attached to the Sabre Conversion Unit Squadron at RAF Wildenrath in the Fifties. What became of this aircraft and why did the RAF need this U.S. import?**

Although Britain was at the forefront of jet aircraft technology in the 1940s and 50s the replacement aircraft for the aging De Havilland Vampire and Gloster Meteor were suffering development problems. This wouldn't have been too much of an issue if the Korean War hadn't broken out, as the RAF would have ridden out the delay with its aging aircraft. However, the introduction of the Soviet built Mig-15 into the Cold War and its operational use by the Chinese in Korea changed the game as it was quickly discovered that the Vampire and Meteor were no match for this new aircraft.

It is ironic that it was the post war British government that sold the Soviets the Rolls Royce Nene jet engines that were copied by the Russians for use in the Mig. The sale was agreed on condition that the engines were exclusively for use in commercial aircraft but, unsurprisingly, Stalin broke his word and used them to develop the Mig. It was rumoured that many of the first Chinese Migs seen in combat were flown by Russian pilots, for whom it would have provided valuable combat experience.

To fill the operational gap the RAF bought the Canadair Sabre 4 aircraft "off the peg". These were a variant of the U.S. F86 but were built under licence in Canada. The RAF bought 430 of them. They arrived too late for operational use in Korea but were deployed with the 2$^{nd}$ Allied Tactical Air Force in Germany where it would again be opposed by the Russian Mig-15. It was still seen as a stop gap until the Hawker Hunter and Supermarine Swift could be introduced, which commenced in 1955.

The F86 Sabre started development in 1947 as the first American transonic jet fighter, although initial design work had begun during the Second World War but was then halted. It was also its first swept wing design. It went into operational service with the United States Air Force in 1949. Keen aircraft spotters will see many similarities between the F86 and the Mig-15. The F86 set its first official World speed record of 670 m.p.h. in September 1948, flown by Chuck Yaegar who was later involved in the American space programme. This was still 32 m.p.h. short of the unofficial record set during the war by the rocket powered German Me 163B.

The Sabre was a popular aircraft with its pilots and the last one was only withdrawn from service with the Chilean Air Force in 1994.

The Sabre started to be taken out of service with the RAF in 1956 and most were refurbished and returned to the U.S.A. because they had been provided very cheaply under the Military Aid Programme (MAP). The U.S.A. then sold them on to other nations, mainly Italy and Yugoslavia. MAP was an American funded programme aimed at bolstering the military strength of allied nations, particularly those of NATO. There is one RAF aircraft remaining, XB812, in the RAF Museum at Cosford.

\* \* \*

**12th February 2014**
**On November 1, 1944, there was a seaborne landing of Allied Troops on the island of Walcheren in Holland. What was the purpose of this operation? Was it a success?**

By October 1944 the British and Canadians forces of 21st Army Group had advanced into the Netherlands as far as the River Rhine. In the process they had captured the port of Antwerp, which was strategically important as it would allow the allies to move their port facilities from now distant Cherbourg into northern Belgium, thereby shortening their supply lines. However, there was one obstacle still remaining; A large concentration of German troops of the 15th Army, along the north side of the River Scheldt, on which Antwerp sat, and in particular on the island of Walcheren where the river met the North Sea. The Germans had had four years to build strong defensive positions as part of Hitler's Atlantic Wall and were capable of shelling any Allied shipping that dared to try to gain access to Antwerp. The assault on Walcheren was the final phase of the Battle of the Scheldt (2 Oct 44 to 8 Nov 44).

By 31st October all the land along the north of the estuary, including the Island of North Beveland and the isthmus of South Beveland , had been cleared of German forces. However, the island of Walcheren was connected to South Beveland by only a narrow causeway across the Slooe Channel, 50 yards wide but a mile long, easily defensible against troops trying to cross it.

The use of assault boats to cross the Slooe Channel from either South or North Beveland was deemed unfeasible as the ground was too muddy to permit the boats to be launched. Under the codename

Operation Vitality the $2^{nd}$ Canadian Infantry Division attempted to capture the causeway but suffered heavy casualties and were repulsed. A foothold on Walcheren was held briefly before the Canadians were once again forced back onto the causeway. A Battalion of the Glasgow Highlanders were ordered to take over the offence from the Canadians but fared no better. The solution, it appeared, was to make a seaborne landing.

The need for a seaborne landing had already been anticipated and the troops who had been selected to carry out the task had started training in mid-October. Codenamed Operation Infatuate, the assault was launched on $1^{st}$ November 1944. It was undertaken by Commandoes from $4^{th}$ Special Service Brigade, made up of 41, 47 and 48 (Royal Marine) Commandoes with No 4 (Army) Commando attached for the operation. There were also troops of French and Dutch from No 10 (Inter-Allied) Commando.

The assault was carried out using armoured amphibious vehicles, known as Buffaloes, which were launched from Breskens on the south bank of the Scheldt and landed between the towns of Flushing and Westkappelle. As each objective was captured by the Commandos they handed it over to regular infantry battalions of the $52^{nd}$ (Lowland) Infantry Division, before moving on to the next objective. The Germans were in no mood to surrender and fought hard to defend the island and it took until $7^{th}$ November to complete the operation.

Because there was no way to evacuate the population of the island, civilian casualties had been high, some of them caused by allied bombing of the sea defences on $3^{rd}$ October and some by artillery fire during the battle.

With the Scheldt river now accessible and the $21^{st}$ Army Group's western flank secure they were able to advance quickly into Holland

and reached the River Waal east of Rotterdam by 15$^{th}$ December. The city itself wasn't liberated until Germany surrendered on 5$^{th}$ May 1945, as the focus for 21$^{st}$ Army Group was switched to the crossing of the Rhine and the subsequent invasion of Germany from the west.

The Canadian units involved in the battle for the Walcheren causeway suffered significant casualties and the Calgary Highlanders were awarded a battle honour for their part in the assault. However, most of those casualties could have been avoided had the decision to take the island by seaborne assault been the first choice strategy. The Canadians eventually had to wait for the Commandoes to secure the island before they could cross the causeway.

After the war, dykes were built at either end of the Slooe Channel and the waters separating Walcheren from Beveland were drained, which means that that Walcheren is no longer an island.

* * *

### 20$^{th}$ February 2014
#### What 'gyrates' on London's Hanger Lane gyratory system?

The definition of the verb gyrate is "to move or cause to move rapidly in a circle or spiral". The definition of gyratory as an adjective is "denoting or involving circular or spiral motion" and as a noun is "a road junction or traffic system requiring the circular movement of traffic, larger or more complex than an ordinary roundabout".

Anyone who has ever used the Hanger Lane gyratory system would probably agree that the definitions provide an almost perfect description of it, and they could also provide a few definitions of their own that are probably not printable.

In short it is the traffic that moves in a circular, or gyratory, motion although probably not at high speed, especially during peak periods.

Located in the London Borough of Ealing, Hanger Lane gyratory system came into being in the early 1980s, primarily to act as an interchange between two of the busiest roads in West London, the A40 (Western Avenue) which runs east-west and the A406 (North Circular Road) which runs roughly north-south. The A40 underpasses the gyratory itself with slip roads providing access to the system. In addition Hanger Lane (A4005) connects to the system at the north west corner and also on the south as part of the A406. Twyford Abbey Road connects on the eastern side. Traffic lights control the entry and exit of traffic to and from the connecting roads and slip roads as well as allowing pedestrians to cross the busy intersections.

The whole system covers about 30,000 square metres, approximately 7.5 acres or about 4 football pitches. It includes access to the London Underground Central Line at Hanger Lane Tube station. It also incorporates a nature reserve which is designated as a Site of Importance for Nature Conservation. This reserve provides natural habitat for local wildlife such as birds.

In December 2007 the Hanger Lane gyratory system was named Britain's scariest junction in a poll held by motor insurance companies.

\* \* \*

## 18<sup>th</sup> March 2014

### Who started the Korean War?

The Korean peninsula was annexed by Japan following the defeat of the Chinese Qing dynasty in 1896. Their grip was strengthened by the defeat of Russia in the Sino-Japanese War of 1904/05 and Korea remained a colony of Japan until the end of the World War II. During the war the Nationalist National Revolution Army and the Communist People's Liberation Army, both Chinese, helped to organise Korean resistance, which helped to establish two competing political movements.

At the Cairo conference of 1943 China, the UK and US agreed that Korea should become an independent state after the end of the war and at the subsequent Yalta conference of February 1945 it was assumed that Moscow would dominate China and Manchuria in political terms, a defacto acceptance of communist dominance in the region. On $9^{th}$ August 1945 Russia declared war on Japan and invaded Manchuria, a last minute political move against an already defeated nation. The Japanese surrendered on $10^{th}$ August to end the war in the Far East.

As part of the agreement between Russia and the USA, a dividing line was drawn across Korea at the $38^{th}$ parallel to demark the Soviet and US spheres of influence on the peninsula, with both sides providing occupation troops within their areas of control. The Russians were in position on the $38^{th}$ Parallel within 3 weeks of the War's end but had to wait a further 3 weeks for the arrival of their US counterparts so that the Japanese surrender on the peninsula could be formally accepted.

In the meantime north of the Korean border the Chinese Civil war had broken out between the Communists and the Nationalists and the North Koreans, with or without Soviet approval, provided considerable materiel support for the Communists as well as providing a safe haven for injured combatants. They went on to provide soldiers for the Communist cause.

Without consulting the Koreans, the Potsdam Conference of July/August 1945 decided that Korea would be a divided between North and South in direct contravention of what had been agreed in Cairo. There was a certain amount of disorder on both sides of the new border, with anti-communist strikes and demonstrations in the North and pro-communist activity in the South. Tensions were high and remained so, with both of the new countries demanding the honouring of the Cairo agreement and the establishment of a single Korean nation. There were a number of military incursions across the border from the Soviet backed north which the weaker South couldn't resist.

Kim Il Sung, the leader of the North Korea, enjoyed considerable Soviet support for his plans to invade South Korea and this was tangible in the form of military equipment. As agreed at Potsdam the Americans had fully withdrawn from South Korea by 1949 and Stalin had exploded Russia's first nuclear weapon, signalling a significant strategic shift in the balance of power between Russia and the USA. This undoubtedly encouraged Kim Il Sung in his invasion plans. With Communist victory in China, ethnic Korean combat units returned to their homeland to provide Kim Il Sung with a battle hardened army to undertake the invasion. In April 1950 Stalin gave his permission for North Korea to invade the South providing the Chinese would provide reinforcements if needed.

The North Korean army crossed the 38$^{th}$ Parallel at dawn on Sunday 25$^{th}$ June 1950 following an artillery barrage. The weak South Korean forces were unable to put up any effective resistance and had to concede territory. Within days the 95,000 strong South Korean army had dwindled to just 22,000 as a result of combat losses and mass desertions. Following a UN resolution on 27$^{th}$ June a US force arrived on the peninsula in July, though their interest was mainly in protecting Japan, which a successful invasion of South Korea might place in jeopardy. This US intervention was essential as it provided a dominance in air power that the North was unable to match. At first it was hoped that this alone might lead to the defeat of the North but this belief quickly foundered as the North Korean army fought on.

The US led UN force, in company with allies such as Britain and Australia, quickly reversed the situation and pushed the North Koreans back over their own border and pushed them to within a few kilometres of the border with China. By October 1950 the North was all but defeated. It was at that moment that China, keeping with its promise to Stalin, intervened on behalf of the North and once again shifted the balance of military power. With over a million Chinese troops committed to battle, the US and their allies were pushed back until the two sides once again faced each other across the 38$^{th}$ Parallel.

An armistice was signed in July 1953 which brought an end to the fighting in Korea but to this day a peace treaty has never been signed and, as recent events have shown, there is still the possibility of hostilities breaking out anew. South Korea reported 373,000 civilian and 137,00 military casualties compared to 215,000 North Koreans killed and the Chinese approximately 400,000 killed, though the Chinese claim they only lost 114,000 men. The USA suffered over 33,000 combat deaths and Britain 1,139 deaths. Actual mortality rates were much higher as non-combat deaths were considerable, caused by both extreme cold and famine.

\* \* \*

## 27$^{th}$ March 2014
**Why was Olof Palme, Prime Minister of Sweden, assassinated?**

Sven Olof Joachim Palme was born on 30$^{th}$ January 1927 in Ostermalm, Sweden. His mother was a German refugee and his father a descendant of a Dutch businessman. Following his mandatory military service Palme studied at Kenyon College in Ohio, USA and graduated in law from Stockholm University. He was recruited into the Swedish Socialist Democratic Party which he eventually led and was serving his second term as Prime Minister of Sweden at the time of his assassination.

Palme's views on the influence and participation of labour in the management of the workplace gained him considerable hostility from the more conservative elements in Sweden, especially big business. He was also responsible for a massive expansion in the Swedish welfare system. With his country hampered by debt, he was seeking a 'third way' for the governance of the country by encouraging more investment from private industry at the same time as maintaining basic socialist policies.

Palme was a severe critic of both left and right wing regimes and his criticism of them earned him enemies both at home and abroad. This, coupled to his socialist policies at home, ensured that he had many political enemies. However there was no person or group that was readily identifiable as being behind his assassination.

Such was the nature of Swedish society that the physical security of its politicians was never a major issue. Palme therefore had no protection when, while walking home from the cinema with his wife, he was fatally shot at around midnight on 28th February 1986. His wife received a minor injury from a second bullet.

After a two year investigation a small time criminal by the name of Christer Pettersen was tried and found guilty of Palme's murder. However the verdict was overturned on appeal and no one else has ever stood trial for the murder.

As with other murders of heads of state a number of conspiracy theories have emerged.

Novelist Steig Larsson, who wrote The Girl With The Dragon Tattoo, is alleged to have sent 15 boxes of papers to the government of South Africa in which he claims a Swedish mercenary by the name of Bertil Wedin carried out the act on behalf of South Africa's former apartheid government. Larsson himself died in 2004.

Other conspiracy theories have pointed the finger at the former Yugoslavia, Kurdish separatists, right wing extremists within the Swedish security services and the aforementioned Petterson, who supposedly confessed to associates and who was also identified by Palme's widow.

No fewer than 130 people have confessed to the murder.

* * *

## 3rd April 2014
**Why does the British national anthem appear in the sound track of the film "The Halls of Montezuma"?**

The film The Halls Of Montezuma was made in 1950 as a celebration of the contribution made by the United Sates Marine Corps to the winning of the Second World War, in the Pacific theatre in particular. The title of the film is taken from the Marine Corps Hymn. The film's plot tells of a tough mission to capture a Japanese held island. It starred Richard Widmark, Karl Malden, Jack Palance and Richard Boone.

One of the pieces of music featured in the film is the hymn "My Country Tis Of Thee", also known as "America", which is an American hymn sung to the tune of God Save The Queen (or King as it was in 1950). The full words are:

1

> My country, 'tis of thee,
> Sweet land of liberty,
> Of thee I sing;
> Land where my fathers died,
> Land of the pilgrims' pride,
> From ev'ry mountainside
> Let freedom ring!

2

My native country, thee,
Land of the noble free,
Thy name I love;
I love thy rocks and rills,
Thy woods and templed hills;
My heart with rapture thrills,
Like that above.

3

Let music swell the breeze,
And ring from all the trees
Sweet freedom's song;
Let mortal tongues awake;
Let all that breathe partake;
Let rocks their silence break,
The sound prolong.

4

Our fathers' God to Thee,
Author of liberty,
To Thee we sing.
Long may our land be bright,
With freedom's holy light,
Protect us by Thy might,
Great God our King.

There were another nine optional additional verses added later.
The hymn was written in 1831 by Samuel Francis Smith, a student at
Andover Theological Seminary, Massachusetts. He based the music
on an extract from Muzio Clemente's Symphony No 3. A friend,

Lowell Mason, asked Smith to translate words from a German song book for use as a hymn but rather than translating the lyrics Smith wrote his own American patriotic version, allegedly in under thirty minutes. Given the patriotic nature of the hymn it must be assumed that Smith didn't know the true origin of the tune he chose to use. The song became one of the defacto national anthems of the USA until 1931 when The Star Spangled Banner was formally adopted.

The tune used for the British national anthem predates the work of Muzio Clemente, having been published in the Thesaurus Musicus in 1744 and then in The Gentleman's Magazine on 15th October 1745. It may date back to a tune written by John Bull in 1615 or to an even earlier work. Both Purcell and Handel had used similar refrains in their work and it has even been suggested that it originated from an old Scots carol, "Remember Oh Thou Man".

Muzio Clemete (24/1/1752 – 10/3/1832) was a prolific writer of music. Born in Italy he adopted the United Kingdom as his homeland. His use of the refrain for God Save The King/Queen in his Symphony No 3 was a tribute to his adopted nationality. Symphony For Orchestra (No.3 in G major), the "Great National Symphony" For Orchestra, to give it its full title, was written between 1816 and 1824. As well as being a composer Clemente was a manufacturer of pianos and publisher of music and is credited with the promotion of the piano as a solo musical instrument, for which he wrote many works.

* * *

## 16th April 2014

**I recently saw a reference to an Australian hand gesture called the Barcoo Salute. What is this?**

The Barcoo Salute is a wave of the hand in front of the face to disperse flies. It is common amongst drovers, farmers and horse riders, all of whom provide a ready target for insects and its often seen on TV news reports from outback locations. The gesture has also been referred to as the Aussie Salute, the Outback Salute, the Bush Salute and the Queensland Salute. All of these may sometimes substitute 'wave' for 'salute'.

The salute is named after the Barcoo River region in Queensland which is particularly well known for the density of its fly population. However, the flies in question are bush flies, genus Musca Vetustissima, which are different from the common housefly and blue bottle with which we are more familiar. The bush fly is particularly attracted to bodily fluids such as sweat, mucus and saliva, which is why all activities involving horses and cattle are likely to increase the level of attraction.

A dismissive wave of the hand will deflect or discourage flies, but once they have landed it is necessary to physically wipe them away as they become trapped in the fluid that attracted them.

Failure to remove them can result in contagion from the many diseases they carry as a result of walking through dung and carrion.

Historically the hat with corks suspended from the brim was created to reduce the amount of waving that was necessary. Modern insect repellents have now replaced the hat as the primary defence.

\* \* \*

## 28<sup>th</sup> April 2014

**Despite not bordering each other, Turks and Afghans refer to each other as 'brothers'. What are the roots of this close relationship?**

While the ethnic roots of the people of both Turkey and Afghanistan are similar, both being descended from the nomadic tribes of central Asia and later from the Mongols who invaded during the 13<sup>th</sup> and 14<sup>th</sup> centuries, this reference to brotherhood is based on the shared nature of the Muslim sects to which the people belong. This too is rooted in history. The two countries are both adherents to the Sunni branch of Islam, while the countries between them, Iraq and Iran, are predominately Shi'a.

The tribes migrating from central Asia to Iraq, Iran, Afghanistan and Turkey were converted to Islam during the 7th and 8th centuries. The form of Islam they followed was Sunni. The split between Sunni and Shi'a Muslims is the oldest in the history of the religion and stems from divisions over who would be leader following the death of the Prophet Muhammad.

The larger group of the religion, those now known as Sunni, chose to follow Abu Bakr, a companion of Muhammad, as the Caliph (politico-social leader) while the minority chose to follow Ali, Muhammad's nephew. These became the Shi'a. The choice of Abu Bakr was more about the political leadership of the fledgling Islamic state of Arabia, while for the followers of Ali the choice was more about religious leadership. The Shi'a had no problem with Abu Bakr providing Ali was acknowledged as the religious leader, which Abu Bakr's followers refused to do.

While there is no basic disagreement about the interpretation of the Qur'an (Koran), Islam's holy book, there are differences in the observation of certain religious practices. The biggest difference, however, remains the age old argument about which is the true line of the descent of the religion from Muhammad.

Abu Bakr's followers were better organised to spread the message of Islam, so the mass conversions that took place between the 7th and 9th centuries were mainly to the Sunni sect. The poorer organised Shi'a were ousted from Arabia and made their base along the Euphrates and Tigris valleys and into Persia, where they established their own schools for the teaching of the religion.

In the 13$^{th}$ and 14$^{th}$ centuries the Tamurid Empire, founded by the Mongol Tamburlaine, swept down from the north to conquer all the lands between Afghanistan and eastern Anatolia in Turkey and as far south as the Persian Gulf. In the 15$^{th}$ century the Ottomans, also Mongols, captured western Anatolia and also the city of Constantinople (Istanbul). With the decline of the Tamurids in the early 16$^{th}$ century the Ottomans spread eastward to fill the power vacuum. Both dynasties, however, had adopted the Sunni religion.

Also as a result of the decline in the Tamurid Empire, the Safavid Dynasty captured Persia in 1501 and ruled until 1722. Although they share the same ethnic origins as both the Turks and the Afghans they preferred the Shi'a school of Islam and made it their official religion when they conquered Persia, thereby splitting the region between the two schools, leaving the Afghan Sunni's isolated from their Turkish Sunni kin. This is the origin of the fraternal feelings between the Turkish and Afghan people to this day.

Between the Sunni Turks and the Shi'a Iranians lies modern Iraq which has a majority Shi'a population but which has been ruled by Sunni's since the days of the Ottomans and which continued all the way into the dictatorship of Sadam Hussein. This split is still evident today in Iraq, where the Shi'a now form a majority in government but some Sunni continue to mount a campaign of terror to try to restore the Sunni's to power.

\* \* \*

## 1$^{st}$ May 2014

### Are all Popes eventually canonised?

Canonisation is the process by which the Roman Catholic Church and the Eastern Orthodox Church create new saints. Their names are then added to the canon, or list, of recognised saints.

The history of canonisation goes back to the earliest days of the church and the original criteria for canonisation was martyrdom. By about the 4$^{th}$ century people who had lived a holy life, professing their faith openly, began to be venerated. Some were given the title of Venerable to denote this quality, such as the British historian and monk the Venerable Bede (672 - 735 AD). Such approval was granted by the local Bishop. However, the burden of proof became more rigid and the requirements for canonisation started to become more demanding than mere martyrdom or living a holy life. Gradually the role of the local Bishop was supplanted by that of the Vatican.

The first papal canonisation was that of St Udlaric, Bishop of Augsburg, by Pope John XV in 993 AD. This is disputed, with some historians believing the canonisation of St Swibert by Pope Leo III in 804 AD was the first such act. Walter of Pontoise was the last person to be canonised by a Bishop, Hugh de Boves Archbishop of Rouen, in 1153.

The present process of canonisation is a number of stages through which the candidate is elevated. Each stage requires a considerable amount of investigation before it is concluded. They are, in order, "Servant of God", "Venerable/Heroic in Virtue", "Blessed" and finally Saint.

In the first instance a commission of investigation is established to gather evidence supporting the candidacy of the subject. This will be started by the local Bishop but is transferred to the Pope for confirmation of the status of Venerable. To become "Blessed" the candidate must have either been martyred or to have performed a miracle while alive. Today most accepted miracles take the form of "cures" as these are the easiest to document: The patient was sick, there is no known cure for their disease, the patient recovered after prayer to the venerable person or at a shrine dedicated to them.

For the candidate to become a Saint two miracles must have been performed after death through the intercession of the candidate following prayers to them.

Including the most recent candidates, Pope John XXIII and Pope John Paul II, a total of 80 Popes out of 269 have been canonised.

The canonisation of Pope John Paul II was a notably speedy process, considering that he only died in 2005. Pope Benedict, as Bishop of Rome, waived the five year waiting period, possibly to satisfy popular demand. One of Pope John Paul II's alleged intercessions to be counted as a miracle was the curing of a French nun of Parkinson's disease. The second alleged intercession was the curing of a 9 year old Polish boy suffering from cancer of the kidney and unable to walk. After visiting the Pope's tomb in the Vatican it was reported that the boy was able to walk again. There is some controversy about these miracles as it is not clear that they are permanent cures, which is necessary to meet the criteria. Relapses are still a possibility.

**Author's note:** My answering of questions related to the Catholic church normally stems from my wife's interest, as she is a Catholic. Having done the work for her I see no point in not then using it, so I submit it to the Daily Mail for consideration.

\* \* \*

## 6th May 2014

**Are there any official memorials to the personnel of UXB (unexploded bomb) units in the UK, many of whom lost their lives in the pursuit of saving others?**

Prior to World War II the British Government had given little thought to bomb disposal (BD), despite the accounts from the Spanish Civil War that told of the risk from unexploded ordnance dropped from the air. When it came to air raid precautions the government focused mainly on the protection of civilians from air attack, and not on what might happen if a bomb failed to explode. When some thought was applied it was suggested that Air Raid Precautions (ARP) Wardens should collect any unexploded missiles and take them to a dump where someone (unidentified, but probably the army) would then explode them. No one sought input from the RAF who would have identified the flaws in this plan. Consideration was later given to providing specialist BD training to ARP Wardens but no actual training ever took place.

It was eventually decided that the Royal Engineers would take on the work of BD, with teams of one NCO and two sappers (junior soldiers) who would dig down to the bomb and then explode it in situ. Clearly no one had considered the collateral damage that this might cause. With the "phony war" between September 1939 and April 1940 dragging on, the teams were almost disbanded because of the lack of work for them to do. The army formally took on the role of BD on 2$^{nd}$ February 1940, with the exception of those bombs that might fall on Royal Navy or Royal Air Force property. The Royal Navy also became responsible for all missiles that fell into the sea or estuaries below the high water mark.

Twenty Five BD sections were established in May 1940. Each section comprised a Lieutenant, a Sergeant and 14 Other Ranks (ORs). They absorbed the earlier working parties that had been formed. With the start of the Blitz in London it soon became apparent that this small number of units wouldn't be able to cope with the demand placed on them and a further 109 teams were formed and by July 1940 had grown to 220. Eventually these units would be reformed into companies and organised into four geographically based BD Groups. Further groups were later established to serve in Africa, Italy and North West Europe.

The methods used to disarm the bombs were initially very crude. German bomb fuses were inserted into the side of the bomb, rather than in the nose or tail as with British bombs. The first methods of defusing the bomb were for the officer to use a hammer and cold chisel to loosen the locking ring so the fuse could be unscrewed and removed. The bomb would then be loaded onto a lorry to be taken away and blown up. The loss of life caused by the accidental triggering of bomb fuses forced more sophisticated methods to be hurriedly developed.

Since the end of World War II the term Bomb Disposal has been replaced with Explosive Ordnance Disposal or EOD. 33 EOD Regiment, Royal Engineers, still remains responsible for the majority of bomb disposal work on the battlefield. However, 11 EOD Regiment of the Royal Logistics Corps is responsible for the disarming and disposal of improvised explosive devices planted by terrorists and also for dealing with any previously undiscovered bombs left over from World War II.

In 2006 a memorial to the Royal Engineers who died while serving with BD units was unveiled at Carver Barracks, Saffron Walden (the former RAF Debden) which is the current home of 33 EOD Regiment. There are two other small memorials; one to the men of the RAF, which is located at Eden Camp, Malton, North Yorkshire and one to the sailors who cleared landmines from the beach at Mundesley in Norfolk.

Eden Camp started life in 1942 as a prisoner of war camp and has now been refurbished as a Second World War museum, opening its doors in 1987. The memorial at Mundesley was dedicated on 2nd May 2004 to honour the men who helped to clear mines from the village's beach and adjacent Norfolk beaches. At least 26 men lost their lives in that operation.

* * *

7th May 2014

**Why is Shamrock so called? Why the particular association with Ireland?**

The naming of this sub-species of the clover family comes from the Irish for "little clover" which is *seamróg*. This is a diminutive of *seamair*, or clover. The word shamrock is merely an Anglicisation of these words.

All shamrocks are clovers, but not all clovers are shamrocks. There are two species that these words can be used to describe: lesser clover or Trefolia dubium and white clover or trefolia repens; *seamair bhuí* and *seamair bhán* respectively.

There was, for many years, some dispute over the precise botanical species that is a shamrock. As well as the two species already mentioned there were three other contenders for the title, all common on the British mainland. The definitive title, however, goes to Trefolia Dubium. This was the species most commonly sold in Covent Garden on St Patrick's Day during the 19th century and which was worn in at least 13 counties in Ireland. Two surveys put the matter beyond doubt. Irish people were asked to send samples of what they considered to be shamrock to Nathaniel Colgan, an amateur naturalist, in 1893 and to E Charles Nelson, Director of the Irish National Botanic Garden, in 1898. Both surveys drew the same conclusions with the Trefolia Dubium being regarded by the Irish as being the true shamrock, though the Trifolium Repens came a close second.

The association of the shamrock with Ireland comes from the legend that St Patrick used the shamrock to teach the Irish the concept of the Holy Trinity. He compared the idea of a single plant having three leaves with the idea of a single God having three forms: Father, Son and Holy Spirit. However, historic Celtic writings don't differentiate between ordinary clover and shamrock and the distinction first appeared in English, in Edmond Campion's work

The Boke Of The Histories Of Irelande (sic). The first visual link to St Patrick is on the St Patrick Coppers or Ha'pennies issued in 1675 and the first written connection doesn't appear until 1681. It seems therefore that the association of the shamrock, rather than just any old clover, with St Patrick was something that was applied retrospectively.

The shamrock doesn't appear as an Irish symbol until the 18th century when it was adopted by some local militias set up to counter the threat of French or Spanish invasion when manpower shortages caused regular British soldiers to be withdrawn from Ireland. It then became a popular symbol amongst other irregular troops raised in Ireland and started to migrate into Irish Nationalist groups when it started to be mentioned in Irish songs. It became an official symbol of Ireland following the Act of Union of 1801 when it was incorporated into the Royal Coat Of Arms of the United Kingdom. It appears united on the same stems as the rose and the thistle, entwined with the Royal motto.

The shamrock isn't unique to Ireland and will grow in most places where clover grows. However, as discussed above, identifying shamrock as a unique species is fraught with difficulty. The variety best known and worn throughout the world on St Patrick's Day has slightly heart shaped leaves and is neither of the competing species but a domesticated American bred hybrid called Oxalis Oregona. In Ireland, though, only Trefolia Dubium will do.

* * *

## 10th May 2015
### Why was it considered shocking, until the Forties, for women to wear red?

Up until the 12th century, images of the Virgin Mary were shown wearing a red cloak or robe, but after that her garb was always portrayed as blue and this may have been the origin of the idea that red was an unacceptable colour for women to wear. Blue was a very expensive colour to manufacture so its later adoption as the colour for clothing images of Mary was an indication of her growing importance to the church.

In Britain this was almost certainly a Victorian taboo based on the idea that the wearing of red made women more sexually attractive, possibly because it was a popular colour amongst actresses, prostitutes and other women of low repute.

There is some modern day research that suggests that the wearing of red does send off a subliminal message regarding sexual availability, which may also be why the wearing of red lipstick is popular. This may have evolutionary origins, as increases in the redness of the skin in some female animals, such as apes and monkeys, during their periods of fertility is known to attract the male of the species.

The Victorians were well known for their prudishness when it came to sexual matters, despite their somewhat hypocritical behaviour behind closed doors. It's therefore likely that Victorian mothers forbad their daughters from wearing red because of its sexual connotations and the taboo would have been passed down through the generations. The converse would be true as well and any woman wearing red would be sending out a clear signal.

Cloth and clothing were rationed during the Second World War so women had to make dresses from whatever was available. With such a shortage a social taboo wouldn't have been sustainable as women used any colour of cloth available to make dresses. More than one pair of curtains ended up as a wedding dress. The same applied to men's clothing as well, of course, and this was the period that saw the introduction of short trousers for schoolboys, the rise of the single breasted jacket and the disappearance of turn-ups from trousers in order to save material.

In the post-war era, as well as continued rationing, there was a shortage of men as a consequence of the war, so in order to be seen as attractive, single women would employ a number of techniques, including the wearing of bright colours, including red, shortening hemlines and wearing more make-up.

\* \* \*

## 15th May 2014

**Henry VII was Earl of Richmond, but was this Richmond in North Yorkshire or Richmond-on-Thames, previously known as Sheen?**

When William, Duke of Normandy, invaded England in 1066 he rewarded his followers with land. This helped him to quickly complete his conquest as his followers spread out across the country to claim their rewards, subduing the populace as they went. One of the contingents of soldiers was from Brittany and this group was awarded lands in North Yorkshire.

The title of Earl of Richmond first appears after "the harrying (or harrowing) of the North" in 1071, the suppression of a revolt against King William which resulted in mass killings, especially in Yorkshire. The first Earl of Richmond was Alan Rufus (1040 – 1093) who was a blood relation of both King William and The Duke of Brittany and was the leader of the Bretons in North Yorkshire who had helped to ruthlessly crush the revolt. In Brittany the title was known as the Compte de Richmonde and the link between Brittany and Richmond was maintained until the 14th century. The Honour of Richmond was one of the most significant in the North and was required to produce 60 knights when called upon to do so by the King. For a long while the area was known as Richmondshire and recognised as being a separate entity from Yorkshire.

The town of Richmond in North Yorkshire takes its name from the first Earl, who founded it. The original town of Richmond was in Normandy, where it was called Richemont.

The town of Richmond in Surrey, now a London Borough, was in an area formerly known as Sheen or Shene (from the Saxon *Sceon*). It takes its name from the palace built by Henry VII in 1501 and named after his Earldom. The town that grew up next to the palace in subsequent years therefore took on the name. It was part of the Parish of Kingston-Upon-Thames and didn't formally become a borough in its own right until 1890, 819 years after its Northern namesake.

The Palace remained in use until the departure of James II into exile, when it fell into decay. The grounds of the house were converted to a deer park for royal hunting and later became Richmond Park. The views from it to the Thames and the City of London are protected by Act of Parliament.

Richmond is the most replicated place name in the world with over 60 locations named after it, but they all stem from the town in North Yorkshire, though many of the inhabitants of these places believe the name originated in Surrey.

In all the title of Earl of Richmond was created and then allowed to fall into disuse 6 times from 1071 until its last holder, Henry VII. It was mainly held by members of the family of the Duke of Brittany, an important English ally. It reverted to the British Crown during the reign of Edward III. The title was briefly held by John of Gaunt, Duke of Lancaster. It was merged with the Crown during the reign of Henry VI, John of Gaunt's great grandson, and remained unused for forty years.

In 1452 Henry VI bestowed the title on his cousin Edmond Tudor, the father of Henry Tudor. Henry was not formally created Earl because his father died before he was born, but he used the title anyway. Henry's mother, Ann Neville, constantly lobbied Edward

IV and then Richard III for recognition of her son's title. It was refused because Ann was a staunch supporter of the defeated House of Lancaster. Henry Tudor formally adopted the title of Earl of Richmond, amongst others, when he defeated Richard III to become King. He was the last holder of the title.

The title of Duke of Richmond and Somerset was created by Henry VIII and awarded to Henry Fitzroy, one of his illegitimate sons. The lands that went with the title were still those in North Yorkshire. The title lapsed but was resurrected by James I with the Somerset element removed. The Dukedom was recreated and then allowed to lapse twice more but was finally awarded to Charles Lennox, an illegitimate son of Charles II, in 1675 and it has existed ever since. The current holder of the title is Charles Henry Gordon-Lennox, the 10$^{th}$ Duke, who was born in 1929.

\* \* \*

## 20$^{th}$ May 2014

### Is the seemingly innocent rhyme "Lucy Lockett Lost her Pocket" about a prostitute?

The handbag or hand held purse didn't make its appearance until around 1830. Prior to that women had to carry their valuables in their pockets. However, these were not the same as the pockets we know today.

The original pocket was a cloth or canvas bag suspended from a tape or ribbon which was tied around the woman's waist, over her petticoats but under her dress. Access to the pocket was then made through an opening in the outer garment, which would have been secured with buttons. A woman might have several pockets arranged around her waist and suspended from a single tape.

To steal a woman's pocket was hazardous for the thief with a high risk of being detected. The best time for such an act to take place was therefore when the woman had removed both the dress and the pocket or pockets. This suggested some sort of immoral conduct was taking place, as no decent woman of the era would undress before any man other than her husband. The rhyme states that the pocket was found empty but with ribbon wrapped around it. This ribbon would have been the one that was tied around the waist, strengthening the notion that the ribbon was voluntarily untied rather than the pocket being cut from it without alerting the owner.

The rhyme seems to have arisen during the 17$^{th}$ or 18$^{th}$ centuries and was in popular use by the start of the 19$^{th}$. It first appears in written records in 1842. When sung it shares a tune with Yankee Doodle, though it isn't clear for which song the tune was composed.

Suggestions are that Lucy Lockett and Kitty Fisher, who found the pocket, were high class courtesans at the Court of Charles II, however there are no verifiable records of that. The name Lucy Lockett first appears in The Beggars Opera written in 1728, giving rise to the idea that the name was well known and possibly notorious. Alternatively Kitty Fisher may have been the courtesan Catherine Mary Fisher, the subject of three unfinished paintings by Joshua Reynolds. She died in 1767. Her name also appears in a number of country dance songs.

* * *

## 29$^{th}$ May 2014

**Were the young Americans killed on Omaha Beach on D-Day conscripts or volunteers?**

In 1940 the American government introduced the Selective Service and Training Act, which was effectively conscription into the armed forces. It required all men between the ages of 21 and 45 to register for conscription. It was the third time conscription, otherwise known as the draft, had been used but the first time that it had been used in peace time.

Earlier drafts had been introduced during the American Civil War and again in World War I. Conscription was by lottery for service of one year. In 1941 this was extended for a further year and when America entered the Second World War following the attack on Pearl Harbour in December 1941 the period of service was further extended to the duration of hostilities.

Between 1941 and 1945, 50 million men were registered, 36 million were classified for service and 10 million were actually inducted into the armed forces. Like most of the soldiers in World War II the soldiers that assaulted Omaha and Utah beaches would have been mainly conscripts with a leavening of professional soldiers and men who had volunteered rather than wait to be drafted.

The casualties for D-Day were unexpectedly light compared to estimates. 2,499 casualties were sustained by the US airborne troops of which 238 died. There were only 197 casualties on Utah beach, with 60 of those listed as missing. Omaha beach suffered heavier casualty rates with about 2,000 casualties. The overall figures for American losses, which included aircrew, were 1,465 dead, 3,184 wounded, 1,928 missing and 26 captured. This figure doesn't include American units, such as Ranger battalions, who were attached to the British and Canadian forces. The figures for the missing are high because the sea claimed many bodies which were never recovered. By comparison the British and Canadians suffered about 3,600 casualties, which includes airborne forces and glider pilots.

Planning estimates for the assault suggested casualty rates of up to 10% of the forces engaged in the assault. With 156,000 personnel committed this suggested over 15,000 would be killed or wounded. The Allies actually lost more men in the two months of operations preparing the way for D-Day, some 12,000 casualties and 2,000 aircraft.

Unlike in many nations Americans were able to register as Conscientious Objectors (CO) providing they could prove that they were not simply trying to avoid the draft. Members of the Amish, Quaker and Mennonite communities and Church of the Brethren members were included in this category but members of all other religious groups were required to serve. During World War II 72,000 men registered as COs of which 52,000 applications were accepted. 25,000 of these men entered the military in non-combatant roles while another 12,000 served in labour camps as an alternative to military service. 6,000 COs were imprisoned because their claims were not considered to be legitimate.

The World War II conscription regime remained in force until 1973 but the last actual conscripts were inducted in 1972 for men born in 1952. Officially conscription still existed and draft priority numbers were issued for men born in 1953, 54 and 55 but were never used. In 1981 President Jimmy Carter issued a Presidential Proclamation requiring American men to once again register for the draft and this order is still in force today. However, no men have actually been conscripted since 1973.

* * *

## 16th May 2014

### What species of duck are Donald and Daffy?

Just as a dog is a species of mammal and a beagle is a breed of dog, ducks are a species of bird and Donald and Daffy are from different breeds of duck.

Donald Fauntleroy Duck, to give him his full name, first appeared in the Disney cartoon film The Little Wise Hen in 1934. He was voiced by Clarence Nash, who gave him his instantly recognisable speech patterns. It was his second outing, in The Orphan's Benefit playing opposite Mickey Mouse, that propelled him to personal stardom. He went on to appear in 130 films over the next two decades. Since then Donald has also featured in books and several TV series, with his nephews Huey, Dewey and Louis having spin off careers. He has a female counterpart, the sweet natured Daisy, as well a miserly uncle, Scrooge MacDuck. One of Donald's many personality traits is the enjoyment he gets from tormenting others, but he quickly loses his temper when the tables are turned on him.

As far as Donald's breed is concerned, his white plumage and yellow bill suggest that he is of domesticated farming stock. His long neck suggests the Aylesbury Duck, however his more uptight posture suggests that he might be either an Indian Runner Duck or an American Pekin Duck, the latter fitting in with his American birth. The American Pekin Duck was originally bred in China from the Mallard. In 1873 25 ducks were exported from China to America, of which only a handful survived the journey to New York's Long Island, a significant number of them having been eaten during the trip. For this reason they were also known as Long Island ducklings. From this start the breed progressed to the stage where they now produce 95% of all duck meat eaten in America.

The equally irascible Daffy Duck appeared four years after Donald, featuring in the Warner Brothers cartoon Porky's Duck Hunt in 1937, playing in a minor role opposite Porky Pig. He is the third most featured Warner cartoon character with 133 outings compared to Bugs Bunny's 166 and Porky Pig's 159. He was voiced by the ubiquitous Mel Blanc until 1989, the world record for a single character voice performance. Daffy was then voiced by five others over the years following Mel Blanc's death. Like Donald, Daffy went on to feature in films of his own and also in TV series.

In terms of his breed, Daffy's origins as a wild duck to be hunted by Porky Pig are harder to identify. The most likely breed is the American Black Duck. While the male does have a thin white collar, like Daffy, the rest of its plumage isn't black, as Daffy's is. It's more of a mottled brown. It breeds in the Great Lakes area of Canada and the USA as well as in the Adirondacks in New York State. The discrepancy in colour may be due to the fact that duck hunters usually see the ducks in the dim early morning light or in silhouette as they fly overhead, both of which will make them appear black rather than brown. The alternative is that he is a Coygana Duck, which breed in the Finger Lakes area of New York State. These ducks are black but don't have Daffy's distinctive white collar. Given the racial tensions of 1930s USA it is unlikely that Daffy is of mixed American/Coygana parentage.

\* \* \*

## 3rd July 2014

**Given that a major is higher in rank than a lieutenant, why does a lieutenant-general outrank a major-general?**

Prior to the English Civil War Britain didn't have a standing army. Armies were raised at need and officers were awarded commissions based on Royal patronage, or commissions were purchased from the Crown in the hope of turning a profit. A person awarded a commission was given the rank of Colonel, deriving from the Spanish Coronellos, or Crown Officers. He would then raise a body of men, known as a regiment, which usually took on the name of the Colonel. For example the first Colonel of the Scots Guards, raised in 1639, was the Marquis of Argyle so the regiment was originally known as Argyle's Regiment.

The Colonel would then appoint subordinate commanders known as Captains, which was derived from the Latin Capitainus, meaning head man or chief. These would each command a company of about 100 men within the regiment.

The term Lieutenant derives from the French words lieu and tenant, literally meaning 'place holding', so a lieutenant was someone who would hold the place of the Captain in their absence. Today we would call them a deputy. In this way we also got Lieutenant Colonels, who were deputies to Colonels and Lieutenant Generals who were deputies to the Generals who commanded whole armies.

The rank of Major derives from that of Sergeant. During the 17th century each Colonel would have an experienced Sergeant who was third in command of the regiment, below the Lieutenant Colonel but above Captains. To differentiate this Sergeant from the lower, non-commissioned rank this senior sergeant was known as the Sergeant Major. In the same way a General would appoint a Sergeant Major General to be third in command of his army, below the Lieutenant General. Over time the position became a commissioned one and the Sergeant prefix fell out of use so the ranks became Major and Major General.

In the 17th century Swedish King Gustavus Adolphous devised a tactical unit he called a Brigade, a mixed formation made up of infantry, cavalry and artillery, which was placed under the command of a Brigadier General. Over time the General suffix was dropped and the rank of Brigadier now sits between a Colonel and a Major General.

Today a Lieutenant Colonel commands a battalion within a regiment, with Majors as company commanders. Captains and Lieutenants command Platoons. A Brigadier still commands a Brigade while a Major General commands a Division of two or more Brigades. A Lieutenant General commands a Corps made up of two or more Divisions and a General commands an Army of two or more Corps. A Field Marshall commands an Army Group made up of two or more Armies. As Britain no longer has an army of that size the rank of Field Marshall is effectively defunct.

The term Sergeant Major came back into use in the late $18^{th}$ century and was awarded to Warrant Officers, senior Sergeants who were awarded a Royal Warrant rather than a commission. Today the Sergeant Major is the most senior non-commissioned officer in a Company or Battalion.

**Author's note:** This question has been asked on more than one occasion and I have submitted the same answer and had it published, on more than one occasion. Recycling isn't just for tin cans!

\* \* \*

## $15^{th}$ July 2014

### Who were the Buffalo Soldiers?

In his song Buffalo Soldier, Bob Marley says that the soldier was taken from Africa and was fighting for survival, and later in the song that the Buffalo Soldier won the war for America. In the first part he is obviously referring to the taking of slaves from Africa and the later words refer to their participation in the Indian (native American) wars caused by the westward expansion of the white settlers and their later service in other wars.

In 1866 legislation was passed in Congress to create six new regiments for the United States army made up entirely of African Americans, with the exception of the officers who would be white. These were drawn from both the northern and southern states and many had been slaves until the Union's victory over the Confederacy. Two of these regiments, the $9^{th}$ and $10^{th,}$ would be cavalry and four infantry, the $38^{th}$, $39^{th}$, $40^{th}$ and $41^{st}$ regiments. In 1868 the four infantry regiments were reorganised into two, the $24^{th}$ and $25^{th}$. Black soldiers enlisted for 5 years and earned $13 a month, far more than a black civilian could hope to earn at that time.

Previously African American army units, such as the 54th Massachusetts Volunteers, had been formed to serve during the American Civil War (1861-1865), but they had been disbanded on the cessation of hostiles and had never been known as Buffalo Soldiers.

Many white officers, including George Armstrong Custer, refused to command the black soldiers and were forced to take lower ranks as a consequence. Custer had been a Major General at the end of the Civil War but was serving in the rank of Lieutenant Colonel at the time of his death. Thanks to the award of an honorary title of Major General he was still able to call himself General but he wasn't paid as one.

The first African American units to be formed were the 9th and 10th Cavalry and their role was to protect the wagon trains of settlers who were travelling west in search of new lands. The units also helped with the building of the infrastructure, such as the telegraph system, that would further assist in the westward expansion. This service brought the units into conflict with those tribes of native Americans that fought against the expansion of the settlers.

The name Buffalo Soldier was bestowed on the cavalry units by the native Americans and there are three possible origins for it. The first is that the soldiers' thick curly hair reminded the Indians of the mane of the buffalo. The second is that their fierce bravery reminded the Indians of the way the buffaloes fought each other and the third because in winter the soldiers wore thick coats made of buffalo hide. No version is held to be the totally correct one. The name later became synonymous with all the African American units.

Over 200,000 African Americans served with the four regiments of the Buffalo Soldiers whose service continued until 1948, when the segregation of military units along racial lines was officially ended.

There is now an organisation named the Buffalo Soldiers of the American West which is a re-enactment group established by John Bell in 1986 to commemorate the role of the Buffalo Soldiers in the expansion of the USA.

\* \* \*

## 28th July 2014

**Assuming you're a warplane, not a civil aircraft, what defences might you have against the Russian Buk missile system?**

There are basically five types of missile guidance systems: wire guided, optical (visual) guidance, heat seeking, laser guided and radar guided. Satellite guidance is also used but this is just a variation of either radar or optical guidance. For each system there are some counter measures that can be adopted but with varying degrees of success.

Combat aircraft carry electronic countermeasures (ECM) pods which identify the threat type and deploy the appropriate counter measures.

The BUK-M1-2, or Beech, missile system is a self-propelled, radar guided system which was developed by the Soviet Union in the 1970s and came into operational service in 1979. In NATO it was allocated with the identifier of Gadfly to distinguish it from other Warsaw Pact missile types. It has been produced in several variants to keep its technology up to date. Most former Warsaw Pact countries were or are equipped with the system.

The radar has two elements carried on different vehicles, the acquisition radar which finds the target and the targeting radar which guides the missile. Each launch vehicle carries four missiles which have an effective altitude between 50 ft and 72,000 ft. Across flat terrain the radar can detect an aircraft flying at 300 ft at a range of 22 miles. The range is extended for each foot of altitude above 300 ft, limited only by the power of the radar.

The whole system is highly mobile. From coming to a halt it can be brought to a state of readiness in just five minutes and if needs be it can be dismantled and ready to move in another five minutes. In terms of reaction time it takes 22 seconds to launch the missile from the time the target is first detected.

The radar isn't capable of distinguishing between aircraft types, however the system is equipped with IFF (identification friend or foe) technology which detects radar transponder signals emitted by friendly aircraft, so the BUK system is also capable of detecting the transponders used by civilian aircraft to identify themselves.

Radar guidance uses airborne or ground based radar signals in a particular frequency spectrum to track the target and provide guidance signals to the missile. The ECM pod on the target aircraft detects the radar signal and sends out jamming signals to disrupt the targeting radar and the guidance signals.

Chaff may also be deployed to disrupt the radar. This is tiny lengths of metal foil which are expelled in a cloud and reflect the radar signals, swamping the radar with false traces. The system was developed during World War II when it was code named WINDOW. It's still in use with the RAF.

To counter the threat of jamming the radar stations often employ "agile" signalling, the rapid changing of frequency to prevent jamming, the counter measure for which is jamming across the whole frequency spectrum.

During the Vietnam War and the Cold War the USA used specialist "Wild Weasel" aircraft to provide ECM cover for whole attacking formations. These would fire radar seeking missiles at the ground radar installations to destroy them. This is a capability retained on modern day aircraft, however, in targeting terms it will always be a race between the launch of the radar seeking missiles and the launch of the ground to air missile.

Radar jamming, chaff and the use of anti-radar missiles are the only effective defences against the BUK weapons system, unless it can be targeted by ground fire from artillery or tanks.

The BUK Missile system is in use with the Ukrainian armed forces as well as with the Russian military. As with all military weaponry this system can't be purchased by anyone other than a sovereign nation, so if it is being used by the ethnic Russian insurgents in the Ukraine then it must have been provided by a friendly nation.

**Author's note:** In 2014 a BUK missile was used to shoot down Malaysian Airlines flight MH17 as it flew through Ukrainian airspace on route from Amsterdam to Kuala Lumpur. The Russians sought to blame the Ukrainians and the Ukrainians blamed the Russians. Forensic examination of the aircraft wreckage, delayed for several weeks by the intervention of Russian separatists, provided evidence to suggest that the missile was from a Russian owned BUK system. The theory is that the Russians intended to shoot down a Russian passenger aircraft and then blame the Ukrainians, in order to provide an excuse for increased military support for Russian separatists. However, an identification error resulted in flight MH17 being shot down instead.

\* \* \*

## 8th August 2014

**My mother, born in 1915, was given the first names St Margaret La Bassee by her father who served in France during World War I. Family folklore says she was named after St Margaret's Church in Folkestone, the town where her father embarked, and the town in France, La Bassee, where he saw**

**action. Are the Church and Town still around today? What action would my grandfather have seen in La Bassee?**

La Bassee is a small town in the Lille arrondissement (district) of the Nord-Pas-de-Calais region of France. After World War I it was re-built and today has a population of about 6,000. Apart from the Battle of La Bassee its main claim to fame is being the birthplace of the painter Louis-Leopold Boilly (1761-1845).

The Battle of La Bassee was one of the earliest of World War I, taking place in October 1914. It was part of the "Race to the sea", the attempt by both sides to outflank each other by capturing the coast of Belgium. The Germans captured the French town of Lille and attacked the British flank at Ypres. Beating the British back they captured the smaller towns of La Bassee and Neuve Chappelle.

The British did succeed in recapturing the town of Givenchy-en-Gohelle but failed to recapture La Bassee. With the arrival of the Lahore Division of the Indian Corps the British were able to keep the Germans at bay until November, when the focus shifted towards Ypres and fighting around La Bassee diminished. The British suffered about 16,000 casualties in the fighting compared to about 6,000 German casualties.

La Bassee was the site of a strategically important crossroads and also a canal. On $14^{th}$ and $15^{th}$ October the British II Corps attacked the canal on both sides of the town. The Germans counter attacked and the British advance stalled. Fighting continued in the area until $2^{nd}$ November but was never conclusive.

There is no record of a St Margaret's church, either Roman Catholic or Church of England, in the Folkestone area. There is a church by the name of St Margaret's of Antioch at St Margaret's-at-Cliffe, which is a holiday area situated between Dover and Folkestone and it is possible that troops waiting for their troopships may have been rested there before marching to the docks in Folkestone itself. It is also possible that it wasn't a church that the writer's mother was named after, but the St Margaret's Girls School in Folkestone which existed from the late 19<sup>th</sup> century until 1968. It occupied a number of premises in Folkestone over the years. Because of their large rooms, schools were often used as resting places for troops

The foundations of the church at St Margaret's-at Cliffe date back to Saxon times but the origins of the present church are Norman. Services are still held in the church at 10.00 am every Sunday.

If the writer's grandfather's regiment can be identified then the regimental war diary may be able to shed more light on the subject. War diaries are usually held in regimental museums, the National Army Museum in Chelsea or by the Imperial War Museum.

\* \* \*

**11<sup>th</sup> August 2014**

**In a TV programme about a small housing estate in Aberdeen, the term 'butt and ben' was frequently used. What does this mean?**

A butt and ben is a colloquial Scottish term for a two roomed cottage. It takes its name from the movement of the occupants from one room to another ("butt" meaning "here" and "ben" meaning "through there"), literally to move back and forth which, in a two roomed house, are the only options for movement between rooms. The two rooms comprised a bedroom and a family room come kitchen. The toilet facilities would be outside.

In the poorer areas of Scotland, other than in cities where tenements formed the mainstay of accommodation, the only affordable housing was a butt and ben and in rural areas they were the traditional homes of crofters and fishermen.

In more recent times refurbished butt and bens have become popular as holiday cottages.

Since 1936 the Scottish newspaper The Sunday Post has published a full page comic strip about an extended family called the Broons (Browns). They live in a tenement in the fictitious town of Kintore and holiday in a butt and ben situated somewhere in the Cairngorms. As there are 11 in the family it must be a bit of a tight squeeze and it must have been a relief when some of the younger members of the family started to holiday in Spain instead.

\* \* \*

### 29<sup>th</sup> September 2014

**What are the Americans referring to when they say 101, as in journalism 101, implying that something is very basic?**

This refers to the method of designating individual units of study, or courses, within a degree programme by subject content and level of academic rigour. It is used throughout the American Higher Education system and has also been used by our own Open University.

This system of numbering provides a simple shorthand for both students and university authorities rather than using long winded and sometimes arcane course titles.

The first digit of the course number indicates the degree of academic rigour required, starting with 1 which is entry level or first year study level, 2 for the next level of difficulty, then 3 and possibly 4.

The second digit normally indicates a specific discipline within a faculty, for example, differentiating between the different disciplines within the Social Sciences, such as Sociology, Psychology, Politics, Economics etc. The use of 0 would mean a broad based multi-discipline level of study in the subject.

The final digit is the version of the course that is in current use, as courses undergo revision and rewriting as the academic understanding of the subject evolves. The use of the 1 in the analogy suggests the first version of the course to be taught.

This gives rise to the Journalism 101 (or other) analogy as it would be the first version of an entry level broad based course of study within the journalism curriculum. Another way of saying this would be 'Day 1, Lesson 1 of journalism', but of course that would take longer to say.

Each course that is studied is worth a number of 'credits' or points which are awarded on satisfactory completion and students who amass the required number of credits are awarded a certificate, diploma, degree or honours degree on that basis. There is also a requirement to earn a number of credits at each level of study so that a student can't graduate just by studying at entry level.

In order to obtain my own Honours Degree with the Open University I studied T101, T291, TM222, T244, D102, DSE202 E206, D307 and D309. The T indicates a technology course while the D was used by the Social Sciences faculty and the E by the Education faculty. M indicates mathematics, S sciences, and A arts. Courses with more than one initial letter indicate that they include course content from more than one faculty, as with DSE202 which included the study of psychology, sciences and education. As can be seen from my list of credits I switched disciplines part way through my course of studies.

The Open University has revamped its course numbering system in recent years though the basic principles remain in place. Post Graduate course numbers start with a higher digit. Studying for an MBA would mean studying courses that that start with the number 8.

\* \* \*

7$^{th}$ October 2014

**What's the difference between the deficit and the national debt?**

The simplest way to think of this is that the fiscal deficit, to give it its full title, is the government's overdraft while the national debt is the government's long term bank loan.

It costs money to run a country, everything from the wages of the MPs and civil servants through to the cutting of grass around a hospital building must be paid for by the public through the levying of taxes. There are several forms of taxation but the two biggest are income tax and VAT. No one living in this country can escape paying one or the other and generally both, though some people do try.

If a government manages its spending in such a way as to have a little of its tax income left in the bank at the end of the year then it is said to run a fiscal surplus which can be used to pay off some of the national debt. If the government overspends then it is running a fiscal deficit. Any deficit remaining at the end of the year is transferred to the national debt which increases the size of the bank loan that the country has.

Tracking the fiscal surplus or deficit and the national debt over a period of time is a simple way to assess how responsibly a government has managed the public finances. For example, the Labour Party claim that the fiscal deficit and national debt that they left behind in 2010 was all the result of the banking crisis, but is this true?

In 1997 the budget was just about in balance and actually ran into a small surplus in 1998 and 99 as Gordon Brown stuck to his promise to adhere to Tory spending plans for his first two years in office. This was actually a false promise that was also made by George Osborne in 2010 and is now being made by Ed Balls. The government financial planning cycle runs over a three year period so that spending plans are pretty much set in stone for the two years following a general election and changing them is very difficult to do. Gordon Brown, George Osborne and Ed balls have little choice about whether or not they adhere to the spending plans of their predecessors.

By 2007, when the banking crisis started, the deficit was already running at £35 billion. For roughly seven years Gordon Brown had been spending more money than he had been collecting in taxes. Over the next three years this deficit ballooned to £156 billion.

Over the same period the national debt also rose considerably, as the overdraft was added to the bank loan at the end of each year. In 1997 it was approximately £350 billion. By 2007, pre banking crisis, it was approximately £500 billion and by 2010 it was approximately £750 billion. The rise from 2007 onwards wasn't directly due to bailing out the banks. That only cost about £65 billion. The rest is down to direct government spending. In other words, with different fiscal policies, it could have been avoided.

In contrast, what has happened between 2010 and the present? The tightening of controls on government spending, known as austerity measures, over the last 4½ years means the deficit is forecast to reduce to about £96 billion by the end of the current financial year. The national debt, however, has risen steadily as the deficit is added in each year and now stands at about £1,400 billion or £1.4 trillion. That is about 70% of Gross Domestic Product (GDP). If the debt gets to 100% of GDP then the nation is effectively bankrupt. This is what happened in Greece.

The national debt can't be reduced until there is a fiscal surplus that can be used to start paying it back. In the meantime, estimating the interest on that loan at 4% per annum, it is costing the taxpayer approximately £56 billion per year in interest. By 2018, when George Osborne hopes to have balanced the budget, the nation will have paid a further £166 billion in interest, more than 1½ times the budget for running the NHS for a year.

When deciding which way to vote at the next election it is critical that we all pay close attention to what the competing parties tell us about what they intend to do about the fiscal deficit if we wish to avoid going the way of Greece. It could still happen.

**Author's note:** Editing this in 2018, Phillip Hammond is now Chancellor, not George Osborne. I checked where we are with the deficit and debt. The deficit for 2018 is forecast to be approximately £37 billion, while the national debt is currently around £1.78 trillion. While government has announced that "austerity" is officially over, many people are still feeling the pinch.

\* \* \*

## 13th November 2014

**I served with the Royal Air Force in Aden from January 1966 to November 1967 and was awarded the General Service Medal. Unfortunately it has gone missing. Can I get a replacement?**

Once medals have been awarded it is expected that the recipient take great care of them. The Ministry of Defence website states that they are expected to be treasured possessions as they have been awarded by the sovereign.

There are circumstances under which medals will be replaced, but only if the loss was beyond the reasonable control of the recipient, such as theft or a disaster such as a house fire.

While travelling to Dieppe for a reunion a few years ago my father passed through Brighton railway station and had his luggage stolen, inside of which were his medals. These had been awarded for campaign service throughout World War II and afterwards. The MoD did replace them, however, unlike the originals they didn't have his name inscribed on them.

Anyone wishing to replace medals lost under circumstances beyond their control should write to the MoD Medals Office,

Innsworth House, Imjin Barracks, Gloucester, GL3 1HW. A copy of the police report covering their loss, plus details on the military service for which they were awarded, must be included.

The MoD Medal Office doesn't hold vast stocks of medals so some may not be replaceable, though most of those issued during World War II and afterwards are still being manufactured in small quantities by The Royal Mint. Replacement medals are marked as such so as to avoid confusion with the originals, should they be recovered. For medals lost under other circumstances the MoD recommends approaching reputable commercial dealers to replace them.

Because replacement medals are being manufactured in the present its probable that those sold by medal dealers will be more 'authentic' than replacement medals.

**Author's note:** I was delighted when, in 2019, I was contacted by a collector of military memorabilia connected to the Middlesex Regiment, my father's regiment, to say that he had purchased my father's medals at auction (through a reputable dealer). He offered them to me for the purchase price, which I was pleased to pay. I also included my father's replacement medals as part of the deal. He had tracked me down through "social media", proof that not everything about the internet is bad.

\* \* \*

## 14th November 2014

In the Royal Navy, we had nicknames for other Forces. Many were self-explanatory, others less so, such as the Fleet Air Arm being known as 'Wafoos', our Army friends were 'Pongoes', Marines were 'Bootnecks' and we called the RAF 'Crabfats'. Does anyone know the origin of these?

All three armed services create slang terms for each other, some less than complementary. For us in the RAF sailors were 'Fish Heads' and an aircraft carrier was a 'Banana boat'.

The origin of 'Wafoo' is believed to be derived from the acronym WAFU meaning weapons and fuel users. In other words they consumed more resources than they could justify. Given the record of naval aviation in its early days this may have been true, but of course the Fleet Air Arm more than justified its existence in later years. There is another version of the acronym which is not fit to print in a daily newspaper.

The term 'Bootneck' for the Royal Marines derives from the high leather stock worn around the neck during the late 18th and early 19th centuries. It was worn by the army as well as marines to hold the head at a suitably military bearing while on parade and it resembled the top of a leather boot, hence the name. While the stock itself went out of service for most regiments during the Napoleonic Wars the slang stuck on board ships where relations between sailors and marines were sometimes strained.

The term 'Pongoes' as slang for the army originates in 19th century music hall. It was used by comedians to get a cheap laugh. With large numbers of draft animals and the need to dig open latrines, armies in the field had a certain odour about them. Off duty soldiers wore uniform during the 19th century, making them easy to pick out from the music hall stage to become the butt of a comedia'ns joke. Typically the unlucky soldier was singled out and the audience were told "wherever the army goes, the pong goes." No doubt the Royal Navy were delighted to latch on to that one and I also remember it from my days in the RAF.

The term 'Crabfats' is probably an extension of the original, 'crabs'. Crabfat was the nickname of an ointment used to treat pubic lice. However, the original use of the term crabs to refer to the RAF doesn't relate to the louse. It is suggested that when a member of the RAF was asked a question they always shrugged their shoulders and shuffled off sideways, like a crab.

The more likely explanation is that the term stems from the way that aircraft sometimes seem to 'crab' across the sky, appearing to move diagonally in order to compensate for strong cross winds, especially when landing. The Royal Navy wouldn't have the same problem as they could position an aircraft carrier so that it was always steaming 'head on' to the wind when aircraft were landing.

The Royal Navy appears to have introduced more slang words than any of the other services and listening in on a conversation between sailors was sometimes like listening to a foreign language being spoken.

**Author's note:** the alternative origin for the slang term WAFU was "wet and all fucked up."

\* \* \*

## 18<sup>th</sup> November 2014

**In the Just William stories, William is hugely embarrassed at being forced to join a Band of Hope meeting. Was the Band of Hope a genuine organisation?**

Not only did the Band of Hope exist, but it still does, though under a new name.

It was inspired by the Rev Jabez Tunncliff, a Baptist minister in Leeds who, in 1847, was disturbed by the tragically young death of a parishioner caused by alcohol abuse. As a consequence Tuncliff and a handful of other believers in abstinence formed the Band of Hope. This became a national organisation in 1855 with branches being established throughout the country.

At the time the drinking of hard liquor was seen as almost a necessity, alongside food and water, partly due to the poor quality of drinking water which was still the source of major epidemics at the time. The water content of alcoholic drinks such as beer and gin had been boiled which killed harmful bacteria. Alternatives such as tea and coffee were largely out of the reach of the poor, while alcohol was relatively cheap. Brewers and distillers actively promoted their beverages as being better for the consumer than water.

The Band of Hope concentrated its efforts on children's activities in the hope of encouraging them to swear off the demon drink before they became adults, though there was little age restriction on the purchase of alcohol at the time. They were the originators of the term 'tea total'. The particular innovation they introduced was 'signing the pledge', a written promise not to partake of alcohol. By 1935 the movement had over 3 million members. In 1935 the UK population was about 46 million so about 6% of the population had signed the pledge, which doesn't include other organisations such as The Salvation Army or other temperance movements.

However, cultural changes led to the demise of the Band of Hope and it transformed into Hope UK and today is more involved in the training of children's social workers in a number of different fields, but particularly in the fields of alcohol and drug abuse and rehabilitation.

Just William, the first by Richmal Crompton, was published in 1922 so the Band of Hope would have been a significant social movement of her time. She died in 1969 and her last William story was published a year after her death. She wrote 41 William books and 7 William plays, as well as 53 children's short stories and books on other themes. Although having a keen eye for the quirky imagination and behaviour of young boys, Crompton never married or had children of her own.

* * *

18<sup>th</sup> November 2014

**Why did Paraguay embark on a near suicidal war against all its neighbours in the mid-19<sup>th</sup> century?**

The Paraguayan War, also known as the War Of The Triple Alliance, was fought between 1864 and 1870 with Paraguay on the one side and Brazil, Argentina and Uruguay on the other.

Its precise cause is vague, with several possible causes being cited, including British expansionism in South America. However, the most likely cause was the combination of the collapse of Portugese and Spanish colonial rule and the ambitions of the Paraguayan President of the day, Francisco Solano Lopez.

The Lopez family had been dominant in Paraguayan politics since 1841 and Solano Lopez was keen to establish Paraguayan dominance along the River Plate. They had more or less isolated themselves from their neighbours, strictly controlled the export of goods and charged high import tariffs on foreign goods, leading to constant trade disputes.

Both Brazil and Argentina had struggled to gain control over the River Plate and its estuary so Paraguay's expansionist policies were seen as a direct threat. Solano Lopez involved himself in Uruguayan politics siding with the ruling National Party, while Brazil and Argentina allied themselves with the opposition Colorado Party. Solano Lopez broke diplomatic relations with Brazil and Argentina and warned that any incursion by Brazilian troops into Uruguay would be seen as an act of war. Brazil had been fighting skirmishes on the border with Uruguayan gaucho famers in areas where control was disputed. Brazilian troops mounted a full scale invasion on 12<sup>th</sup> October 1864 to start the war, though a formal declaration wasn't made by Paraguay until 13<sup>th</sup> December.

A lot of the early conflict focused on maritime battles along the River Plate, which was Paraguay's lifeline to the sea. Whoever controlled the estuary controlled the flow of goods and weapons, into Paraguay. The war see-sawed back and forth for three years until the combined forces of Argentina and Brazil were able to gain the upper hand. They affected a land borne invasion of Paraguay, forcing them into fighting a guerrilla war which went on until the death of Solano Lopez on 1st March 1870.

It took decades for Paraguay to recover and the civilian population suffered considerably through food shortages and disease. Final Paraguayan casualties are unknown but estimates of casualty levels suggest as many as 90% of the male population were killed of which 150,000 were troops. Estimates of alliance casualties suggest 200,000 Brazilians, 3,000 Uruguayans and 30,000 Argentinians died.

As a consequence of the war Paraguay's boundaries were redrawn, losing them over 154,000 sq km to Argentina and Brazil. The country suffered very poor economic development for most of the rest of the 19th century. In Brazil the army became a significant political force, effectively ending the reign of Emperor Pedro II. In return for service in the army slaves were freed by their owners, which started the gradual move towards the ending of slavery in Brazil which came about in 1880.

\* \* \*

28th November 2014

**How did the German Worker's National Socialist (ie Nazi) Party come to be viewed as far right? Surely if they were Socialist they were Left-wing? Where did the idea of Left and Right-wing politics come from?**

The terms Left and Right to describe political positions originated in France at the time of the French Revolution when the members of the National Assembly split into supporters of the King and supporters of the revolution, thus dividing into clear parties. Those supporting the King stood to the right of the President of the Assembly and those of the revolution to his left. It was a significant declaration of political interest which hadn't existed up until then.

Since then the political stances have traditionally been those of change and revolution being Left wing and those of stability and order being Right wing. Those who adopt less extreme standpoints are said to be in the centre and the term Centrist is used to describe them. There are even sub divisions of Centre Left and Centre Right to indicate that while there may be a bias in one direction there isn't support for the more extreme views suggested by the terms Left and Right.

Taking that concept into the 19$^{th}$ and 20$^{th}$ centuries it's is easy to see how communism, with an emphasis on the overthrow of existing regimes, came to be seen as Left wing while totalitarian regimes, such as the Nazi's, were seen as Right wing. There is no doubt that the Nazi's stood very much for order and any attempt at dissent was treated harshly.

The fact that the title of the Nazi party included the term 'socialist' doesn't mean they believed in Socialism. In this context the term meant that the party was driven by what the party's founders perceived to be the interests of the people, not those of the establishment. Of course as the party developed and grew the needs of the people became less and less influential on party policy as the central figures took total control.

There was an element of social reform built into the Nazi party manifesto. Article 7 of the Nazi Party declaration of 1920 states 'We demand that the State shall above all undertake to ensure that every citizen shall have the possibility of living decently and earning a livelihood.' Unfortunately it then goes on to demand that 'aliens' (non-Germans) be expelled to allow the fulfilment of that article.

Article 9 states that all Germans have equal rights and duties. In article 14 there is a demand for profit sharing from industry.

While those requirements may appear socialist in nature many of the other requirements in the 25 point declaration are far more totalitarian, in particular those relating to nationality and 'Germaness'. Article 4 of the declaration states that Germans can only be of pure blood. Therefore Jews cannot be German. Article 5 then goes on to say that anyone who is not 'German' can only live in the country as a guest. This was the excuse used for shipping millions of Jews eastwards to their ultimate death. Article 8 demanded the forced repatriation of immigrants. None of those demands would fit well with Socialism, which believes in pan-national egalitarianism.

With regard to income, article 10 demands that all income must be derived from work, so Article 11 demands that all income not derived from work (including welfare income) be removed. Only the old age pension was excluded from that requirement. The declaration is very much in favour of small business ownership, but demands the break-up of large businesses so that small businesses can flourish. True socialism, on the other hand, favours state ownership of business and this was put into practice with the nationalisation of a number of industries by the post War Labour government in Britain.

In the title of the National Worker's Socialist Party the emphasis was very much on the Nationalist part of the name and far less on the Socialist.

\* \* \*

## 23rd December 2014
**Did cannonballs explode as they do in The Pirates Of The Caribbean films?**

Although the exploding shell was in use at the time in which the Pirates of The Caribbean films are set it is unlikely that they would have been used in naval warfare.

The purpose of the exploding shell is to maximise casualties by spreading shrapnel, fragments of hot metal, around the battle field. A solid shot doesn't do that. The original exploding shells were fired over walls to land in the streets of a fortress or town. The fuse would then burn out and the shell exploded, the purpose being to kill the defenders rather than to damage the walls.

The first recorded use of a fused, exploding shell was at the Siege of Wachtendonk in 1588. The term 'shrapnel' originates from Lieutenant Harry Shrapnel, a British army officer who invented an exploding shell for use by the British in 1784. This type of shell was designed to explode in mid-air, propelling its load of 'shrapnel' down into the enemy ranks. This is the earliest date at which such shells would have come into common use and is somewhat after the period depicted for most pirate epics.

The golden age of piracy is considered to be between 1690 and 1730, with most Caribbean piracy starting to die out after that as the colonial powers gained more control over the seas around their new territories, although there are records of piracy continuing in the region into the 19th century. Although no precise date is given for the "Pirates of the Caribbean" films, the style of clothing depicted fits with the generally accepted hay-day of the pirates.

Solid artillery shot were originally made from stone and later from cast metal, usually iron. Their purpose was to batter at a defence until it crumbled. Artillery was primarily a siege weapon used to bring down walls. The use of solid shot on the battlefield was of secondary importance as it might take out a file of men or a horse but little else, making it very inefficient. Heavy artillery was used much more as a demoralising agent, chipping away at formations of soldiers from a distance. For battlefield use the preferred ordnance was 'case shot'. This was a container filled with musket balls which split open as it left the muzzle of the gun. Working in a similar way to the modern shot gun cartridge the shot would spread out causing multiple casualties. However, the use of case shot reduced the effective range of the guns which led to the introduction of Horse Artillery to get the guns closer to the enemy.

In naval warfare the aim is to disable the enemy ship as quickly as possible and the exploding shells available at the time wouldn't have achieved that. Exploding shot are fired in a high arc to explode above the target so that they can spread their shrapnel. There has to be a guaranteed level of accuracy so that the shell explodes at the correct time and the correct place and that can't be achieved from the deck of a rolling ship. Even today the accuracy of gunnery has to be controlled by computers to compensate for the ship's movement.

Solid shot were used in order to try to hole the ship's hull near the waterline so it would start to take on water. Alternatively 'chain shot' might be used, two projectiles joined by a length of chain intended to carry away masts and rigging and prevent the ship from manoeuvring. The small swivel mounted guns that are often seen at the front of the quarter deck would be loaded with 'grape shot', handfuls of musket balls that worked in the same way as case shot and would be used to repel boarders.

If a commander wanted to set fire to an attacking ship they might use heated shot. The round shot would be put into a forge until it was glowing red hot and would then be inserted into the barrel of the gun. A wet rag would be used to insulate the shot from the gunpowder, preventing it from prematurely setting off the propellant charge. This was often used by shore batteries to repel an invading ship or ships, though it was also used in sea engagements. If a heated shot were to penetrate the gunpowder magazine it would set off a devastating explosion, but in ships that contained a lot of tarred ropes and dry canvass sails it would be more likely to start fires, which the sailors had to extinguish, distracting them from fighting duties.

Impact fused high explosive shells, which explode on contact with a hard surface, didn't come into being until about 1870. Unfortunately neither round shot nor chain shot caused the sorts of explosions beloved of Hollywood directors so they have used some poetic licence.

**Author's note:** Exploding shells form the core of several questions I have answered for some reason, and the answer is always pretty much the same. The siege of Wachtendonk has featured many times in the column, as has Lieutenant Harry Shrapnel.

\* \* \*

## 9th January 2015

**Could Robin Hode of Wakefield, a 14th century supporter of Thomas, Earl of Lancaster, be the real Robin Hood?**

Apart, perhaps, from King Arthur there is no figure in English legend about whose identity there has been so much speculation as Robin Hood or Hode. There are many candidates for the name, as well as variations such as Robyn and Robert. Unfortunately the names Robert and Hood and their variants were quite common, so proving that any one of that name was the legendary figure is fraught with problems.

Although film and TV have placed Robin Hood firmly in the times of King Richard the Lionheart he first makes his historical appearance during the rule of Richard's Great Great Nephew, Edward II. There was a rebellion against him led by the Duke of Lancaster and the first stories of an outlaw by the name of Robin Hood appear at that time.

In a ballad called A Gest of Robyn Hode a "comely King" named Edward meets and pardons an outlaw by the name of Robyn Hode and he enters the King's service. Robyn later becomes bored and returns to his outlaw life. The King is believed to be Edward II.

Research by a 19th century clergyman by the name of Joseph Hunter identifies a Robyn Hode in the service of Edward II in 1323-24 and he was in the right place at the right time to match with the ballad.

Hunter then speculates that this was the same Robert Hood who had been a tenant in Wakefield who is mentioned in 1316-17. Wakefield is only 10 miles from Barnesdale which has strong connections with the Robin Hood legend. Robert's wife is Matilda which is given as the real name of Maid Marion according to two Elizabethan plays.

The final "proof" is the suggestion that Robert of Wakefield became involved in the rebellion against Edward, which could have led to him becoming an outlaw. If so then the King is supposed to have pardoned Robert during a visit to Nottingham in 1323. However, there is no proof that Robyn and Robert were the same person or that either had been involved in the rebellion. Robyn Hode was already in the King's service in 1323 and therefore couldn't have been pardoned by him at the same time.

There are other candidates for the title of Robin Hood. The records for the Yorkshire Assize of 1225-26 mention a Robin Hood, fugitive, and records his chattels. The same outlaw turns up in later years under the nickname of Hobbehod and also Robert of Wetherby, the hunting down of whom cost a total of 68 shillings, plus another 2 shillings for a chain on which to hang his body. Although all this took place in Yorkshire, because of his connections to Nottingham Eustace of Lowdham, captor of Robert, might have been known as the Sherriff of Nottingham. He had actually held the post of Deputy Sherriff of the county.

Even the village or Manor of Loxley is not a known quantity. It has been placed in Yorkshire, where it might be associated once again with Barnesdale, but may also refer to Loxley in Warwickshire. There never was a Loxley in Nottinghamshire. The first references to Loxley don't appear until about 1600. As it was mediaeval practice to associate the names of people with their residences, as with Robert of Wetherby, the name of Loxley would have been expected to have emerged much earlier.

In the 16th century Robin is elevated to the rank of Earl before being outlawed. The real Earls of Huntingdon were very wealthy and influential and were directly related to the Kings of Scotland. This element of the story emanates from a play by Anthony Munday written in 1599. The play allies the outlawed Earl with Richard I against his brother John.

There are a number of other candidates for recognition as the real Robin Hood, some stronger than others. It is also possible that the real Robin Hood (if he existed) was actually known by another name or may even have been an amalgamation of several real people. There are so many legends surrounding this character that it's almost impossible to identify a definitive truth.

**Author's note:** I have recently discovered a new novel about Robin Hode (or Hood). Anyone interested in reading about Robin Hode the villain, might like to try "Outlaw" by Robin Saint.

\* \* \*

## 10th January 2015

**Why, in 1956, did a Vulcan bomber crash at London Airport killing four aircrew?**

Vulcan bomber XV897 was on a round the world flag waving trip when it crashed in bad weather at London Heathrow Airport on 1st October 1956. Because of the nature of the flight Heathrow was selected as the arrival airfield rather than a military airfield. The aircraft was the first of its type to enter RAF service and the first to crash.

Although Heathrow was already a busy international airport by 1956 it wasn't unusual for military flights to use it.

The Captain and pilot of the aircraft was Squadron Leader (Sqn Ldr) D. R. Howard and the co-pilot no less a figure than the head of Bomber Command, Air Marshall Sir Harry Broadhurst. The rest of the crew were Sqn Ldr Stroud, Sqn Ldr Eames, Sqn Ldr Gamble and a representative of the aircraft's manufacturer, Avro, Mr Bassett. The ranks of the crew members give some indication of the prestige nature of the exercise. Far more junior crew members, including NCO Aircrew, would be normal.

After visiting Australia and New Zeeland the aircraft had left RAF Khormaksar, Aden, at 02.30 hrs GMT and made a routine flight to the UK on the last leg of its trip. The Captain had been given a weather forecast for Heathrow and possible diversion airfields before departure and these were updated en-route, the last update being given as the aircraft passed over Epsom. The aircraft had ample fuel to divert if necessary.

The Captain decided to make landing attempt at Heathrow, which he started at about 10.04, setting a "break-off" height of 300 ft should he decide that the weather was unsuitable to continue the attempt. He was "talked down" using the Ground Controlled Approach (GCA) radar system which was typical of the technology of the era.

For some reason altitude information from the "talk down" was inaccurate after the aircraft had reached a distance of about ¾ of a mile from touchdown. With altimeters becoming less accurate as they got closer to the ground and the weather at its worst an error was made which resulted in the aircraft hitting the ground prematurely damaging the undercarriage and the trailing edge of the wings. It bounced back to a height of about 200-300 ft where it was found that control had been lost because of the damage.

The Captain ordered the aircraft be abandoned before using his own ejector seat. Air Marshall Broadhurst also ejected. Both survived. The remainder of the crew and the passenger were unable escape before the nose and starboard wing of the aircraft tilted down and the aircraft crashed and burst into flames. All four were killed. At this time there were no ejector seats fitted for the use of the "back seat" crew.

It emerged that the GCA controller had advised the pilot that he was 80 ft above ground but not that he was below the correct glide path and therefore in danger of touching down prematurely. This no doubt contributed to the crash, but it has to be recognised that the pilot had ignored his own "break-off" height for a poor visibility landing. The crash was therefore avoidable.

There have been allegations made that Air Marshall Broadhurst overrode three radio instructions from Bomber Command HQ to divert to another airfield with better weather conditions and that this was concealed to prevent embarrassment to such a senior officer. However, these allegations have never been investigated.

**Author's note:** The Vulcan was a marvellous aircraft with an excellent safety record. The story around this is an interesting one and there are several sources on the internet that claim to be eye witnesses who insist that the aircraft was ordered to divert to another airfield, but that the order was ignored or over-ruled. I doubt, however, that the truth will ever be known now that the significant participants are all dead.

\* \* \*

**12<sup>th</sup> January 2015**

**What became of Maglev, which was supposed to revolutionise rail travel?**

The word maglev is derived from "magnetic levitation" ie the use of the properties of magnets that make similar poles repel and can therefore "levitate" an object. By reversing the polarity in neighbouring pairs of electro-magnets to make them attract or repel it is then possible to make a vehicle move forwards or backwards. This is known as a "linear motor". Because of the lack of friction between the vehicle and the surface over which it travels exceptionally high speeds can, in theory, be achieved. However, at low speeds this is countered by the high energy input required to make the vehicle levitate in the first instance, up to 15% of the total power consumption.

The first patent for a linear motor propelled train was granted in the USA to German inventor Alfred Zehden on 14th February 1905, so this technology is far from new. However, its development into operating trains has been a bumpy ride, even if the trains themselves run smoothly.

The first full size working model of a linear motor was developed in the 1940s by Eric Laithwaite, a Professor of Engineering at Imperial College, London. Several demonstration models were developed after that and appeared at international exhibitions.

The first commercial linear motor powered train was introduced in 1984 on a 600m long track between Birmingham International Railway Station and Birmingham International Airport. Problems with reliability resulted in it ceasing operations in 1995. Its cars are on display in railway museums in Peterborough and York. The current system in use at Birmingham Airport is known as Skyrail and was opened in 2003 using cable and winch technology with load bearing wheels in full contact with the track, which was built on top of the old maglev track.

Perhaps the best known linear motor trains are in use in Japan, operated by Japan Airlines and the Central Japan Railway Company. This latter train, the JNL ML500, set a world record speed of 517kph (321 mph). The current speed record stands at 581 kph (361 mph) set in Japan by an experimental model MLX01.

Part of the problem with maglev trains is that they can't operate on existing track, which means they require brand new infrastructure which requires very high levels of investment. This has encouraged rail companies to concentrate on developing faster conventional trains, such as the French Train à Grand Vittesse (TGV), the Eurostar and the Harmony CRH380A, the world's second fastest train which operates on the Shanghai-Hangzhou intercity line at speeds of 380 kph (237 mph). The world's fastest commercial train is the Shanghai Maglev. Some of the latest experimental conventional trains have been able to attain speeds close to that of the record setting Japanese JNR ML500.

There are currently three maglev train systems in commercial operation. The Shanghai Maglev system operates 115 daily trips along a 19 mile track, covering the distance in 7 minutes. The Linimo system operates along the 5.6 mile Tobu-kyuryo track in Japan. In South Korea a domestically developed model operates in Daejeon along a 0.62 mile track between the Expo Park and the National Science Museum.

There are currently six maglev systems of varying designs and lengths being built: in Georgia, USA; Beijing; Changsha, China; Tokyo; Tel Aviv and Incheon Airport in South Korea.

A number of maglev systems have been proposed for Australia, China, Italy, UK and USA, but with varying levels of support many of these (the2005 UK proposal to connect London to Glasgow, for example) may never come to fruition.

* * *

**28th January 2015**

**In the first episode of Wolf Hall, Thomas Cromwell arrived home to find his wife and daughters had died of a fever which appears to have killed them in a few hours. Is this based on fact? What would this illness have been?**

Elizabeth Wykes, wife of Thomas Cromwell, was the daughter of a shearman (a cutter of cloth) and she was the widow of Thomas Williams, a Yeoman of the Guard. Thomas and Elizabeth were married in 1515 and had three children: Gregory, Ann and Grace.

Elizabeth died in 1528 during an outbreak of "sweating sickness" which was known to be capable of killing its victims within hours. Ann and Grace didn't survive to adulthood, however the cause and dates of their deaths are unknown. Cromwell had yet to start his climb to power and so attracted little attention from historians of the day, however it is believed that the two girls didn't survive long after their mother. It is likely that either author Hilary Mantel or the makers of the TV drama Wolf Hall have used a little bit of poetic licence to place all three deaths on the same day.

Sweating sickness was common in Britain between 1485 and 1551, though little is actually known about it. The disease is associated with the arrival in Britain of Henry Tudor when he returned to challenge Richard III for the throne, though there is no evidence that it was present in his troops when they landed at Milford Haven. Henry arrived in London on 28th August 1485 and the first recorded outbreak of the disease in the city was on 19th September. The disease is blamed for the death, in 1502, of Arthur Prince of Wales, the elder brother of Henry VIII.

It has been suggested that sweating sickness originated in the Americas, but as Christopher Columbus didn't set sail until 7 years after the first outbreak this would seem to be a red herring.

Over the first half of the 16$^{th}$ century the disease spread widely across England, Wales and Ireland, but failed to reach Scotland. At that time Henry VIII was expanding English rule in Ireland, but there was little direct involvement with Scotland, save for the short war against James IV won on Henry's behalf by Catherine of Aragon at the Battle of Flodden. Henry himself was campaigning in France at the time.

After a few outbreaks in Europe the disease disappeared without trace in 1551, never to reappear. Gregory Cromwell survived his father's political downfall and execution, was created 1$^{st}$ Baron Cromwell of Rutland and married Elizabeth Seymour to become brother-in-law to Henry VIII. He too died of the sweating sickness during its last outbreak.

The disease has similarities to the Picardy Sweat, which had outbreaks in France between 1718 and 1918. An outbreak in 1906 was subject to in depth study and attributed to either fleas or field mice but this theory remains unproven. Poor sanitation is just as likely a cause.

There are many similarities between sweating sickness and hantavirus pulmonary syndrome which is one variety of the hantavirus, others are known as Black Greek Canal virus, New York virus and Sio Nombre virus, all named after the places where outbreaks occurred. Symptoms include fever, cough, myalgia, headache, lethargy and shortness-of-breath which leads ultimately to respiratory failure. There is no medical cure for the virus and survival depends on patients having their breathing assisted by ventilators. Early recognition of the symptoms gives the best chance of survival.

Given the random nature of its spread it doesn't appear that sweating sickness could be passed directly from an infected person to someone else, which makes it unlike influenza and many other viruses. If Ann and Grace died from sweating sickness then it's probable that they didn't catch it from their mother.

**Author's note**: Having recently read Wolf hall myself, Hilary mantel makes it clear that Cromwell's daughters survived the initial outbreak of the "sweating sickness" and lived for several more weeks, though they did eventually died together on the same day.

\* \* \*

## 30th January 2015

**What is the origin of the term 'barnstorming', sometimes used to describe rugby players making line-breaking runs?**

The earliest reference to barnstorming is in political campaigning in rural America. With public meeting halls being in short supply political candidates would often use a farmer's field to hold their hustings. If the weather turned inclement, such as a storm breaking, the farmer might allow the meeting to be moved into his barn, hence barnstorming. There is also a connection to groups of travelling actors putting on performances using country barns in lieu of theatres.

However, the term rose to wider prominence with the advent of air shows put on by pilots in the wake of World War I. Pilots would move from town to town offering aeroplane rides and then putting on shows, performing aerial stunts that had never been seen before. In some cases more than one aircraft would be involved and these became the original flying circuses.

How the term transferred from politics to air displays isn't clear, but with the pilots using farmer's fields to take off and land and using barns for overnight parking of the aircraft, as well as a place for the pilot to sleep if he couldn't afford to stay in a hotel, the connection can be made.

Early aircraft pioneers such as the Wright brothers and Glenn Curtiss put on the first air displays to demonstrate their new machines, but the real phenomenon didn't start until the 1920s, with many out of work former World War I pilots and the government selling off large numbers of training aircraft left over from the war, notably the Curtiss JN-4s, known as Jennys. An Army surplus Jenny originally costing $5,000 could be bought for as little as $200. There was also a rapid expansion in aircraft production with many small companies springing up, which introduced stiff competition into the market.

However, custom didn't expand as quickly as manufacturing and many aircraft were limited in use to mail carrying, barnstorming and smuggling, with pilots often drifting back and forth between the three occupations.

In order to continue to attract crowds, barnstormers had to develop ever more dangerous tricks, including wing walking. The more skilled and daring barnstormers became household names, attracted big crowds and also aggressive competition between pilots. This increased the level of accidents and the American government was forced to intervene and regulate the industry.

The new regulatory standards that barnstormers were required to meet were uneconomical for most of them and the industry began to decline towards the end of the 1920s, but there are records of shows continuing until 1941, when America entered the Second World War.

Barnstorming has featured in a number of books and films, such as "Those Magnificent Men In Their Flying Machines" and "The Great Waldo Pepper".

Air displays have never gone out of fashion and there are teams flying replica bi-planes who recreate the barnstorming days, but mainly as part of bigger events. In modern use the term barnstorming can be used to describe any performance executed with panache.

* * *

3$^{rd}$ February 2015

**With all the controversy about fracking, could we have extracted all the gas currently said to be underneath us from the coal mines we closed down in the Seventies and Eighties?**

The answer to this question is a theoretical yes and a practical no. While apparently similar, coal gas is different from the natural gas (NG) retrieved from under the North Sea and from the many other places around the world. These differences mean that the appliances that burn the gas are slightly different, especially the size of the jets that they use; the point at which the gas is released from the pipe to mix with air and ignite.

When NG was introduced in the 1960s every house in the country that used gas for cooking or heating was visited by gas fitters to modify the equipment, an exercise that was carried out at considerable public expense. Industry also had to modify much of its gas burning equipment.

The switch-over was made progressively over a number of years, with gasworks closing as their distribution pipes were connected up to form a national pipeline network.

Coal gas is a mixture of hydrogen, carbon monoxide and methane. It was produced by a process of carbonisation, subjecting coal to high temperatures forcing it to release its gas content. It is inherently inefficient to produce as it requires fuel to be burnt in one form in order to produce it in another, just as producing electricity by burning gas or coal is similarly inefficient.

Most large towns and all cities had their own gasworks and the gas was stored in giant tanks, called gasometers, until it was needed. Some of these gasometers, such as the famous one next to the Oval cricket ground, are still in use to store a reserve of gas for use in response to peaks of demand. The production process also produced a number of by-products such as coke, coal tars and ammonia, which were sold on.

The coal gas found in coal mines is produced by the natural release of gas from the coal while it is under pressure below the ground. Capturing coal gas without digging up the coal wouldn't produce enough to make it commercially viable unless the gas can be forced out under pressure. This is the process we know as fracking. However, as discussed, the gas isn't compatible with the current equipment. The fracking proposed for Lancashire and other locations is to produce NG.

NG is predominately methane and was discovered under the North Sea by the drilling rig Sea Gem on 17$^{th}$ September 1965. This effectively sounded the death knell for coal gas, or "town gas" as it was also known. With the spiralling price of deep mined coal NG, even taking into account exploration drilling and infrastructure costs, was far cheaper. The decision was taken by Harold Wilson's government to switch the nation's gas supply to NG. Most of the other countries in North West Europe made similar decisions at about the same time and it had a similar effect on their coal mining industries.

For the two systems to exist side by side would have necessitated the construction of a new distribution network for NG which would have resulted in some parts of the country using expensive coal gas while others enjoyed cheaper NG. Although the national price would have been averaged out it would have increased the price of gas overall. Because the two types of gas need slightly different equipment to burn them it isn't possible to mix the two types of gas in the same pipe, just as you can't mix paraffin and petrol in a car even though they are similar products. Modern engineering designs might be able to resolve this issue but it wasn't considered viable back in the 1960s; or perhaps even considered at all.

There were two final elements in the differences between coal gas and NG. Coal gas contains carbon monoxide which makes it poisonous and there were many deaths each year resulting from minor gas leaks, as well as its deliberate use to commit suicide. NG can't kill in that way, though it does still create carbon monoxide when it is burnt so rooms where it is used have to be ventilated. There are still some deaths from carbon monoxide poisoning caused by defective equipment.

The second factor was environmental. NG is considerably cleaner as far as its production is concerned while producing coal gas was extremely dirty, as anyone who lived near a gasworks could attest. As any former coal miner will tell you there are also severe safety implications involved in the deep mining of coal, including risks to health from diseases such as silicosis.

Theoretically Britain's coal mines could be re-opened to provide coal gas once again, but replacing the infrastructure necessary to mine it and produce gas in commercial quantities would make it uneconomical compared to finding other sources of supply for NG. In the meantime we are now dependent on the foreign supply of NG which makes up 63% of total gas usage. To reduce this dependence on foreign gas it is essential to find new sources of domestically produced NG, which is why the fracking argument is so critical. The day when we can rely totally on renewable energy sources is still a long, long way away.

\* \* \*

## 3rd February 2015

**When Tony Benn was Postmaster General in the sixties did he try to have the Queen's head removed from British postage stamps?**

Tony Benn was born a minor aristocrat, the son of the 2nd Viscount Stansgate, though he adopted very strong Labour principals and was elected to Parliament as a Labour MP. He had to campaign for a change in the law to allow him to renounce his peerage and sit in the House of Commons.

On 15<sup>th</sup> October 1964 Tony Benn was appointed Postmaster General in Harold Wilson's government, a post he held until 4<sup>th</sup> July 1966. During this time he conducted some major reforms of the postal and telecommunications services. One project was the overseeing of the building of the Post Office Tower in London, at the time the country's tallest building.

In terms of the Post Office and Royal Mail services he introduced the Post Bus, which was a vehicle used in rural areas , driven by a postman but carrying fare paying passengers. He also founded the National Giro, later to become Girobank, which was meant to be a rival to the High Street banks. However, Girobank didn't offer a number of services that were offered by its competitors, such as loans, mortgages and overdrafts, so it never gained massive popularity. Consequently Girobank became uncompetitive and was sold off to the Alliance and Leicester Building Society in 1989. The Girobank brand was subsequently dropped though one of its financial instruments, the Giro, is still used to make welfare payments.

Tony Benn did indeed suggest removing the Sovereign's head from postage stamps but the idea was dropped in the face of opposition from the Queen herself. Instead the size of the image of the Sovereign's head was reduced and became a cameo rather than a portrait. It's the day to day design that remains in use for non-commemorative stamps.

The title of Postmaster General can be traced back to February 1512 when a person by the name of Tuke was paid £100 to be Master of the Posts. This title was changed in 1517 to Master of the King's Posts. The title of Postmaster General came into being through an Act of Parliament in 1657. It was therefore older by far than the title of Prime Minister, which didn't enter common usage until about 1805.

The role of Postmaster General was abolished in 1969 when the post was held by John Stonehouse MP. The relevant legislation made the Post Office a publicly owned corporation rather than a department of government and inadvertently sowed the seeds for the eventual privatisation of both British Telecom and Royal Mail. The telecoms arm was split off from the Post Office in 1981 and privatised in 1984. Royal Mail was privatised in 2013 leaving only the High Street Post Offices in public ownership.

After the demise of the Postmaster General the oversight of the Post Office Group, as it became, fell under the remit of the Secretary of State for Trade and Industry (now Business, Innovation and Skills) where the rump of the corporation remains.

**Author's note:** I somehow think that Tony Benn would have been horrified to think that he had paved the way for the privatisation of Royal Mail, but the process started with the changes he made to the Post Office. The law of unintended consequences strikes again!

\* \* \*

## 4<sup>th</sup> February 2015

**The film Pearl Harbor depicts many black US Navy ratings. Is it true that a strict colour bar operated in the US Navy during World War II and that the film is wrong?**

Segregation did exist in the United States Navy when the USA entered the Second World War but it was a segregation based on the jobs that African American sailors were allowed to do, rather than segregation of the ships in which they served. It was never a full colour bar as African Americans did serve in all branches of the Armed forces.

African American sailors were restricted to menial duties, mainly as cooks and mess hands. As sailors that worked together usually also bunked together this also led to a physical segregation within ships. No doubt this was seen as a pragmatic state of affairs as mixing African American sailors with those born in the Southern states might well have caused friction. The restrictions on the nature of duties that African American sailors were allowed to undertake was based on the prejudiced views about the capability of African American people to handle more complex tasks, despite the extensive evidence to the contrary.

This state of affairs was a consequence of the "Jim Crow Laws" that had been passed in the Southern states, the former Confederacy, in the aftermath of the American Civil War. These laws mandated equal but separate treatment of African American people, similar to the apartheid laws that would later be introduced in South Africa. As history reflects, the treatment of African Americans was anything but equal. Despite the wishes of the egalitarian North, the South was able to maintain sufficient pressure on government to ensure the armed services remained segregated while appearing, from the outside, to be integrated.

During the Japanese attack on Pearl Harbor a black mess hand by the name of Doris Miller manned an anti-aircraft gun and kept up steady fire on the attacking aircraft despite having no training in how to use the weapon. For this action Doris Miller was the first African American to be awarded the Navy Cross. This was undoubtedly the inspiration behind some of the scenes depicted in the film Pearl Harbour.

There was similar segregation within the other branches of the United States armed services, where African American servicemen were given only the most menial tasks. However, following on from African American units formed after the American Civil War, the so called Buffalo Soldiers, there were a number of all-black combat units in the Army which served with distinction in all theatres of the Second World War.

Benjamin O Davis was the commander of a unit of the United States Army Air Corps known as the Tuskegee Airmen. These were African American airmen including pilots, navigators and bomb aimers who made up the $332^{nd}$ Fighter Group and the $477^{th}$ Bombardment Group. Their name stems from Tuskegee military airfield, Alabama, where they were trained. Benjamin Davis was the first African American to rise to General rank in the armed forces of the United States.

In all, eight African Americans were awarded the Congressional Medal of Honour during the Second World War, the highest American military honour and the equivalent to our Victoria Cross. All but one of the awards was made posthumously.

Racial segregation in the United States Army, Navy and Air Force didn't come to an end until $26^{th}$ July 1948 when President Harry S Truman signed Executive Order No 9981 which mandated equality of treatment and opportunity to all members of the American armed forces. Segregation based on duties was ended immediately, but the ending of all-black units took longer and the last one wasn't disbanded until 1954, after the Korean War.

\* \* \*

## 5<sup>th</sup> February 2015

**I recently read 'Bronislav Kaminski's RONA made the Nazis look like choirboys'. Who were they?**

Bronislav Vladislavovich Kaminski was born on $16^{th}$ June 1899 in the Vitensk Governate of the Russian Empire, now Polatsk Raion, Belarus. His father was of Polish descent and his mother German. During the Soviet Revolution Kaminski served in the Red Army before returning to study at St Petersburg Polytechnical University where he trained as an engineer, specialising in the distilling industry.

During Stalin's Great Purge Kaminski was accused of belonging to a counter-revolutionary group and put on trial. In 1941, after serving a prison term, he was ordered to move to the Lokot area, which was a part of Belarus designated for people who weren't permitted to return to their own homes. The area was overrun when the Germans invaded in 1941, leaving many disaffected former Soviet citizens behind German lines.

Kaminski and others approached the Germans with a proposal to form a police militia to maintain order in the area. Kaminski was appointed as deputy to the new unit's head, Voskoboinik. This unit, known as the Lokot Autonomy Militia, originally numbered no more than 200 men, but during 1942 expanded to 400-500. Voskoboinik was wounded during anti-partisan operations and Kaminski took over as leader. He renamed the unit the Russian National Liberation Army or *Russkaya Osvoboditelnaya Narodnaya Armiya*, (RONA).

The unit grew in size and by mid 1943 numbered between 10 to 12,000 personnel. Using captured Russian tanks and equipment they were formed into a Panzer Division and operated alongside regular German troops and SS units. After taking part in the Battle of Kursk they were withdrawn to Belarus to take up anti-partisan duties once again. Here they were responsible for many atrocities. The Soviet advance into Belarus in early 1944 caused the unit to be withdrawn into Poland and, with combat losses, had reduced in size to about 4 – 5,000.

In June 1944 RONA was absorbed into the Waffen SS and withdrawn from operations with a view to being retrained and re-equipped for combat. When the Russians advanced as far as the Vistula River the Polish Free Army staged an uprising in Warsaw and RONA was moved to the city to restore order. The atrocities committed during this time are a matter of record.

In 63 days of fighting around 15,200 Polish insurgents were killed or listed as missing, 5,000 wounded and 15,000 taken prisoner. Of the civilian population around 200,000 were killed, another 70,000 wounded and 55,000 were sent to concentration camps, of which 13,000 went to Auschwitz. Not all of those deaths can be laid at the door of RONA, as there were several other German units involved, mainly Waffen SS. The Germans /RONA lost 16,000 dead, 9,000 wounded and 2,000 prisoners.

After this Himmler was anxious to distance himself from what had happened in Warsaw and placed the blame on RONA. He had Kaminski executed on 28th August 1944, but RONA were told that he had been killed by Polish partisans and were shown faked proof of it; a bullet riddled vehicle smeared with goose blood.

The remainder of the RONA were withdrawn into Slovakia in September 1944 to help quell the Slovak National Uprising and were then absorbed into Alexandr Vlasov's Russian Liberation Army or ROA. After being used to try to combat the Prague uprising, which started on 5th May 1945, the ROA surrendered to Patton's 3rd Army, after which many of its members were forcibly extradited to Russia.

Not realising that the ROA now also contained elements of RONA, the Americans allowed some to "escape" into American controlled areas. Most of the extradited ROA were sentenced to terms in prison camps while Vlasov and other leaders were hanged. Other repatriations to Russia took place during the years after the war and many former members of RONA were arrested by the Russians, tried and executed. The last known RONA member was executed in 1978.

RONA's atrocities weren't just confined to Russians, Poles and Slovaks. There were also reports of rape being committed against German nationals. Exactly how many war crimes RONA committed isn't known but they had a fearsome and apparently well-deserved reputation for brutality.

\* \* \*

## 12<sup>th</sup> February 2015
### Are any real pirates mentioned in Robert Louis Stevenson's Treasure Island?

To answer this question it is necessary to separate Pirate Captains, names that have been passed down through history, and members of their crew, which haven't. Both are used by Stevenson but in different ways.

Five known pirate Captains are named in the book but don't appear as characters: William Kidd, Blackbeard (Edward Teach), Edward England, Howell Davies and Bartholomew Roberts.

Captain Flint, the pirate who is supposed to have buried the treasure and the name of Long John Silver's parrot, wasn't a real pirate. He was created by Stevenson but his name is used in at least three other books by different authors: *Porto-Bello Gold* by A D Howden-Smith, *Peter and Wendy* by J M Barrie and *Swallows and Amazons* by Arthur Ransome. Flint also appears in the 2014 TV series Black Sails, which was created as a prequel to Treasure Island.

William Kidd is supposed to have buried a treasure horde on Gardiner's Island and it is the hunt for treasure such as this that forms the backdrop to the story of Treasure Island. In reality the authorities recovered Kidd's treasure not long after it was buried.

Within the story the names of two known pirate crew members are used for crewmembers aboard the Hispaniola, the ship hired by Squire Trelawny to sail to Treasure Island. These are Israel Hands and John Silver.

The real Israel Hands, also known as Basilica Hands, was a member of Blackbeard's crew who Blackbeard maimed by shooting him in the knee just to ensure that the rest of the crew remained in terror of him. As a consequence. Hands was taken ashore to have his wound treated and was therefore not present for Blackbeard's last fight at Ocracoke Island. This saved him from the gallows as Blackbeard's surviving crew were captured and put on trial. Blackbeard himself was killed in the fight.

Hands was later captured and transported to Virginia. He was given a pardon in exchange for testifying against corrupt North Carolina officials who had collaborated with Blackbeard. From there Hands disappears from history.

John Silver is believed to have been a ships' surgeon from Bartholomew Robert's crew. He is supposed to have amputated his own leg in order to save his life. Not much more is known about him other than that he was hanged at Cape Coast Castle, a British fort on the Gold Coast of Africa.

There has been a lot of speculation as to the location of Treasure island. Its outline is similar to the Isle of Unst in the Shetland Islands. The outline of La Isla De La Juventud off the coast of Cuba also has a similar shape. The fictional Ben Gunn names an island in the South West Caribbean that could be Tobago. Norman Island in the British Virgin islands was visited by Stevenson as a young man and has a Spyglass Hill, a location named in the book. There are other possible candidates.

Ben Gunn first appears in The Adventures of Ben Gunn, a fictional work by R F Delderfield, a contemporary of Stevenson's.

Treasure Island was first published in 1883 but started its life in serial form in a magazine titled "Young Folks" published from 1881-82. The use of ambiguous morality in a story aimed at children caused quite a stir at the time. It was popular because of its use of "authentic" pirate vocabulary and characters. It is one of the most dramatised stories for film and TV and has even made the transition into space on the 2002 Disney animation Treasure Planet. Our popular view of pirates, portrayed in many books and films up to and including the Pirates of the Caribbean, comes from Stevenson's book rather than from real life.

**Author' note**: Space pirates feature a lot in my Magi series of books and I always use the names of real pirates where possible. Some of the names go all the way back to the Roman era and as far afield as China.

\* \* \*

## 13<sup>th</sup> March 2015

**My wife's grandfather was with the Experimental Squadron at Martlesham Heath in 1916. What was the purpose of this unit?**

On 16<sup>th</sup> January 1917 the Experimental Aircraft Flight of the Central Flying School was moved from Upavon in Wiltshire to Martlesham Heath in Suffolk, thereby opening up the new airfield. The unit was renamed the Aircraft Experimental Unit, Royal Flying Corps.

The purpose of the unit was to test out new aircraft types to establish their usefulness to the military. As well as test flying the aircraft they also carried out testing on new innovations in aerial combat, such as the method of synchronising the firing of machine guns with the rotation of the propeller so that the machine gun could fire through the propeller arc without destroying the blades.

All of the aircraft that came into use during World War I, from 1917 onwards, would go through the Aircraft Experimental Unit first to ensure that they were fit for purpose.

In 1924 the unit changed its name to the Aircraft and Armament Experimental Establishment (A&AEE) and in 1939 transferred to RAF Boscombe Down, Hampshire, where it has remained ever since. However, as a result of organisational changes since 1992 the unit is now split in two. The government owned part is now the

Defence Science and Technology Laboratory (DSTL). The other part is now a privatised company trading under the name QinetiQ, which carries out work on behalf of the government.

RAF Martlesham Heath remained in service as an RAF station with 11 Group, Fighter Command, providing a base for RAF units and in 1941 it was briefly the home of 71 Squadron, the American Eagles, which was made up of American pilots who had volunteered to fly with the RAF. In 1943 the station was assigned to the 8$^{th}$ Air Force of the United States Army Air Corps, who operated both fighters and bombers from the airfield.

The Americans departed on 10$^{th}$ November 1945 and the airfield reverted to RAF ownership. It once again became home to an experimental unit, the Bomb Ballistics and Blind Landing Unit, which was re-named the Armament and Instrument Experimental Unit in 1950. From 1958 to 1961 it was also home to the Battle of Britain Memorial Flight, who moved out when the station closed. The Air Ministry finally disposed of the airfield in 1963.

* * *

19$^{th}$ March 2015

**Players in the Six Nations rugby appear to have a raised rectangle on the back of their shirts, just above the number. What is this?**

This modern innovation allows the use of "real time" monitoring of a range of physiological aspects of a player's body and performance while at the same time tracking the player's movements around the playing park, using the same technology as that used for satellite navigations systems.

The small device sewn into the players kit records heart rate, breathing, body temperature etc and then relays the information to a computer via satellite. The information is then used by both the rugby coaches and by TV sports commentators.

TV stations are given limited access to the data to allow them to track the movement of players around the park for use in their match analysis. This has resulted in a far greater use of complex graphics showing how players move and position themselves as well as providing information on yards covered, tackles made etc. In the past this was done by assigning a TV camera to an individual and then using that camera to follow the player for the whole match. Using computers, distance covered over time aspects such as running pace could be assessed. However, that was expensive in terms of the numbers of cameras (and camera operatives) required, so the use of this radio frequency (RF) tracking system is far more economical.

The team coaches use the information in real time to analyse players' performance and vital physiological information. The information is displayed on the laptop computers that are seen when the TV cameras cut to a shot of the coaches. Amongst some of the tactical decisions this allows coaches to make are those related to substitutions, by monitoring the fatigue levels of players so coaches can decide if they are maintaining their performance.

After the match the data can be used to analyse individual and team performances, such as "set plays" where the players were expected to make a particular manoeuvre. By analysing the collected data the coaches can assess if the play worked or not and why it may not have worked. They can also use the data to analyse good and poor periods of team performance so that they can improve team tactics.

Based on the physiological data gathered coaches can tailor the training regimes of individual players to ensure that they get the right training for the role they perform. For example, forwards use a lot of muscle strength but don't get involved in long, surging runs. The opposite applies for centres and three quarters. By measuring the body's performance "in play" it is easier to see if personal training regimes are effective.

The RF transponders, as they are called, are positioned so that they are less likely to cause injury when a player falls or is tackled and, similarly, are less like to suffer damage themselves. The system is also used in top flight club matches such as those in the Aviva Premiership, as well as at international level. Similar systems are also used by football clubs and in other sports, such as cycling though the positioning of the transponders can be more discrete and therefore not so obvious to the observer.

\* \* \*

## 8<sup>th</sup> April 2015

**The enormous USS Theodore Roosevelt has more than 80 combat aircraft crowded onto her four-and-a-half acres of deck. How soon can she get any of them into the air?**

The flight deck of an aircraft carrier is a busy place and it would require only a minor error by a pilot landing his aircraft or taxiing for take-off to cause an accident that might cost millions of dollars to repair. Therefore aircraft are only parked on the flight deck for display purposes, such as during courtesy visits to foreign ports, or in readiness for flight. Although there may seem to be many aircraft on the flight deck there is usually only small number at any time while at sea.

Under normal circumstances the aircraft are parked on a hanger deck beneath the flight deck. This is also the place where routine maintenance is carried out before and after sorties and where refuelling and re-arming is carried out. As well as providing a storage and maintenance space for the aircraft it also provides weather protection. Salt water can be very damaging to an aircraft, even if it is on a deck that is 100 ft above the waterline. Photographs of aircraft carriers at sea often show spray breaking over the front of the flight deck.

The aircraft are raised and lowered between the flight deck and the hanger deck by large, open sided elevators. An aircraft carrier will have at least two of these, one towards the forward end of the ship to deliver aircraft for take-off and one further aft to remove aircraft after landings. The Theodore Roosevelt has four elevators, one on each side towards the aft and two on the starboard side in front of the accommodation island.

On board the carrier there are several different aircraft types. Fighters for both defensive and offensive operations, supplemented by airborne early warning aircraft such as the E18 Growler or E2 Hawkeye. There will also be helicopters for anti-submarine patrols and to rescue downed aircrew. The F18 variants currently in use by the United States Navy are multirole and therefore conduct both defensive and offensive operations, though their armament mix will vary depending upon need. From 2018 the Lockheed F35 Lightning II will start to replace the F18 in US Navy service.

When an aircraft carrier is in a combat zone, or when international tensions are high and a surprise attack may be a risk, there will be a variety of operational patterns that might be flown to protect the carrier group itself or to mount offensive operations. For defensive purposes there will usually be one pair of aircraft airborne and operating under radar guidance from an airborne early warning aircraft.

Back on the ship there may be two more aircraft on "immediate readiness" which means they can be launched as soon as the order is given and there may be two more aircraft on 5 minute readiness. This means the aircraft will be in position on the flight deck but the crew aren't actually sitting in the aircraft, but will be in a "ready room" close by. If an attack is believed to be imminent, forewarned by the airborne early warning aircraft, then the number of aircraft airborne or on immediate readiness may be increased until the threat has passed.

The USS Theodore Roosevelt is a Nimitz class carrier, the fourth to be built. Her keel was laid in 1981 and she was commissioned on 25<sup>th</sup> October 1986. Her flight deck is 1,088 ft long and 257 ft at its widest. From keel to masthead she is 257 high and weighs in at 91,300 tons. She can sail at 35 kts powered by 2 nuclear powered reactors driving 4 steam turbines turning 4 propeller shafts. Her endurance is theoretically unlimited, dependent mainly on food and other logistical limitations. The total ship's company is 3,200 of which 2,400 make up the air wing.

\* \* \*

## 14<sup>th</sup> April 2015
### Is Malaysia's King elected?

The Malaysian federal King, or Yang diPertaun Agong, is elected but not by popular vote. Agong means King and Pertuan means Lord. The political government is democratically elected under a system similar to that of our own Parliament.

The country we now know as Malaysia, formerly Malaya, had previously been made up of a number of small Kingdoms or Sultanates. The British formed these into a single colonial administration which also included Singapore. The Act of Parliament passed in 1947 that paved the way for Malaysia's independence proposed a federation of states under a central government. In 1957 this became the modern state that we know.

The nine states that make up the mainland of Malaya have traditional rulers that we might refer to as Kings. The Malaysian constitution limits eligibility to males of Muslim descent from the royal families. In the states of Kedah, Kelantan, Johor, Perlis, Pahang,

Selangor and Terengganu the rulers are hereditary and the title of Sultan is used.

In Perak the role of monarch is rotated between three branches of the royal family based on seniority and is known as Rajah. In Negiri Sembelan the monarch is elected from eligible candidates by hereditary tribal chiefs. He takes the title Yang diPertuan Besar, meaning 'Great Lordship'.

Every five years, or when a vacancy occurs, the rulers of the nine states meet in what is called the Matis Raja-Raja, or Conference of Rulers. This conference then selects the Yang di-Pertuan Agong, who becomes the federal monarch and Malaysia's constitutional head of state for a five year period.

The nine rulers fulfil the role of constitutional monarch for their own state. They are also the nominal head of the Muslim religion in their own state. The Yang diPertuan Agong performs a similar function in terms of the federal government and is also symbolic Commander-in-Chief of the armed forces. As with all constitutional monarchs the amount of power he is able to wield is strictly limited and his functions are mainly religious, ceremonial and diplomatic.

There are four states that don't have their own ruler: Penang, Malacca, Sabah and Sarawak (Sabah and Serawak are in northern Borneo) so the federal ruler also performs the function of head of the Islamic religion for those four states as well as his own.

The current Yang diPertuan Agong is Almu'tasimu Billahi Muhibbuddin Tuanku Alhaj Abdul Halim Mu'adzam Shah Ibni Almarhum Sultan Badlishah, Sultan of Kedah, born 28$^{th}$ November 1927 and the 14$^{th}$ to hold the title. He took office on 11$^{th}$ April 2012 and previously held the office between 1971 and 1976. He is the only one to have held the post twice, no doubt a benefit of longevity.

Singapore was also a member of the Federation of Malaysia when it was established in 1957. However, the predominantly Chinese population of Singapore felt that their place wasn't within a federation that was ruled primarily by Muslim politicians. In 1966 the recently deceased Lee Kwan Yew took the island out of the Federation to become a nation in its own right.

\* \* \*

## 17<sup>th</sup> April 2015

### When was the term no-man's-land first used?

While this term is most strongly associated with the trench warfare of World War I it dates back to at least 1320 and probably earlier.

The Oxford English Dictionary cites the term nonesmanneslond being used to describe a disputed patch of land over which there was a legal disagreement. Over the years the term has evolved into its present form and has been used for a number of purposes, including the name of an area outside the north wall of the City of London where executions were carried out and to describe part of the forecastle of a ship where ropes and tackle were stored.

At the outbreak of WWI the term wasn't widely used in the British Army. In the early days of the war the terms "between the trenches" and "between the lines" were the commonly used and approved terms.

The first known use in relation to trench warfare was by soldier and author Ernest Swinton who employed it in his short story The Point Of View. He also used it in his correspondence from the Western Front, especially in relation to the "Race To The Sea" in which the British and the Germans attempted to outflank each other before either side could get to the natural barrier of the English Channel. The failure to achieve a decisive result in this race was what condemned the warring nations to four years of trench warfare.

The Christmas Truce of 1914 brought the term to popular attention and after that it started to be used in official communiques, news reports and personal correspondence.

As might be expected, there is no defined width to No Man's Land. During World War I it could be as much as several hundred yards or, on occasions, as little as ten yards.

In 1949 an armistice agreement signed between Israel and Jordan officially designated stretches of land as 'no man's land' between the territories of both sides in Jerusalem and other parts of what is now referred to as The West Bank. Since 1967 all of this land has fallen under Israeli control.

**Author's note:** While visiting the World War I battlefields in August 2018 I discovered just how narrow No Man's land could be. On Hill 60, to the East of Ypres, metal strips show the positions of the front line trenches in early 1915. In places they were just a few feet apart. The soldiers in one trench could have touched the bayonets of soldiers in the opposing trench.

\* \* \*

### 6th May 2015
#### Who invented the compass?

The Norse (often inaccurately referred to as Vikings) are often attributed with having been the first to use a compass like device. It is reputed that they suspended a piece of magnetic rock, called a lodestone, from a thread and found that it always aligned itself on a north-south axis. This explanation is used to account for their great seafaring skills, which took them to Iceland, Greenland and possibly as far as Newfoundland.

However, the compass is much older and dates back to the ancient Chinese and the achievements of the Norse may have been more due to the direction of the winds than to a navigational device.

Those same winds are what took Columbus to the Caribbean and the British to Virginia. The further north each one started the further north they were when they arrived, but always south west of their start point, pushed there by the prevailing winds.

The compass was first used in China during the Han dynasty, $2^{nd}$ to $1^{st}$ century BC, however, its purpose wasn't navigational, it was used in fortune telling of a particular type, called geomancy. This is the art of throwing handfuls of small rocks, gravel and sand to see what sort of pattern they form and then interpreting that pattern to foretell the future. It was discovered that a form of magnetised rock, which we called a lodestone, which is a form of the mineral magnetite, tended to align itself on a north-south axis.

This magnetic property was later incorporated into other fortune telling devices similar to Ouija boards. From this developed the idea of aligning one's house in certain directions, the art we now know as feng-shui.

It was later discovered that by stroking a piece of metal, perhaps a needle like sliver, with a lodestone the magnetic properties would be transferred to the needle. When the needle is floated on a bowl of water it will point north-south. This is an experiment modern day children still conduct in their science classes and is the origin of the navigational compass.

There is a theory that in Mesoamerica, now called Central America, the tribes used similar techniques as far back as 1000 BC, but this has yet to be verified. Even if it is true there is no way that it could have been introduced from there to either China or Europe as the existence of Central America wasn't established by outsiders until the $15^{th}$ century.

The Chinese appear to have started to use a compass for navigation around the $9^{th}$ or $10^{th}$ centuries AD. The skill of making magnetic compasses was transferred to Europe, probably by Arab traders, and starts to appear in the late 12<sup>th</sup> century, where they are recorded for the first time in the texts De utensilibus and De naturis rerum, written between 1187 and 1202. It may have been about this time that the Norse were given credit for the use of compasses as an explanation for their apparent sea faring skills.

Persian texts refer to metal fish like object being used for navigation in 1232. A fish was a common shape used by mariners. However, the fact that this is after the recorded use of such devices in Europe doesn't signify that their introduction to the Arab world was later. Navigators were notoriously secretive about their methods of navigation as it gave them a trading advantage. They made their own charts and books of navigational notes and guarded them with their lives, passing them from father to son. More significantly the use of compasses is mentioned in India in the 4<sup>th</sup> century AD, so Arab traders would almost certainly have come across it at that time, though it hadn't started to be used for navigation.

**Author's note:** Since the publication of this letter archaeologists have now confirmed that the Norse did reach Newfoundland and they suspect that they travelled farther south and are now seeking evidence to support this theory.

* * *

## 11<sup>th</sup> May 2015

### Was the Green Howards regiment named after two different people called Howard?

While the name most associated with the 19<sup>th</sup> Regiment of Foot is the Green Howards, it wasn't their original name. They were raised in 1688 in Devon. not Yorkshire, the county they are normally associated with. In keeping with the practice of the day, they were named after their Colonel: Luttrel's Regiment. As such they changed their name when they changed their Colonel. They saw their first action in 1680 fighting with King William III at the Battle of the Boyne.

It was in 1744 that the regiment got its new name. At that time there were two regiments commanded by Colonels with the name of Howard. To distinguish between the two they were called by the colour of the facings on the collars and cuffs of their red coats: Howard's Buffs (Thomas Howard), eventually just The Buffs and the Green Howards (Charles Howard). Although not officially recognised, the nicknames caught on.

In 1751 the army changed the system for identifying regiments, adopting a numbering system. The Green Howards became the 19th Regiment of Foot and Howard's Buffs became the 17th Regiment.

At this time regiments had no geographic affiliations and would recruit from wherever they were garrisoned at the time. This changed in 1782 and the Green Howards became the 19th (First Yorkshire North Riding Regiment) of Foot. Howard's Buffs were affiliated to Kent and became, over a period of time, the Royal East Kent Regiment, but always known as The Buffs. It is where we get the saying "Steady, the Buffs", supposedly from their commanding officer exhorting his men to remain steadfast as the enemy attacked.

In 1873 the town of Richmond, North Yorkshire, became home to the Green Howards. By 1902 they had gone through a couple of name changes and had become Alexandra, Princess of Wales Own (Yorkshire Regiment). It wasn't until 1920 that for the first time The Green Howards were officially called by that name. This was a reward for their service during the First World War.

Unlike many regiments the Green Howards survived several re-organisations to retain their regimental identity right up until 2006. In that year they were amalgamated with the Duke of Wellington's Regiment and the Prince of Wales Own Regiment of Yorkshire to become the Yorkshire Regiment. They had been one of only five regiments to have survived for so long without being amalgamated or merged. The others were the Royal Scots, The 22nd (Cheshire) Regiment, the Royal Welch Fusiliers and The Kings Own Scottish Borderers.

\* \* \*

## 6th May 2015

**Science tells us that a streamlined shape is more fuel efficient. So why do most European truck manufacturers produce trucks with a flat front?**

The shape of European lorries is governed not by the need for fuel efficiency, but the maximisation of cargo carrying capacity. This is where cost and profit is generated in the trucking industry.

Under UK law the maximum length of an LGV (large goods vehicle), commonly called an articulated lorry, is 18.75 metres (60ft 11 in) with a maximum loaded weight of 44 tonnes. The length is measured from the foremost point of the towing unit to the rearmost point of the cargo carrying space. This means that if the front of the vehicle is extended to provide streamlining then the length available for cargo carrying must be reduced by the same amount. For this reason a flat front to the lorry is the preferred option.

In order to justify the sacrifice in cargo space caused by streamlining there must be sufficient fuel saving to make up the difference in lost revenue or increased costs. As the streamlining effect makes only marginal savings in fuel the sacrifice isn't financially viable. To accommodate the length restrictions the engines of LGVs are mounted in the middle of the cab, between the driver and passenger seats and extending rearwards. To access the engine the whole cab tilts forward.

The government could legislate to improve fuel efficiency through streamlining, however there would be a cost to this. If current maximum vehicle sizes were to be maintained then there would be a loss in cargo carrying capacity, which would put more lorries on the road to compensate, which would make overall fuel efficiency worse, as well as increasing traffic volumes on already crowded roads. It would also increase the cost of everything we buy, as transport costs are part of purchase prices.

Increased lorry lengths could be introduced to allow for more streamlining but this would mean them taking up more room on the road at a cost to other road users. It isn't just the number of vehicles on the road that contribute to congestion, it is also their overall size. To illustrate: a 5 ft increase in lorry length would be the equivalent of adding one extra lorry for every 12 currently in use, but without the benefit of adding any additional cargo carrying capacity. At current transport levels this would be the equivalent of putting in excess of 23,000 more lorries onto our roads.

Operators do value any fuel saving that can be made from streamlining, providing it isn't gained by sacrificing cargo carrying capacity. For this reason many lorries are fitted with air deflectors of varying styles and some innovative shapes have been introduced for trailers. However, this also increases manufacturing costs and again there will always be a trade-off between cost and fuel efficiency.

In the USA the lengths and weights permitted for lorries varies from state to state, starting from 53 ft (Mississippi, New Jersey) to 75 ft (Alaska, Iowa). The average appears to be around 65 ft. However, most states specify a maximum trailer length of around 40 ft, which is about the same as that used in the EU, which allows the extension of the towing unit for streamlining in those states that allow larger vehicles. As may be imagined, where shorter vehicles are a legal requirement they tend to be flat fronted.

Typically in the USA, the lorry's engine is mounted in front of the driver's cab and this allows for improved streamlining. For example, the 75 ft total length specified for Alaska limits trailer size to 40ft, which allows for a towing unit of 35ft, over half the length allowed for the whole lorry in the EU. Some of the extra space is also used for sleeping accommodation as some owner/drivers practically live in their vehicles.

\* \* \*

### 1$^{st}$ June 2015
#### Who was the first pilot to take off and land on an aircraft carrier?

The first take-off of an aircraft from a ship occurred quite soon after the development of heavier than air flight. The Wright Brothers flew their aircraft for the first time on 17$^{th}$ December 1903. On 14$^{th}$ November 1910 Eugene Ely became the first pilot to take off from a ship, the USS Birmingham.

Ely was born in Williamsburg, Iowa on 21$^{st}$ October 1886. He later found himself working as a car salesman for E Henry Wemme who purchased a 4 cylinder Curtiss aircraft and acquired the airmail franchise for the Pacific North West. Wemme was unable to fly one day so Ely offered to pilot the aircraft, thinking it would be no harder than driving a car. Needless to say he crashed, but Wemme was forgiving and allowed Ely to use the rebuilt Curtiss to learn to fly and he went on to become a demonstration pilot for the Curtiss organisation.

Captain Washington Chambers of the US Navy had been appointed to investigate the possible naval uses of aviation and Ely was introduced to him. This resulted in the pilot launching a Curtiss pusher aircraft from a temporary platform on the bow of the USS Birmingham. The aircraft plunged from the deck towards the sea and actually dipped its wheels into the water before struggling skywards. Ely was so shaken by the experience that he promptly landed on the beach rather than at the Norfolk Naval Yard as planned.

Two months later on 18<sup>th</sup> January 1911 Ely successfully landed the same Curtiss pusher on a platform erected on the USS Pennsylvania, anchored in San Francisco Bay. Thus he became the first man to achieve both feats of taking off and landing an aircraft from a ship.

The next development in naval aviation wasn't in aircraft carriers, however, it was in sea plane tender ships. A sea plane would be lowered over the side of the ship to take off and land on the water, before being recovered back onto the ship. The French Navy were the developers of this idea, with their ship, the Foudre.

The first use of a ship borne aircraft for a combat mission was made by the Japanese Imperial Navy on 6<sup>th</sup> September 1914 when a French built Farman Experimental aircraft was launched from the Wakamiya to undertake a bombing mission against the Austro-Hungarian cruiser Kaiserin Elisabeth (Queen Elizabeth) which was in Qiaozhou Bay, China. The Wakamiya's planes were also used against German and Austro-Hungarian shore based targets in the area. The Wakamiya was a seaplane tender converted from a merchant vessel.

In 1918 HMS Argus became the first aircraft carrier proper, being capable of both launching aircraft from its deck and landing them again. Film from two cameras showing 'alighting trials' in 1918 show an RAF Sopwith 1½ Strutter flown by Lieutenant-Colonel Richard Bell-Davies VC, DSO, making a take-off at the second attempt, with bad weather preventing the first landing attempt. The second attempt was successful. Although not officially recorded as such, the filming of these attempts suggests that they were the first time such flights had been made.

The Argus was converted from an ocean liner that had been under construction at the outbreak of World War I. Her design became the pre-World War II standard, with a single long deck for take-off and landing and all her navigation and accommodation positions being mounted below the deck. The original design had called for two islands, one on either side with the deck passing between them, but this design was abandoned when trials on another ship, the Furious, had revealed that the islands caused air turbulence which endangered landing aircraft.

This problem wasn't overcome until after World War II when the higher approach speeds of jet aircraft countered the turbulence, while at the same time the landing deck was angled in relation to the ship's fore-aft axis.

Smoke from the Argus's boilers was ducted aft and cooled before being expelled from beneath the deck on either side, while the ship was navigated from a position below the deck at the prow of the ship.

HMS Argus was commissioned too late to take part in World War I and first served as a trials ship for naval aviation. Her only operational use at this time was in the Dardanelles during the Chanak Crisis (a war scare between Britain and the newly formed Republic of Turkey) in 1922. After serving on the "China Station" for several years HMS Argus was reclassified as a training ship. During the Second World War she served in operational roles where she ferried aircraft until she reached a point where they could be launched and were then able to land at airfields, mainly in Malta and North Africa. She also served as a convoy escort carrier on several occasions. Towards the end of the war she was finally decommissioned and sent to Chatham dockyard to provide accommodation for sailors. HMS Argus ended her days at Inverkeithing where she was broken up in 1946.

\* \* \*

**5th June 2015**
   **Why is Bluetooth so called?**

Bluetooth has become a generic term for a range of similar products from different manufacturers. The same happened with the use of Hoover to represent vacuum cleaners and Jacuzzi to represent whirlpool baths.

In 1996 a number of technology companies were looking for ways to connect electronic devices together wirelessly. This included the use of wireless technology to connect mobile phone handsets to earpieces for hands-free use.

As new systems of low power radio frequency (RF) connection developed the jargon associated with them became complicated by naming issues. The Intel Corporation referred to their system as Biz-RF, Erricsson as MC-Link and Nokia as Low Power RF. A number of companies got together in Lund, Sweden, at the headquarters of the Erricsson company to set up a special interest group (SIG) to work on the subject of system standardisation, which included naming. The project became known as Project Bluetooth, which was expected to be a working title until the marketing arm of the SIG could get together and work up a marketable name.

The name was taken from the 10<sup>th</sup> century King of Denmark Harold Blaastand, nicknamed Bluetooth. It was common for the Danes and other Norse peoples to name their heroes after physical attributes. A Danish King of Dublin was named Citric Silkbeard.

A technology specialist by the name of Jim Kardach of the Intel Corporation claims credit for the introduction of the name. A hobby of his is the study of Norse history and he claims that he came across the name Bluetooth after a conference in Toronto which was also attended by Sven Matheson of Erricsson. Each was pitching to have the new RF systems named after their own company's preferred titles. Both proposals were rejected.

During social activity after the conference, Kardach and Matheson were discussing Norse history when the name of Harold

Bluetooth was mentioned. From this the working title for Project Bluetooth was later suggested.

What had started out as a working title has become the globally recognised name for technology that is connected wirelessly by low power RF signals.

\* \* \*

## 22nd June 2015

**Who coined the nickname 'Bomber County' for Lincolnshire and when did it originate?**

The term "Bomber County" comes from World War II and refers to the sheer number of Bomber Command airfields that there were in the county. From Goxhill in the north to Sutton Bridge in the south the county housed 48 RAF bases, most of which were home to bomber squadrons.

Lincolnshire offered the RAF two advantages. Firstly the flat nature of the countryside made it ideal for the construction of airfields. However, it was also far enough away from German occupied territory to make attack by the German fighters a minimal risk. As well as RAF squadrons the county was also home to many squadrons of the United States 8th Air Force. Yorkshire, particularly the area along the Humber Estuary and in the Vale of York, was also heavily populated by Bomber Command and the 8th Air Force.

Quite who coined the phrase "Bomber County" is lost in the mists of time but it is likely to have been a media invention, probably first used by one of the larger circulation daily newspapers of the day.

Folk Singer Mike Harding has done his bit to preserve the term in popular culture, using the phrase in his song Bomber's Moon, recorded in 1984.

Today four of the airfields used during World War II remain in use. These are RAF Scampton, from where the Dambusters raid was mounted, RAF Waddington, RAF Coningsby and RAF Cranwell, home to the RAF College. None of these are used by the modern day 'bombers' of the RAF, the Tornado. Those are based at RAF Lossiemouth in Scotland and RAF Marham in Norfolk.

**Author's note**: Since writing this answer the Tornado has gone out of service, to be replaced by the F35 Lightning II.

\* \* \*

## 22nd June 2015

**How many of the regiments that took part in the Battle of Waterloo are still with us today?**

There are three regiments of infantry and one of cavalry that existed in their current form at the time of the Battle of Waterloo and even those have changed their names. There is also one regiment of artillery.

The 1st Regiment of Foot Guards was awarded the name of the Grenadier Guards in honour of their victory over Napoleon's Grenadiers of the Imperial Guard at the battle. All regiments had a Grenadier company who were made up of the biggest and strongest soldiers and who acted as 'shock troops' to overpower the enemy. The Light Company of the battalion also took part in the fighting at Hougemont Farm.

The 2nd Regiment of Foot Guards, now the Coldstream Guards, were in the thick of the fighting at Hougemont Farm which anchored the right flank of Wellington's army. The ferocity of the fighting was commemorated with a new memorial as part of the recent 200th anniversary celebrations.

The 3rd Regiment of Foot Guards, now the Scots Guards, were billeted near Brussels in 1815 and after a march of 27 miles they engaged in the lesser known battle at the crossroads of Quatre Bras on the evening before the Battle of Waterloo. This small battle engaged the advance guard of Napoleon's army, delaying him and giving Wellington time to prepare for the main battle the following day. The Light Company of the 3$^{rd}$ Regiment were then engaged at Hougemont Farm while the remainder of the battalion were positioned on a ridge behind the farm..

As for the remainder of the infantry regiments engaged in the battle it is true to say that none of them are now present in the British Army and it is also true to say that all of them are present. Since Waterloo, regiments of the British Army have rarely been disbanded. Instead they were merged to create new regiments as a way of preserving their rich histories. As an example it is possible to trace the lineage of two of the regiments present at the Battle of Waterloo through to the modern British Army.

The 33$^{rd}$ (1$^{st}$ Yorkshire West Riding) Regiment served in the line at Waterloo. As a young man the Duke of Wellington had served as an officer with the 73$^{rd}$ Regiment of Foot which was merged with the 33rd. In 1881, after the Cardwell reforms, their name was changed to the 33$^{rd}$ (Duke of Wellington's) Regiment in honour of the Duke's connection. Their name was later changed to The Duke Of Wellington's Regiment. In 2004 this regiment was merged with the Prince of Wales Own Regiment of Yorkshire and the Green Howards to form the Yorkshire Regiment.

The 14$^{th}$ (Buckinghamshire) Regiment fought at Waterloo and were later merged to form the West Yorkshire Regiment which later became part of the Prince of Wales Own Regiment of Yorkshire and then the Yorkshire Regiment. Similar military genealogy can be traced for most of the British regiments that were present at the Battle.

The Life Guards were present as part of Wellington's Cavalry Corps. The 1$^{st}$ and 2$^{nd}$ Life Guards formed the first two ranks that broke the French Cuiraissiers and saved the British centre at the battle. They now make up one of the two regiments of The Household Cavalry, along with the Blues and Greys.

With regards to the other cavalry regiments, like the infantry regiments they too have been merged over the years. One of the regiments present at the battle were the Royal Scots Greys, depicted in the famous painting by Elizabeth, Lady Butler, who were merged in 1971 to become the Royal Scots Dragoon Guards who are still in existence.

The presence of other cavalry regiments at Waterloo can be inferred from their modern day regimental name of the Royal Dragoon Guards. At the time of the battle the cavalry regiments were designated Dragoons, Light Dragoons or Dragoon Guards. The term dragoon originates from the short carbine that they carried, called a dragon. Four dragoon regiments were allowed to use the title of 'Hussar' in parentheses from 1805 onwards. The 10th (Prince of Wales Own) Light Dragoons (Hussars), present at the battle, were therefore one of the forefathers of the present day Kings Royal Hussars.

Of course the presence of the Royal Artillery can't be overlooked and they played a major part in the battle, providing batteries of guns as well as the more mobile horse artillery. The only regimental designation in the British Army that remains unchanged to this day is The Royal Horse Artillery, who were attached to the Cavalry Corps. The other major corps that existed then and were present at the time was The Royal Engineers.

There are just 5 regiments who, because of the date of their founding, can't claim any lineage to Waterloo. These are: The Royal Gurhka Rifles (1816), The Irish Guards (1902), The Welsh Guards (1915), The Royal Tank Regiment (1916) and The Parachute Regiment (1940).

Just as the Queen can trace her lineage back to William The Conqueror, so the regiments of the current British Army can trace their lineage back to Waterloo and many to even earlier battles.

* * *

**2rd July 2015**
**Apart from being there, was there any planned French military involvement for the D-Day operations in June 1944, covert or otherwise?**

While the involvement of French military personnel on D Day wasn't extensive, the Free French forces took part in land, sea and air operations.

There were four British built navy ships present that had Free French crews. These were: the light cruisers Montcalm and the Georges Leygues which were positioned in front of the coastal artillery battery at Longues-Sur-Mer, between Gold and Omaha beaches; the destroyer Roselys was off Omaha Beach and the destroyer La Combattante off Juno beach. These ships engaged shore installations and provided artillery support for the troops engaged in the landings.

Air operations conducted between 5 and 6th June, under the codename Operation Neptune, involved 3 Squadrons of Free French fighter aircraft and 2 of Free French bombers.

For the army there were two separate engagements. The first was the participation of 4 sticks of 8 paratroops of the Free French Army who were dropped over Brittany. These were members of the Special Air Service Brigade dropped behind enemy lines to conduct sabotage operations. The first Frenchman to be killed on D Day is recorded as being Cpl Emile Bouétard who died at Plumelec in Brittany.

The second involvement was 2 Troops of French commandoes from No 10 Inter-allied Commando who were attached to No 4 Commando of 1<sup>st</sup> Special Service Brigade. They went ashore on Sword Beach with a total of 176 men. They captured the heavily defended Riva Bella Casino in Ouistreham, before moving forward to join the rest of the 1<sup>st</sup> Special Service Brigade on the River Orne, where they anchored the left flank of the 6<sup>th</sup> Airborne Division, captors of Pegasus Bridge.

The contribution made by the French Resistance must not be overlooked. Acting on orders from London, hundreds of acts of sabotage were carried out on communications networks, the railways and other infrastructure vital to the German war effort. These were high risk operations as any Resistance member captured would be automatically sentenced to death, a sentence that wouldn't be carried out before they had been tortured for information.

By 1944 the Free French forces numbered about 400,000 soldiers, sailors and airmen. The majority were involved in operations involving the French colonies that were either under the control of the Vichy government or threatened by it, especially those in North and Central Africa. Following on from D Day there was a considerable commitment of Free French troops in France, where they were involved in the break out from the Normandy beachhead and spearheaded the advance on Paris.

* * *

## 6<sup>th</sup> July 2015

### Can a Welshman still be hung from a tree if caught in Chester after dark?

It is an urban myth that a Welshman might ever have been be hanged if found in Chester after dark. This belief stems from an order issued by Henry, Prince of Wales (later Henry V) in 1403.

At the time there were a number of border skirmishes going on between Welsh lords and their English neighbours. To quell the fears of the citizens of Chester, Henry authorised the removal of all Welsh people from the city, on pain of death if they remained. It was something of a knee jerk reaction to the situation and was never enacted as a law. As far as history recalls it also seems that no Welshman was ever executed under this order.

The myth was made popular once again in 2006 when Coronation Street actor Adam Rickett made an unsuccessful attempt to stand for Parliament. In his election campaign he promised to use his position as an MP to repeal a law that didn't exist.

There are a number of similar myths or urban legends about the law. For example it has often been said that it is illegal to affix a postage stamp to a letter upside down. This belief stems from the 1848 Treason Felony Act which made it an offence to "deprive or depose" the monarch of the "imperial crown of the United Kingdom", but it makes no mention of stamps. Royal Mail, who print and issue the stamps, states that "It's a myth and not true. There's nothing to say you can't put a stamp upside down."

A rather bizarre myth that relates to Christmas is that it is illegal to eat a mince pie on Christmas Day. This stems from laws passed under Oliver Cromwell, who did ban Christmas festivities other than as a religious observance. However, when King Charles II was restored to the throne most of Cromwell's laws were repealed, including those relating to Christmas. Of the 11 laws made by Cromwell that remained on the statue books, none relate to mince pies.

These myths remain in circulation because it is assumed that a law must be repealed for it to no longer apply. In most cases laws aren't repealed, they are simple subsumed or modified by new legislation. There has been very little genuinely new legislation for over a hundred years. Most modern Acts of Parliament modify existing law, usually by closing loopholes or creating new offences under the terms of an existing law. For example the Dangerous Dogs Act of 2012 added additional offences to those covered by the 1991 legislation and tightened up the definition of a dangerous dog. However, the 1991 legislation wasn't repealed, it was subsumed into the new act.

If it had ever been legal to hang a Welshman in Chester it would have become illegal when capital punishment was abolished in the UK in 1965 (1973 in Northern Ireland). With regard to capital punishment it is a belief held by many that you can still be executed for committing arson in Her Majesty's Dockyards. This too is untrue. That exemption to the abolition of the death sentence was itself abolished in 1971. The death penalty for espionage, which some people also believe still exists, was abolished in 1981.

**Author's note:** One act of Parliament that does have to be repealed is The European Communities Act (1972). It was never envisaged that we would one day decide to leave the EU so no provision was written into the Act for us to do so. To leave the EU, Parliament must therefore repeal the Act and pass new legislation. I wouldn't recommend affixing a postage stamp sideways. It would mean that the sorting machines couldn't correctly read the phosphorous strips on the stamp that differentiate first and second class mail, which might delay the letter's arrival. Affixing the stamp upside own, however, doesn't affect the stamp's readability.

*　*　*

**21st July 2015**

**How does an unmanned spaceship manage to dock with the international space station?**

There are currently two docking systems in use, both Russian, one for an unmanned capsule docking with a manned space station and one for use when both the space station and the capsule are unmanned.

The system used for the unmanned capsule to dock with the manned space station is called TORU (*Телеоператорный Режим Управления* - Teleoperated Mode of (spacecraft) Control). In this system the personnel aboard the space station use remote control to guide the capsule into position to dock with their own craft.

The technology isn't new and is basically a more advanced version of the systems that model aircraft enthusiasts have been using for decades to control their models. Similar technology is used to control remotely piloted military aircraft, or drones as they are more commonly known.

The "pilot" on board the space station can observe the unmanned capsule through a port, as well as in TV images produced by externally mounted cameras. He or she then uses two controllers which send radio commands to the capsule to guide it towards their own craft, one controls the angle and direction of approach while the other controls speed. Lugs and receptors on the two craft guide the nose of the capsule into its final resting place, where electrically operated clamps then secure it. The system also uses a TV camera mounted on the capsule to allow the pilot to observe proceedings from the viewpoint of the unmanned craft.

Toru was used by the Salyut space station, the Mir space station when it was manned and currently the International Space Station. Its first public use was in 1997, when it allowed the docking of the Progress M-34 capsule with the Mir station. This docking resulted in a near fatal collision between the two craft, so the skill of the pilot is clearly a factor.

The system used to guide an unmanned capsule to dock with a space station which is also unmanned is called KURS (Ukrainian and Russian: Kypc, *Course*) which is a radio telemetry system. This system broadcasts radio signals from the capsule which are reflected back from the space station to various antennae. The variations in signal strength between the different antennae are analysed and calculated to adjust the course, attitude and speed of the unmanned capsule to guide the craft into its docking position. This was first used on the Mir space station, which wasn't kept permanently occupied.

The Kurs system is also used when the capsule is transporting cosmonauts to an unmanned space station, as the restricted space inside the capsule would make it difficult for the cosmonauts to operate controllers even if they were fitted.

Theoretically it is possible to guide an unmanned capsule from a control room on Earth, just as military drones are guided from half a world away. However, delays between the time radio and TV signals are transmitted and then received, sometimes several seconds depending on how far way the space craft is and how many communications satellites it must be routed through, make it a very complicated method of docking and the other available systems are therefore preferred.

* * *

## 22$^{nd}$ July 2015

**How are images transmitted back from Pluto? How long do they take to travel the distance?**

The photographs taken of Pluto use similar digital photographic techniques to those used in digital cameras and the cameras installed in mobile phones. The different intensity of light reflected from the planet, or dwarf planet as it is officially designated, on a scale from pure white to pure black (the absence of light) is converted into a digital code. This digital code is then used to "modulate" a radio signal.

This is a more advanced version of the facsimile (fax) technology used to transmit weather maps and black and white photographs using radio waves, which dates back to the 1950s.

In simple terms the digital code is used to make minute variations to the frequency of a radio signal in a way that can be decoded when it is received. In order to speed up the transmission of a complete photograph the digital code can be broken up and different sections used to modulate several radio signals at the same time. The decoded signals are then re-combined when they are received. In essence it is no different to the way that digital photos are uploaded from a mobile phone to Facebook, Twitter or Instagram. The only real difference is the distance the signals must travel.

Radio signals are electro-magnetic waves and as such they travel at the speed of light. If the distance between Earth and Pluto is known then it is quite a simple calculation to work out how long it takes using the formula: time = distance/speed.

The speed of light in a vacuum (space) is 299,792,458 metres per second. With the current relative positions of the two planets Pluto is about 4.7 billion km (2.9 bn miles) from Earth, or 4,700 billion metres, so it takes the photographs approximately 15,960 seconds or 4 hours 26 minutes to reach Earth.

The orbit of Pluto around the sun is extremely eccentric. At one point it actually passes closer to the sun than its nearest neighbour, Neptune, and its furthest point from the sun is about twice the distance of its nearest point. It takes 264 of our years to complete its orbit. At its closest Pluto is 4.2 billion km from Earth and its furthest, when they are on opposite sides of the Sun, is 7.5 billion km.

New data gathered by the New Horizons mission shows that Pluto is slightly larger than originally thought at 1,473 miles in diameter. This compares to 7,926 miles at the equator for Earth.

**Author's note:** The previous two answers both relate to technology that people believe is new but, in fact, has been around for much of the last 100 years. What is new is the tiny size of the components that are now doing the work, and the increase in transmission speeds that have been attained by increasing signal bandwidth through the use of the higher end of the radio frequency spectrum.

* * *

## 11ᵗʰ August 2015

**Can a nuclear device be small and light enough to be concealed in a suitcase?**

The size of a nuclear weapon is dependent on a number of factors, but the most important one is the "critical mass" of the fissile, or nuclear, material.

Critical mass is defined as the minimum amount of fissile material needed to maintain a nuclear chain reaction. However, this can be varied by a number of factors, such as the shape of the material, the temperature, adding other elements to affect its molecular properties, or adding a neutron reflector which prevents the escape of neutrons prior to it going critical.

The fissile material which requires the smallest amount to make it go "critical" is Californium-252. The critical mass is only 2.73 kg, the equivalent to less than three bags of sugar, forming a sphere about the size of an apple. This is a manmade element created by bombarding Curium with Helium-4 ions. There are another six elements with a critical mass of 10 kg or less that might be used in a small sized bomb. This is about half the baggage allowance for a single suitcase set by the majority of airlines.

Californium-252 and the other elements aren't the sort of materials that can be manufactured in a garden shed but, theoretically at least, could be used to manufacture a nuclear weapon small enough to fit inside a large suitcase. The remaining components are simply those that would be required to bring about the nuclear explosion: the containment chambers, conventional explosives, power supply (batteries), triggers and timing controls.

Nuclear weapons are prevented from going prematurely "critical" and causing an explosion by dividing the fissile material into halves and keeping them apart. The halves are then brought together by firing them at each other, using conventional explosives, which will combine the mass and cause the chain reaction which causes the nuclear explosion.

A small weapon means a small nuclear yield, probably no more than one kiloton or the equivalent of 1,000 tons of conventional explosives. The major threat to life, however, isn't from the explosion, it is from the spread of radioactive material which will poison anyone who ingests it. Only a small amount, perhaps a few molecules, is needed to cause illness with a significant likelihood of death. The lethal dose of radioactive polonium administered to Russian journalist Alexander Litvinenko was probably no larger than a pin head.

The problems of manufacture would arise from the design requirements rather than from the physical size of the components. That is the shape required to fire the two halves of the fissile material at each other in such a way as to cause the nuclear reaction, while storing them far enough apart to prevent the reaction occurring prematurely.

A more likely scenario for would-be terrorists is to construct what is known as a "dirty bomb". This is a conventional improvised explosive device (IED), or bomb, packed around with radioactive waste. The nuclear industry produces tons of radioactive waste each year and its safe storage and disposal is a major headache.

A dirty bomb doesn't create a nuclear detonation, but will spread radioactive contamination across a large area, threatening the lives of people some distance, perhaps miles, from where the bomb was actually placed. Such a weapon could be fitted into a container much smaller and lighter than a suitcase. In 2008 Al Qaeida terrorist José Padilla (aka Abdullah al-Muhajir) was imprisoned for 17 years in the USA for plotting to explode a radiological, or dirty, bomb. This is an idea I explore further in my novel The Warriors: Mirror Man.

**Author's note:** Californium-252 costs about $27 million per gram to manufacture, so it would be a very expensive bomb to build, about $74 billion for the smallest viable device. The other 10 synthesised elements are also expensive, but not quite as expensive as Californium-252

* * *

## 14th August 2015

**Why is St Christopher, patron saint of travellers, no longer considered a saint? Have any other saints suffered a similar fate?**

It is something of a myth that St Christopher and many other saints are no longer regarded as such. This is a misinterpretation of events. The Roman Catholic church has no procedure for de-canonising a saint, as saints are canonised by the Pope and the Pope is infallible. For a saint to be de-canonised would be an admission that Popes weren't infallible.

Prior to 1234 AD there was no formal process for recognising someone as a saint and it was common for Bishops to name people as such. It was the acknowledgement that some saints who had been created might not be worthy of the title that led to the Vatican taking control of the process.

On 14<sup>th</sup> February 1969 Pope Paul VI issued the Mysterii Paschalis, an apostolic letter, which reorganised the liturgical year for the Roman Catholic Church. This is essentially a calendar of the various holy days and celebration days throughout the year and the forms of worship for them. In doing so he removed the celebration days for a large number of saints.

Over the years it had also been the habit of monarchs to insert into the church calendar celebration days for saints they favoured. Once inserted no one wished to cause offence to the monarch's descendants by removing them. St Thomas à Beckett would almost certainly fit into that category.

Three classes of saint were created as a result of the changes. The lowest class was that of saints over whom there were historical doubts. Perhaps they had never really existed or perhaps the claims for their acts were unsubstantiated. Saint Cecelia was saved from inclusion in this lowest category because of her veneration by the public.

The second class of saints were those who it was known existed, but about whom very little was known other than their names. Many of the Roman martyrs of the 1<sup>st</sup> to 4<sup>th</sup> centuries fell into this category, as did many Celtic and Anglo Saxon saints. St Christopher also fell into this category. Again St Cecilia was saved from inclusion because of her popularity.

The final group, those whose names are commemorated in the current liturgical calendar, were those whose provenance, as far as the church was concerned, was proven. Amongst those saints that were "saved" were the most popular and the most revered. A balance was also maintained in terms of their chronology and geographic dispersion so as to avoid accusations of an Italian bias. For this reason some of those saints who were "demoted" may have been unjustifiably treated, while others may have been elevated beyond their true worth.

In 1988 285 Saints were included in the liturgical calendar, down from around 1,800. The true numbers of saints was difficult to establish as some were known by more than one name. Under Pope John Paul II 485 new saints were canonised and under Pope Benedict XVI. a further 45 were added, making 810 in all. On 27th April 2014 both Pope John Paul II and Pope John XXIII were canonised by Pope Frances. However, only those saints listed by Pope Paul VI have specific celebration days in the liturgical calendar.

Not only was the celebration of certain saints removed from the church calendar, but also some feast days disappeared. These were different from Holy Days such as Christmas and Easter. As the name implies, these days allowed the clergy to break from their vows of fasting and abstinence, which made them popular amongst those in holy orders. The original Tridentine calendar, created by the Council of Trent (1545 – 1563), had only two feast days, Corpus Christi and The Feast of the Holy Trinity, but over the centuries a further 18 were added, the last of which was in 1955. Pope Paul reduced this number to 6.

The story of St Christopher comes from the 3rd Century AD. Legend has it that he was a Canaanite (part of modern day Lebanon) by the name of Reprobus, noted for his large stature. He decided to go and serve the "greatest King there ever was" and went off to search him out. After trying several kings and finding them wanting, Reprobus found a king who feared the Devil so he went to find the one the King feared. He fell into the company of a band of robbers, the leader of whom referred to himself as the Devil. However, this leader was seen to avoid a wayside cross and was clearly fearful of the power of Christ.

Reprobus then found a Christian hermit who taught him about Christ. The hermit said that if he helped people to cross a certain river his service would be pleasing to Christ, so Reprobus took up that duty. It is then reputed that he helped a child to cross, who turned out to be a reincarnation of Christ and who blessed him for his work. The meaning of the name Christopher is said to be "Christ Bearer". The image of Christopher carrying a child is the one most commonly associated with the saint and is used on medallions and other jewellery.

As well as being a patron saint of travellers St Christopher is also patron to archers, bachelors, bookbinders, gardeners, mountaineers and transportation workers, as well as many others.

It is likely that Saint Christopher is based on a real martyr who died in Antioch (in modern day Syria) during the Christian purges initiated by the Emperor Decius in the 3$^{rd}$ Century AD. There are also strong similarities to an Egyptian martyr, St Menas, who also died in Antioch in the 3$^{rd}$ century and who is patron saint of travellers in the Coptic tradition.

\* \* \*

## 17$^{th}$ August 2015

**What is the origin of the "-sex" in Sussex, Essex, Wessex and Middlesex? What became of North-sex?**

The "sex" suffix to county names derives from the original Saxon kingdoms that were established during the Anglo Saxon invasion of the British Isles. It is a contraction of 'seachs', the old English word for Saxon. The name of England itself derives from the 'Anglo' part of that of that invasion and was originally applied only to areas of eastern England: Norfolk, Suffolk, Cambridgeshire and southern Lincolnshire, that had been occupied by the Angles.

The arrival of the Anglo Saxons wasn't a co-ordinated invasion, but a 'land grab' by opportunist warlords from those parts of Holland and Germany (the Saxons) and Denmark (the Angles and

Jutes) that had a North Sea coastline. Each warlord that arrived established their own 'kingdom'. These warlords were mainly the second and third sons of kings who wouldn't inherit their fathers' kingdoms. They raised armies with the promise of wealth and went off to seek lands of their own to rule. They were as prone to fighting each other for dominance as they were the native Britons they sought to conquer. The invasion started as soon as the Roman era ended.

The Saxons first started raiding around 395 AD. In 402 AD Emperor Honorius removed the last troops from Hadrian's Wall in order to defend Roman territories on the European mainland and no Roman coinage dating after that has been found in Britain, suggesting that was the effective end of Roman rule. With the North Sea being so treacherous the raiders tended to follow the coastline as far as what we now call the Straights of Dover before crossing to the English coast, which is why they established themselves in the south first, even though they originated further north.

The areas we now know as Sussex, Essex and Middlesex were originally far larger kingdoms meaning the East Saxons, Middle Saxons and South Saxons. Wessex, or the West Saxons, was the largest of these kingdoms and covered the whole of southern England south of the Thames, starting west of London and extending all the way to the Severn estuary and then to the border with Cornwall. Winchester was its capital, which later became the case for the whole of England until the 12$^{th}$ century.

To the north of Wessex and Middlesex was another Saxon Kingdom called Mercia. If there had been a 'Northsex' this would have been it. The origin of the name 'Mercia' is from the old English Mierce or Myrce meaning 'border people'. This border gradually worked its way northwards until it made up the whole of the area we now know as The Midlands.

Wessex annexed Mercia in the 10th century and set up the shire counties that now make up the centre of England. These are recognisable from that date as the county town gave its name to the county as a whole, which is not the case in Wessex itself. The county we now know as Cheshire was called Chestershire by the Saxons as Chester was the county town.

To the north of Mercia was the Kingdom of Northumbria, whose southern border was a rough line from the Mersey estuary to the Humber estuary and bounded to the north by Hadrian's Wall, though this was fluid. This was the last part of England to be occupied by the Saxons, but fell to the Danes (Vikings) when they started to colonise in the $8^{th}$ century, rather than just raiding as they had in earlier times.

Pockets of Saxon resistance persisted, such as the area of Northumberland around Bambrough with its easily defended castle. When the Danes invaded and settled the northern lands they started to extend southwards and Mercia became a disputed and much fought over territory. Towns and villages in Northamptonshire and Warwickshire whose names end with the suffix 'by' (Badby, Barby, Corby) mark the southerly extent of the invasion as this suffix was only used by the Danes.

The county of Kent was taken from the name of the Cantiaci tribe, meaning those who lived on the edge, meaning the edge of the country. This area was ruled by the Jutes, close relations of the Angles, from the $5^{th}$ century and was known as Cantwara, with its capital at Canterbury.

With the rise of Alfred the Great the other kingdoms were gradually drawn under the rule of Wessex, mainly by conquering the invading Danes who had previously captured the territory.

In the $9^{th}$ century Alfred the Great (849 – 899) led the resistance against the Danes but never ruled over a fully united England. That didn't come about until the rule of Æthelstan in 927 AD but it was a fragile thing and the Danes continued to contest

Saxon rule until the Norman invasion of 1066. For an entertaining, if fictional, account of Alfred's rule try Bernard Cornwell's series of books set against the backdrop of Alfred the Great's campaigns.

As part of their conquest the Normans dismantled Wessex as the heart of the Saxon kingdom and its name ceased to have any administrative meaning, unlike Essex, Sussex and Middlesex.

Middlesex ceased to be a county under local government reforms that came into effect in 1965, transferring its local government authority mainly to the newly formed Greater London Council and the rest to Hertfordshire, Buckinghamshire, Berkshire and Surrey. Essex and Sussex are the only counties left to remind us of the days when we were ruled by Saxon Kings.

**Author's note:** When this letter was published the whole of the second half was omitted, that relating to the founding of Northumbria and what followed. While I recognise the need to make space for other letters, some interesting historical information, relevant to the question, was lost.

\* \* \*

## 24<sup>th</sup> August 2015

**Was Margaret Thatcher once on a pop music panel on a children's game show?**

The children's TV programme Saturday Superstore ran from October 1982 until April 1987, hosted by BBC Radio presenter Mike Read. Also among the presenting team were Keith Chegwin, Sarah Greene and John Craven. The programme had evolved from Multi-Coloured Swap Shop which ran from 1976 to 1982 which had also featured John Craven and Keith Chegwin as presenters alongside Noel Edmonds.

During the show, celebrities would be invited on and would take part in a question and answer session with the studio audience of young people and also by telephone. They would also take part in a feature where they would listen to newly released records and give their opinion of them.

The celebrities that were invited were usually popular musical acts and actors and presenters from TV programmes aimed at young people. However in 1987, in the run up to the general election of that year, Prime Minister Margaret Thatcher appeared.

It isn't clear if the show's production team invited the Prime Minister onto the show, or if the production team were persuaded to invite her by the Conservative Party's election campaign manager.

During the show Mrs Thatcher appeared alongside TV zoologists Terry Nutkins and Chris Packham, presenters of he Really Wild Show, neither of whom would regard themselves as being well disposed towards Mrs Thatcher and the Conservative Party and have said as much in subsequent interviews about the programme; though it didn't stop them from appearing anyway.

Mrs Thatcher took part in the question and answer session as expected. The presenter for the segment was John Craven. One persistent young questioner phoning in to the programme, asked her "Where will you be if nuclear war breaks out?" Mrs Thatcher avoided answering it, turning the question into one about the effectiveness of the independent nuclear deterrent instead. However, the young questioner, clearly a Jeremy Paxman in the making, wasn't to be diverted and asked the question several more times with similar results.

Mrs Thatcher then took part in the music panel segment alongside Gordon Kaye in his 'Allo, 'Allo character of René Artois. She watched the video of Heartache by Pepsi and Shirlie which she didn't seem to enjoy, describing it as lacking melody. The record went to No 2 in the UK charts. She then watched Beautiful Imbalance by Indie band Thrashing Doves, which she said she enjoyed. The record only made it to No 50 in the UK charts. Did the Prime Minister's views on the music influence the records' chart performances? No one can be sure.

Video extracts of Margret Thatcher's appearance on the show are available to view on YouTube.

**Author's note:** Since writing this answer I have become aware that presenter Mike Reid has emerged as a supporter of UKIP. Back in the 1980s, before UKIP was formed, it might be assumed he was a Conservative and Thatcher supporter. This may have been the reason that the Prime Minister was invited on the show.

\* \* \*

## 25<sup>th</sup> August 2015

**Did a German official called Gunther Schabowski inadvertently cause the tearing down of the Berlin Wall?**

This would seem to be a case of history occurring by accident rather than design.

Although a journalist by profession, Gunter Schabowski became a senior member of the Socialist Unity Party of Germany (SED), the ruling party in the German Democratic Republic (GDR) or East Germany as it was known in the West. In 1985 he became First Secretary of the SED and a member of the Politburo, the equivalent of our Cabinet, meaning that he was no minor functionary.

In October 1989 there was something of a 'Palace Coup' inside the SED, replacing hard line Chairman Erich Honecker as party leader and long-time head of the GDR. His place was taken by Egon Krenz.

As Schabowski was an experienced journalist he became the SED's unofficial spokesman and held several press conferences each day in an attempt to manage the media reporting of the events that were happening in East Germany following Honecker's replacement.

Just before a press conference on 9<sup>th</sup> November 1989, Schabowski was handed a note stating that East Germans would be allowed to cross the border into West Germany providing they had the proper permission. The note contained no further details. The arrangements had only just been agreed by Egon Krenz and border guards had yet to be instructed on the new procedures.

At the end of the press conference, when Schabowski had concluded his pre-arranged agenda, he read out the note, which brought a flood of questions from the assembled media. Without any detail Schabowski made the mistake attempting to ad lib answers. In response to a question about when the new regulations would come into effect he answered that as far as he knew it was "sofort, unverzüglich"- immediately, without delay.

When asked if the regulations applied to exit from East Berlin to West Berlin he said that they did, though they hadn't been mentioned in the note. There were different rules applied to Berlin compared to the rest of East Germany because the Russians still considered it to be an occupied city and controlled one of the crossing points in the Berlin Wall; Checkpoint Charlie where NATO and Warsaw Pact military personnel passed to and fro through the wall as tourists, shoppers or on the business of government.

At 7.17 pm West German TV station ZDF broadcast an extract of the press conference as part of a news bulletin. This was followed at 8 pm by ARD, another West German station. Both stations were widely viewed in East Berlin.

As the evening progressed thousands of East Berliners started to assemble at the six border crossings between East and West Berlin, demanding to be let through. The caveat in Schabowski's announcement about having the 'correct permission' in order to exit had gone unheard even though it had been broadcast in both TV bulletins; the story had grown in the telling, fuelled by rumour and gossip

The border guards initially tried to resist the crowds, stalling for time while they sought clarification and orders. However, the huge crowds threatened to overwhelm them and at 11.30 pm Stasi (East German security police) officer Harald Jäger opened the gates at the Bornholmer Strasser crossing point to allow people into West Berlin. What followed is now a matter of historic record and signalled the beginning of the end for East Germany and also for the Cold War.

Germany became a reunified country on 3$^{rd}$ October 1990, less than 12 months after the Bornholmer Strasse gate was opened.

After reunification Schabowski turned on his former colleagues and denounced the policies of the government of the GDR. He is the only senior ranking member of the East German Politburo to have done so. However, it didn't save him from prosecution for the murder of East Germans who had died attempting to cross into West Germany, but because of his denouncements he received a prison sentence of only 3 years and was released after 1 year following a pardon by Berlin's Governing Mayor Eberhard Diepgen . Now aged 86 Schabowski lives quietly in a nursing home in Berlin, suffering from poor health.

**Author's note**: I was stationed in West Germany with the RAF in 1989. Seeing the Berlin Wall come down triggered my first major career change in over 20 years as I realised that in order to justify the maintenance of armed forces a nation needs to have an enemy. Britain's enemies of 40 years were busily dismantling themselves. I decided to leave before I was pushed. The RAF is now about 1/3 the size it was in 1989. Gunter Schabowski died just a few months after my answer was published, on 1$^{st}$ November 2015.

*  *  *

## 2<sup>nd</sup> September 2015

**During World War II, East Anglia probably had more than 100 airfields, with something like 1,000 bombers. How were these airfields re-supplied with fuel?**

As a former RAF officer responsible for the supply of aviation fuel for a major operational station in the late 1980s/early 90s I can tell you that the logistics of fuel supply has barely changed since the earliest days of powered flight. There has only been one significant innovation in all that time.

At the outbreak of World War II fuel was moved from oil refineries to regional distribution centres by rail, using tanker cars. From there it was distributed to airfields by road tanker.

As may be imagined, fuel supply was a major logistics operation in East Anglia, Lincolnshire and Yorkshire where most of the RAF's bombers were based.

A Lancaster bomber required around 20,000 lbs of fuel, about 2,000 gallons (9000 ltrs), for a single sortie. 12 aircraft made up a squadron and there were usually between 2 and 4 squadrons operational at each airfield. Taking the lower number, that meant that 48,000 gallons of fuel were required per day of operations. However, it was unusual to fly operations 7 days a week, so assuming 4 days of flying per week that meant a week's supply of fuel would be about 190,000 gallons, though a reserve was also held in case a surge in operations was ordered.

A typical road tanker of the era would have a capacity of about 3,000 gallons, so this meant that 64 tanker loads of fuel per week were required, or approximately one delivery every 2½ hours, day and night. That was for just one airfield! The chances of getting stuck behind a fuel tanker on a narrow country lane in Lincolnshire were quite high.

Once at the airfield the fuel was stored in Bulk Fuel Installations (BFIs). These are arrays of horizontal cylindrical tanks with a capacity of about 10,000 gallons for each tank. There would be a number of these, dispersed around the airfield and buried to protect them from air attack. A typical BFI array would comprise between 6 and 12 tanks, complete with pipework, pumping equipment and dispensing points. Fuel would be delivered to one installation while it was dispensed from a different one to ensure a regular turnover of fuel in the tanks. The fuel was transferred from the BFI to the aircraft by fuel bowser, much as it still is today at many airports.

The innovation referred to earlier was the creation of the Government Pipeline and Storage System (GPSS). Prior to World War II the government realised that the supply of fuel to RAF airfields would be of major strategic importance. In 1936 planning commenced to establish a pipeline to connect selected storage depots to RAF airfields using a pipeline. The first part of the system was the establishment of a pipeline between Liverpool docks, Stanlow oil refinery and Avonmouth docks. This meant that regardless of which port the crude oil was delivered to, it could be transferred to Stanlow by pipeline.

In 1939 the government started building underground storage depots, which were connected together and to the oil refineries. The building was undertaken at night in order to avoid detection by the Luftwaffe. The interconnected system eventually extended into Kent and westwards from the Thames estuary as far as Oxfordshire and Wiltshire and northwards into Essex, Suffolk and Norfolk and eventually Lincolnshire.

RAF and USAAF stations were connected to the pipeline by spur lines with fuel flows being controlled by valves. Initially the valves were manually operated but later innovations included remotely controlled electrically operated valves. Eventually a "ring main" was established forming a rough quadrilateral from Liverpool to the Humber and south to Bristol and the Thames. However, airfields further from the pipeline were never connected and continued to be supplied by road tanker. This is still the case today for some RAF stations.

On 10<sup>th</sup> March 2015 the government sold GPSS to the Spanish company Compañía Logística de Hidrocarburos (CLH) for £82 million, at the same time signing contracts to maintain the supply of fuel to the RAF stations that are still served by it.

While serving in Germany in the late 1980s we had 4 Tornado squadrons on our base. Under NATO operating rules we were required to hold 7 days supply of fuel so our 4 BFIs had the capacity to hold about 10 million litres of aviation fuel (about 2.2 million gals). Fortunately we were connected to the NATO fuel pipeline for re-supply.

The 1980s saw the installation of 4 giant 2 million litre tanks to bring our airfield's storage capacity up to the NATO requirement. These were vertical tanks and when covered in soil and grass resembled man made hills. The last of these was completed in 1989, just before the fall of the Berlin Wall and just ten years before the station closed.

Our "Plan B", in the event of the NATO pipeline being destroyed, was to bring fuel in by rail tank car to our local railway station and transfer fuel to the airfield by road, taking us back to the logistics of the 1930s.

**Author's note:** I turned "fuel pipeline geek" for this answer so I'm not surprised that the editor curtailed most of the latter part of this letter.

\* \* \*

**29<sup>th</sup> September 2015**

**William Webb Ellis has been credited with inventing rugby by running with the ball during a football game at Rugby School.**

**In his lifetime, is this something he personally claimed, confirmed or at any time talked about?**

William Webb Ellis was a clergyman who attended Rugby School between 1816 and 1825. He was born on 24th November 1806 in Salford, Lancashire, the son of a soldier who died at the Battle of Albuhera in 1811 and he was raised by his mother until he was sent to Rugby. He died on 24th February 1872, about fourteen years before his name was first linked to the game of rugby.

It is said that William Webb Ellis "with a fine disregard for the rules of football as played in his time, first took the ball in his arms and ran with it" in 1823. However, this account entered the public arena some 53 years after the event through the writings of former Rugbeian Matthew Bloxham, who indicates that the information came to him via an unidentified third party. In other words it may never have actually happened and if it did it hadn't been previously remarked upon. But it has certainly become part of the legend of the game of rugby.

Bloxham, the son of an assistant teacher at Rugby, had attended the school but left 3 years before the alleged event, though he still lived in the town as an articled clerk to a local solicitor and remained there, becoming a noted antiquarian.

There is ambiguity with regard to the term "played in his time" as this almost certainly refers to how the game was played at Rugby School, rather than how it was played in the country at large.

Football as a sport in Britain goes back at least as far as 1170, where an account refers to groups of youths going into a field for a game of ball. However the Greeks and Romans were both known to have played ball games that involved the feet. The first formalised rules of rugby weren't published until 1845, 22 years after William Webb Ellis's alleged infringement of the rules.

The game of rugby came to be seen as a sport in its own right only when, in 1863, Blackheath Football Club decided not to join the newly formed Football Association, preferring their own version of the sport which adhered to the rules of rugby. The rules for Association Football were formally published on 3$^{rd}$ December 1863 and, as we know, outlawed the use of the hands other than by the goalkeeper.

The establishment of the Football Association defined the difference between the game played by rugby clubs and the game as it was played everywhere else. The Rugby Football Union was formed 8 years later in 1871. The Rugby League wasn't formed until 1895 when the Northern Rugby Football Union broke away from the RFU over disagreements about professionalism in the sport.

Until the rules of rugby and association football were established matches were played either following local traditions or by agreement between the two sides. These rules may or may not have allowed the use of hands when playing the game, depending on these local traditions. Football and rugby clubs as we know them didn't exist until the mid 19$^{th}$ century and so the rules for various games were established mainly within public schools and varied from school to school. The various rules for the game may have had obvious similarities but they also had their differences. It is likely that there were vast differences in rules in different parts of the country, as before the arrival of the railway players wouldn't have travelled far to play the game, which meant that different versions of the rules also didn't travel.

It is likely that the form of football created at Rugby School was spread through competition with other schools. The first established rugby club was the Guys Hospital Football Club founded in 1843 by former Rugby School pupils, two years before the rules of rugby were formalised. The oldest non university or school club is the aforementioned Blackheath Rugby Club founded in 1858. Notts County Football Club are claimed to be the oldest football team in the world but weren't formed until 1862, before the name Football Association came into being.

\* \* \*

### 16th October 2015

**Lt George Knowland was a former pupil at Elmwood Junior School in Croydon, Surrey, where my son goes to school. Knowland was awarded the VC. What was his story?**

Lt George Arthur Knowland was born on 22nd August 1922 in Catford, Kent, (now in the London borough of Lewisham) and attended Elmwood Primary School. Little is known of his later schooling. In 1940 he joined the Royal Norfolk Regiment with the rank of Private but within a year he had been commissioned as a Second Lieutenant, which suggests at least a Grammar School education. He then volunteered for the Army Commandos and served in Burma with No 1 Commando.

The action for which he won the VC was the Battle for Hill 170 in Kangaw, Burma. On 31st January 1945 George Knowland was in command of the 24 men of No 4 Troop when they came under attack by around 300 Japanese. When one of his forward Bren gun team was wounded Knowland moved forward to take his place. The enemy were less than 10 yards away, lying below the level of the rim of his trench, so Knowland had to stand up to fire the gun. He continued to maintain fire in this exposed position while casualties were evacuated and two more Bren gun teams were moved up to provide more fire support.

Later in the battle he was seen to fire a 2 inch mortar from the hip directly into enemy positions and when his rifle jammed he grabbed a 'Tommy gun' to continue to rain fire on the enemy. He died later in the day from wounds sustained during the fighting.

Despite suffering 50% casualties the troop were able to hang on to their position until relieved, after being under constant fire for 12 hours, preventing any Japanese advance through their positions.

The Battle of Hill 170 was fought between 3$^{rd}$ Commando Brigade, part of XV Indian Corps, on the British side and the 54$^{th}$ Infantry Division on the Japanese. The objective for the Brigade was to seize the Arakan Peninsula in Burma as part of the overall operation to force the Japanese out of Burma.

The Battle of Hill 170 was a counter attack by the Japanese in an attempt to eject the British from the peninsula. It was part of the larger Battle of Kangaw.

The commanding General of VX Corps, Sir Phillip Cristison, said of 3$^{rd}$ Brigades' part in the battle "The Battle of Kangaw had been the decisive battle of the whole Arakan campaign and that it was won was very largely due to your magnificent defence of Hill 170"

Lt George Knowland's grave is in the Taukkyan War Cemetary, Burma.

**Author's note**: I am always inspired by the stories of winners of the VC and this is just one of a number of answers I have submitted on the subject. Others may be found in "I'm So Glad You Asked Me That", the predecessor of this book. It is my ambition, one day, to put together a history of all 1,358 winners of the medal. In the meantime, you can find out more about the Army Commandos and their heroics in my book "A Commando's Story".

\* \* \*

## 21$^{st}$ October 2015
### Do mobile phone signals reach space?
All radio signals, which includes mobile phone signals, are electromagnetic waves and have the capability to reach space if they

exceed a certain frequency. That frequency is determined by the ionosphere, which acts to either reflect or refract signals, just as light is reflected by a mirror or refracted by a prism. Light is just a visible form of electromagnetic wave. The ionosphere is one of the highest layers of the atmosphere, starting at around 60 km (37 miles) above the Earth.

Radio waves travel in straight lines and can't follow the curvature of the Earth, so this property of the ionosphere was exploited by early radio pioneers to send radio signals around the world long before the communications satellite was invented. Radio signals below 3 Mhz tend to be reflected by the ionosphere while signals between 3 and 30 Mhz are refracted. Low frequency radio signals are also bent by gravity to a limited degree, so the combination of these properties is the reason why so called 'long wave' signals, such as that used by Radio 4, can be heard hundreds of miles beyond the horizon.

Generally any radio signal above 30 Mhz is refracted by too small an amount to be diverted and therefore will escape into space. Without that property the communications satellite wouldn't be possible and we wouldn't have Sky TV or GPS. Mobile phone signals operate in the frequency range 850 Mhz to 1,900 Mhz (1.9 Ghz), many times that needed for them to pass unimpeded through the ionosphere.

The strength of the radio signal will determine whether or not it is usable once it has been detected. A typical phone handset will emit a maximum of 2 watts of power when transmitting.

Radio signals obey an 'inverse square' law with regard to their signal strength. This means that every time the distance travelled is doubled you 'lose' half the power in the signal. So if a 2 watt signal is 1 watt in strength after travelling 1 metre it will be ½ a watt after 2 metres, ¼ of a watt after 4 metres etc. However, because of this same law the signals never actually reach zero power. They effectively go on forever, however weak in strength.

Space is generally regarded as starting at a height of 100 kilometres or 60 miles so the signal will be extremely weak by the time it gets there. Very sensitive equipment would be needed to be able to detect it. However 'satellite phones' are available which work like mobile phones, at a similar low power output and at similar frequencies, but connect their calls via satellite rather than through ground based radio masts.

* * *

## 29th October 2015

On holiday in the Nord-Pas-de-Calais district of France, staying in the small village of Caumont, south of Hesdin, we discovered the headstones of four British Airmen who had died on the same day, March 31, 1944. Who were they and what had happened to them?

There are, in fact, eight graves of British and Canadian servicemen in the cemetery of the church at Caumont, six together and two in the North West corner of the cemetery. One of these is of Private Thomas Hartley of the Queens Own Oxfordshire Hussars who died on 27th December 1916, during the First World War. The second is that of Sqn Leader Patrick Thornton-Brown who died on 21st December 1943. Of the six that are together, five are members of the RAF and one of the Royal Canadian Airforce (RCAF) who all died on 31st March 1944.

They are: Flying Officer Peter Munnery RCAF, Flight Sergeant Albert Brice, Sgt Frederick Boyd, Sgt William Gibson, Sgt Graham McNeight and Sgt Victor Rhaney. All six were members of 158 Sqn RAF.

At the time of their deaths they were flying a Handley Page Halifax Mk III bomber serial number HX322 from RAF Lisset in Yorkshire. The seventh crew member, wireless operator Sgt Kenneth

Dobbs, was taken prisoner. Dobbs had only just transferred in from 78 Sqn as part of the crew of a replacement aircraft and he hadn't been scheduled to fly on the raid, being a late replacement (and a volunteer) for the regular radio operator who had gone sick that day.

RAF records show that on the night of 30th/31st March 1944 the RAF mounted an attack on Nuremburg which resulted in the heaviest loss of aircraft and aircrew of the entire war. Of the 795 bombers dispatched 95 failed to return.

Having suffered some damage from anti-aircraft fire over the target area, the pilot took the aircraft on a southerly route so as to avoid a lengthy sea crossing in a damaged aircraft. HX322 was on the last leg of its journey when it was intercepted by Hauptman Earnst-Willhelm Modrow in a Heinkel 219 of I/NJGJ1, a night fighter squadron, who shot it down over Caumont, strafing it from nose to tail. It is thought that most of the crew were killed by the cannon fire rather than the crash. Sgt Dobbs had no recollection of leaving the aircraft. He regained consciousness in the back of a German army truck suffering from a broken leg, broken ribs, head injuries and a cannon shell wound to his thumb. He discovered later that he had been found in the rear of the aircraft's wreckage. His survival of such a crash can only be described as miraculous.

158 Sqn records show that HX322 was the only aircraft the squadron lost that night. A full sized replica of a 158 Sqn Halifax bomber can be seen at the Yorkshire Air Museum at Elvington near York.

On 21st December 1943 Sqn Leader Patrick Thornton-Brown (aged 24) was leading a flight of six Typhoon aircraft of 609 Sqn based at RAF Manston in Kent, accompanying a force of USAAF Martin Marauder light bombers on a daylight raid over Northern France. After the Typhoons had fired their rockets at ground targets they were attacked in a 'friendly fire' incident involving both RAF Spitfires and USAAF Thunderbolt aircraft. Despite the Typhoons and Marauders firing flares to give the recognition signal for the day the attacks continued, downing the Typhoon of Fg Off Miller as well as that of Thornton-Brown. Sqn Ldr Thornton-Brown was seen to bail out of his damaged aircraft and it is believed that he was killed by fire from German troops on the ground. Sqn Ldr Thornton-Brown was awarded a posthumous DFC.

There are no records as to how Pvt Hartley died or why he is buried at Caumont rather than in one of the larger Commonwealth War Graves cemeteries in the area. Although his headstone records his rank as private, his Graves Registration Report (Army Form W3372) gives his rank as Lance Corporal. At the time of his death the Queens Own Oxfordshire Hussars were based at Vaulx, just a short distance from Caumont, but there is no evidence of any combat operations taking place in the area at the time, so his death was likely to have been the result of an accident or illness. Other records show that he was born in France and his burial in Caumont cemetery may be a recognition of this, laying him to rest in 'French' soil rather than in 'Commonwealth' soil.

\* \* \*

## 14<sup>th</sup> December 2015

**Is it true that the letter 'X' was added to Naval Ratings' service numbers following the Indian Mutiny to indicate they hadn't participated.**

The letter X was added to Royal Navy service numbers as a result of pay cuts that led to a mutiny, but it was The Invergordon Lower Deck Mutiny, not the Indian Mutiny.

In 1931, in their efforts to deal with the Great Depression, the National Government of Ramsay MacDonald introduced massive public spending reductions. Part of these included pay cuts of between 10% and 25% for Royal Navy personnel, depending on their pay scales at their date of enlistment. Longer serving sailors had the larger cuts imposed, affecting them more than newer recruits. Similar cuts were also imposed on the Army and RAF.

Sailors of the Atlantic Fleet arriving back from sea at the port of Invergordon in the Firth of Cromarty on 11th September 1931 learnt of the pay cuts from newspapers. Some reports were suggesting that the pay cut was 25% across the board. Not surprisingly the sailors reacted badly to this news. The Admiralty issued a formal announcement by telegram on 12th September by which time some sailors were already agitating for some form of action.

Ten warships arrived in Invergordon on 11th September, these were the flagship HMS Hood, Adventure, Dorsetshire, Malaya, Norfolk, Repulse, Rodney, Valiant, Warspite and York. Now having access to newspapers some sailors started to organise and met on a football field on 12th September to vote on strike action. Speeches were made at the canteen on shore the following evening. The Officer of the Patrol, effectively the Guard Commander, called for reinforcements and the canteen was closed early, the crews leaving peaceably. More speeches were then made on the pier

Five more ships, the Nelson, Centurion, Tetrarch, Shikari and Snapdragon all arrived in port on the 14th September while the Warspite and Malaya left to conduct exercises.

While the officers of the fleet were being entertained to dinner by Rear Admiral Tomkinson there were further disturbances at the shore canteen and also in the open air. Although the crowds of sailors were broken up many returned to their ships to continue their protests.

On 15th September HMS Repulse sailed on time to carry out exercises, but crews on the other four capital ships had already started to refuse to obey orders. Acting on their own initiative, the crews continued to carry out essential safety patrols and some other harbour duties but refused to go to sea. Officers who tried to give orders were ignored or ridiculed and the mutiny spread to the remaining ships in port.

In the hope of quelling the mutiny, Rear Admiral Colvin was dispatched to the Admiralty to present the sailors' complaints, but it appears that they were not taken seriously. Minor concessions were made on the reduction of pay on condition that the sailors returned to normal duties. The Admiralty did eventually put new proposals to the Cabinet while giving orders that all ships should put to sea immediately to join their squadrons. These orders were obeyed and the mutiny was ended without bloodshed.

In the end the ratings who were expected to receive the largest pay cut of 25% were only given a 10% pay cut and beneficial changes to marriage allowances were also made. As a punishment the organisers of the mutiny were jailed and 200 sailors were discharged from the service. Across the Navy as a whole another 200 sailors were discharged for attempting to incite similar unrest. Len Wincott, one of the organisers at Invergordon, became active in the Communist Party and defected to Russia in 1934 and served at the Battle of Stalingrad. He returned to Britain only once, in 1974 and died in Moscow in 1983.

At the time of the Invergordon mutiny Royal Navy service numbers were made up of 6 digits with a prefix letter J, K, L or M to indicate in which branch of the service the sailor served. J was for seamen and communicators, K for stokers, L for officers' cooks and stewards and M for all others. In 1931 the letter X was added after the initial letter for those personnel who had their pay adjusted as part of the pay settlement that led to the Invergordon mutiny, but it didn't indicate whether or not they had participated as it applied to all personnel affected by the pay cut.

\* \* \*

15<sup>th</sup> December 2015

**What is the story behind Camp Century, a giant underground bunker in the Arctic belonging to the U.S.?**

Project Iceworm was the codename used for a major construction project initiated by the United States military with the intention of concealing medium range ballistic nuclear missiles under the ice of Greenland without the knowledge of the Danish government. Greenland is Danish sovereign territory. The project was started in 1959 and abandoned in 1966.

To test the concept of building missile silos in this remote and inhospitable environment a smaller project, known as Camp Century, was started. This was explained to the Danish government as a feasibility study for affordable military outposts in Arctic conditions and was sanctioned by the Danes on that basis. It was even discussed in an article in the Saturday Evening Post in 1960, without mention of the more secret elements. The construction site was in North West Greenland 150 miles from The US Air Force base at Thule. This would place the USSR within range of the missiles. The radar station and airfield had been in use at Thule since 1951 as part of a NATO agreement with Denmark.

Camp Century was built by digging 21 trenches in the ice, totalling slightly under 2 miles in length and then erecting arched roofs above to form tunnels. The tunnels were made up of a main central tunnel with side tunnels branching off.

Prefabricated buildings were installed, connected together by the tunnels. Amongst the buildings were a full medical centre, a theatre and a church as well as living accommodation, laboratories and workshops. From 1960 to 1963 the electricity supply was provided by the world's first portable nuclear reactor while fresh water was provided by tapping into water melted from the icefield on which the camp sat. At its peak Camp Century housed 200 military personnel.

Although the Greenland icecap looks like a vast sheet of solid ice it actually moves. Ice core samples taken from the glacier on which Camp Century was built showed that the ice was flexing and moving. This would cause the ice to shift over time and destroy the tunnels, which made Project Iceworm unfeasible. Camp Century was abandoned in 1966.

In 1995, following the release of previously classified information about a B-52 bomber crash at Thule in 1968, the Danish government opened an inquiry into the storage of nuclear weapons in Greenland by the Americans which, after decades of secrecy, brought to light the information about the real purpose of Camp Century. Had the plan gone ahead Project Iceworm would eventually have consisted of 2,500 miles of tunnels through the ice to house 600 nuclear missiles in silos and it would have encompassed 52,000 square miles of the Greenland icecap.

A 1963 documentary about Camp Century, but not Project Iceworm, can be viewed on YouTube. It is presumed that the documentary was designed to prove that the U.S.A. had nothing to hide while at the same time it was hiding the real purpose of Camp Century.

* * *

### 21st December 2015
**Is the Ski Sunday theme tune a parody of Bach?**

Most people who know the theme tune to Ski Sunday know it just by that pseudonym, but the answer to this question becomes immediately apparent when it is discovered that its correct title is "Pop Looks Bach". It was written by Sam Fonteyn (real name Soden), a British musician and composer, born in 1925 and who died in 1991.

While the word "parody" might be used to describe Fonteyn's work, as a musician he might prefer the term "inspired by". Fonteyn wrote a number of short pieces of music with titles that hinted at the style that inspired the piece, hence the Ski Sunday theme was inspired by Bach. "Galloping Gertie" and "Dirty Work At The Crossroads" are reminiscent of the sort of piano tunes that were used to accompany silent movies of the slapstick and melodrama genres respectively. Galloping Gertie in particular is often used when old silent movies are shown on TV or when a pastiche of silent movies are used for comic effect.

Sam Fonteyn was primarily a jazz musician, a career he followed throughout the 1950s and 60s. He was a regular at the popular London jazz venue The Black Sheep Club, where his audience might include people such as Robert Mitchum and Judy Garland. He also wrote the theme tunes for the TV comedy "Please Sir" and the more serious "Training Dogs The Woodhouse Way", which was presented by the slightly eccentric dog trainer Barbara Woodhouse.

However, Fonteyn didn't write specifically for the TV media. His music was purchased by Boosey and Hawkes, a music publishing company and music library, who recorded tunes and licensed them for use in film, radio, TV and theatre. That is how both the themes for Ski Sunday and Please Sir were discovered. Fonteyn's son Nicholas recalls that his father was always taken by surprise when he watched a TV programme for the first time and heard his music being used as the theme tune.

The Ski Sunday theme has been voted a national favourite in a number of polls and has also been used to introduce the Winter Olympics coverage on the BBC. Nicholas Fonteyn recalls that his father said that if he had known Pop Looks Bach was going to become so popular he might have called it something else.

* * *

## 22nd January 2016

### Why do the Jewish and Muslim religions prohibit the consumption of fish that don't have scales?

One of the names applied to Moses was "Law Giver". It wasn't just because he brought the Ten Commandments, as given by God, down from Mount Sinai. He also acted as a channel for God to provide the Children Of Israel with many, many more laws.

These laws may be found in the Book of Leviticus, the third book of the Pentateuch, or Torah; the first five books of what we call the Old Testament and the theological basis for the whole Jewish religion.

In the main these laws are about how to go about the worship of God and include forms of worship, sacrifice, cleanliness, punishments for sin etc. It also lays down the laws of marriage, which include prohibiting certain sexual relationships. It is Leviticus Ch18 v22, for example, that prohibits homosexuality. If you find that harsh then Ch19 v19 says you can't wear cloth woven from two different types of material and v28 says you mustn't put tattoo marks on your body.

The whole of Ch11 is devoted to defining Jewish dietary law, often referred to as Kosher. Basically any meat from animals that have cloven hooves and which chew the cud are "clean" and OK to eat: sheep, cattle, deer etc but meat from animals without cloven hooves or which don't chew the cud is unclean and can't be consumed. Horse is off the menu because it doesn't have a cloven hoof, as are pigs which have cloven feet but don't chew the cud. Why this should be so isn't stated in Leviticus. These were given as laws but without explanation.

When it comes to water creatures vs 9 and 10 state "Of all the creatures living in the water of the seas and the streams you may eat any that have fins and scales. But all creatures in the seas or streams that do not have fins and scales—whether among all the swarming things or among all the other living creatures in the water—you are to regard as unclean."

This may be a matter of observation, as most of the creatures that fall into this category are "bottom feeders" that live off the waste of other creatures, which would breach all the Jewish laws on cleanliness. Tainted sea food was also a common source of food poisoning and this, too, may have been observed.

With regards to Islam, almost all their dietary laws are also based on the book of Leviticus. This isn't surprising as the Jews had a lot of influence across the Middle East and the prophet Mohamed, as a trader, will have visited many cities with Jewish communities and will have traded with the Jews. Medina, where Mohammed lived after being forced to flee from Mecca, was a Jewish town seized by Mohamed and his followers.

As a keen observer Mohamed may have noticed that Jews suffered less from food poisoning than non-Jews and may have attributed this to their dietary laws. As well as food poisoning caused by tainted sea food, for many centuries pork was known to cause an illness known as trichinosis, which we now know was caused by a type of roundworm. This parasite has been eradicated in modern pork farming. The Halal and Kosher practice of draining the blood from animals before eating is laid down in Ch17 of Leviticus, which prohibits the consumption of blood.

Because Christianity grew out of Judaism the laws laid down in Leviticus were originally followed by the new religion. However, Christians began to differentiate between the "old covenant", God's promise to the Hebrews, from the "new covenant", Jesus's promise to his followers. Consequently they decided that many of the laws of Leviticus no longer applied to Christianity. This trend seems to have started following the Council of Jerusalem (approx. 50 AD) when the apostles first started to preach Christianity outside of the Jewish communities. However, Christianity does seem to be have been selective about which of the laws they kept and which they abandoned. For example, a Christian can eat calamari (which don't have scales), have tattoos and wear cloth made from two different types of material, but still can't be gay.

**Authors note:** One of the (many) issues that throw doubt on the authenticity of the Book of Genesis is Ch 7 v 2 which instructs Noah to select animals for the ark based on whether they were "clean" or "unclean". If they were clean he was to take 7 pairs but if they were unclean he was to take only one pair, so the animals may have gone in two-by-two, but that doesn't mean there were only two of each species. However, it wasn't until Leviticus was written, which would have been several centuries after the events described in Genesis, that the status of clean and unclean animals was defined. This suggests that Genesis may have been "reverse engineered", at least in part, to comply with the laws laid down in Leviticus.

\* \* \*

## 24<sup>th</sup> January 2016

**Driving past the M6 junction for Tebay, Cumbria, my car radio suddenly picked up a Spanish station broadcasting from a holiday resort. How might this have happened?**

Radio signals are an electro-magnetic wave which can only travel in straight lines. This means that they can't follow the curvature of the Earth, they have to have some form of assistance, either natural or artificial, if they are to be heard more than about 20 miles from their point of origin. This property allows the same VHF frequency to be allocated to different radio stations in different countries, providing they aren't close neighbours, as there shouldn't be a clash of frequencies.

To broadcast signals in the commercial VHF band (80 Mhz to 110 Mhz) broadcast aerials are positioned on tall masts built on high points, which can double or even triple their range, depending on the exact height of the aerial and the flatness of the surrounding terrain. The BBC has a network of 39 aerial masts to provide its national VHF coverage. Each aerial is able to cover a circular area between 40 and 120 miles in diameter. However, to extend the range of a radio signal sufficiently for a Spanish radio station to be heard in Cumbria requires nature's help.

For a VHF signal to be heard so far from home requires a condition known as "Sporadic E". Above our normal atmospheric layer, known as the troposphere, is the ionosphere, which is made up of various layers of ionised atmospheric gases. The ionosphere acts like a prism to refract, or "bend", radio waves and return them to Earth some distance from the point at which they were broadcast. This is the way "shortwave" radio signals (3Mhz to 30 Mhz) can be received around the world without the aid of communication satellites. The degree of ionisation of the atmosphere is governed by solar activity and is seasonal; in the Northern Hemisphere the ionosphere is "thicker" in summer than in winter.

Under normal circumstances VHF signals are too high in frequency to be bent very far off course by the ionosphere and will continue to pass through it and out into space. However, under certain circumstances the E layer of the ionosphere, the lowest layer, can be subject to thicker "clumps" of heavily ionised atoms which allows VHF signals to be refracted back to Earth thousands of miles from their point of origin.

As the ionisation is extremely localised the area where the signals are received will be quite small and the effect may last for only a few minutes before the ionised cloud moves on or it breaks up. However, the phenomenon is quite common and people have reported hearing radio stations from across Western Europe in seemingly random locations. The effect is more common in summer and during periods of increased solar flare activity.

\* \* \*

8<sup>th</sup> February 2016

**A recent episode of War and Peace featured a cannonball rolling along the grass with a burning fuse which subsequently ignited the explosive inside. When did cannonballs change from a solid ball of iron to such a device?**

It is certainly historically accurate that fused shells were in use at the time of the Battle of Borodino, the battle shown in the episode of War and Peace.

There were three types of artillery ordnance in use at the battle of Borodino and other battles of the Napoleonic era.

Solid round shot, better known as cannonballs, were still in use and remained so until the 1860s, when rifled barrels were introduced to make artillery more accurate. This was around the time of the American Civil War. They were the most common type of munition, used to blast defences apart as well as to kill soldiers. They were replaced by shells which were hollow metal cylinders filled with explosive and triggered by a percussion fuse in the nose.

In the late 1700s, the case shot was developed for use with ordinary field artillery. These were light metal canisters packed with musket balls. The case burst after firing to pepper the enemy with projectiles.

The first recorded use of an exploding shell was by the Spanish at the siege of the Dutch fortress of Wachtendonk in 1588. These early shells were hollowed-out metal cases filled with gunpowder, lit by a fuse. The shell was propelled over a defensive wall using a high angled cannon, such as a mortar or howitzer.

In 1784 a British artillery officer, Lieutenant Harry Shrapnel, invented a fused shell for the same purpose. It was first used at the Battle of Maida in 1803. The shell could be fused accurately enough to be made to burst either directly in front of, or above, enemy infantry. Shrapnel's name came to be synonymous with all metal fragments propelled from an explosion.

While it wasn't uncommon for soldiers to see the flight of the round shot that would kill them it was while it was in flight, not on the ground. Round shot would often hit the ground and roll and inexperienced soldiers would sometimes try to stop them with their feet, like a football, which usually caused their foot to be amputated.

However, showing the shell landing and spinning in the manner depicted in War and Peace is a bit of poetic licence. No gunner would ever fuse a shell so badly that it hit the ground and fizzed for several seconds. Fused grenades, smaller than a shell but otherwise similar in appearance, had been in use for over a century and one of those might have behaved as depicted. These are archetypal "bombs" shown in the hands of cartoon assassins.

The use of exploding shells is recognised in the American national anthem, "The Star Spangled Banner", where the line "the rockets bright flare/shells bursting in air' refers to the War of 1812 against the British.

Napoleon started his military career as an artillery officer and consequently valued he contribution of artillery on a battlefield. One Russian messenger at the battle of Borodino recalled that the continual bombardment caused him to have to keep his mouth open in order to equalise the pressure in his head, such was the effect of the cannon firing. This phenomenon, caused by mass artillery fire, was well known during World War I, but this may have been the earliest reference to the need for a countermeasure.

\* \* \*

## 9th February 2016

**Were all Roman gladiators former captives, or did citizens volunteer?**

It is thought that gladiatorial contests date back to around 264 BC when the heirs of a Roman aristocrat arranged for slaves to fight to the death in order to honour the memory of Junius Brutus Pera. This ceremony of remembrance was known as the munus, or duty. The idea caught on and contests grew in size and spectacle until they became the arena event that we are familiar with. The name gladiator derives from the gladus, the short Roman sword.

Most gladiators were slaves, mainly captured in battle but when peace caused a shortage of candidates they were purchased in the slave markets that were common throughout the Roman Empire. Others were criminals who had their citizenship stripped from them as a punishment and were made into slaves, some of whom ended up in the arena as gladiators. They were trained in Gladiator Schools (ludus, pl. ludi) where they lived a reasonably pampered existence. The school owners understood the relationship between the welfare of their gladiators and their performance in the arena.

From around 60 AD female gladiators began to appear. Their use was received with mixed feelings with some regarding it as a 'harmless' novelty while other believed it ridiculed a noble art. Their use was banned in 200 AD.

Some gladiators were volunteers. There was a financial incentive, as the volunteer was paid a cash bounty on taking the gladiatorial oath, which was a convenient way of paying off a debt. Volunteers of this sort were also permitted to transfer money and property to their families before entering the arena in order to prevent them being left in poverty. Other volunteers were simply in it for the adventure. The oath gave the gladiator's 'owner' the final decision over the life or death of his charge.

Gladiators were the sporting heroes of their day, along with charioteers, and gathered huge followings of supporters. Gambling on the outcome of a contest was also a major pastime. Gladiators could become quite rich on a share of the prize money or through gambling. In order not to upset either fans or gamblers a complex set of rules and regulations evolved to govern contests. Each fight also had an umpire and it was he who stayed the hand of the victor, preventing a killing blow, until the sponsor of the games decided whether the loser should live or die.

Frequently this decision was reached by gauging the reaction of the crowd. A loser who had put on a good show was likely to be spared, while one that had performed poorly (or had lost people a lot of money) was almost certainly condemned to death.

As may be expected, the life expectancy of a gladiator was short, with few surviving more than 10 combats or living past the age of thirty. Each gladiator might fight 3 or 4 times a year. With around 400 arenas across the Empire it is estimated that 8,000 gladiators died each year. A gladiator who had a "good" death (didn't show any weakness or beg for mercy) was treated with honour and their graves were marked by headstones that proclaimed their prowess, unlike the graves of ordinary slaves.

The greatest reward for any gladiator was to be granted his freedom, signified by the award of a wooden training sword (*rudis*) by his owner or the sponsor of the games. A gladiator by the name of Flamma was awarded this 4 times but each time refused his freedom and kept on fighting. His headstone in Sicily records his record: Fought 34, won 21, drawn 9, lost 4. He died at the age of 30.

The decline in gladiatorial contests mirrors the decline in the staging of games and the rise of Christianity in the Empire. With money needed for the defence of the Empire from around 300 AD onwards there was little to spare for games, which had become ever more expensive. Constantine, the first Emperor to officially recognise Christianity, banned gladiatorial contests in 325 AD though they did return. In 393 the Emperor Theodocius adopted Nicene Christianity and banned pagan festivals, which effectively ended the legality of gladiatorial contests, though they continued sporadically until around 530 AD.

Although most closely identified with Rome it is known that the Aztecs engaged in gladiatorial style contests as part of their religious ceremonies and this was witnessed by the Spanish during their conquest of Mexico in the early 16<sup>th</sup> century.

**Author's note:** As a keen readers of historical fiction set in the Roman era (try Simon Scarrow and Robert Fabbri) this is another type of question that I'm drawn to.

\* \* \*

## 11<sup>th</sup> February 2016

**I have been told that Gatwick Airport has a second runway but, over the years, it has been allowed to be overrun by grass. If true, and this runway was recovered, would it still be in a fit state to be used for today's aircraft?**

In the early days of flight wind direction was an important factor. Slow moving aircraft relied heavily on a headwind in order to generate additional lift for take-off. The forward motion of the aircraft and the opposing force of the wind created a combined lift that wasn't attainable by the aircraft alone. On landing this same head wind would help to maintain lift as the pilot slowed the aircraft ready to touch down.

At first airfields didn't have runways. Aircraft just taxied out onto the grass and took off in the best direction commensurate with the wind. The purpose of the "wind sock", the orange fabric tube that flies from a pole on the airfield, was to indicate wind direction and speed for the pilot. It's continued existence is largely a matter of tradition in these modern times. Only when aircraft became heavier and risked sinking into the grass were runways built.

The first runways were just compacted earth topped with grass, sometimes covered with a steel mesh to improve grip, but over the years there was a transition to concrete in order to support ever more heavy aircraft. In order to accommodate differing wind directions it was common for RAF airfields to be built with at least two runways, configured in an X and intersecting somewhere near the middle. As the wind changed direction so the runway in use would change.

As aircraft with more powerful engines were built, take-off speeds improved and the need for this X formation was diminished. Typically airports now only have one runway, though it will still be aligned to take advantage of the prevailing wind. For this reason most runways in Britain are aligned between East-West and North East – South West.

Gatwick airport started life in the late 1920s when land adjacent to Hunts Lane Farm, along Tinsley Green, was purchased for use as an aerodrome. It was next door to a racecourse which has since been absorbed into the airport. It opened on 2$^{nd}$ August 1930 as the Surrey Aero Club, a private club for flying enthusiasts. The Air Ministry granted a license for commercial flights in 1933 and Hillman's Airways (a predecessor of the modern day British Airways) commenced commercial flights in 1934 to Paris and Belfast. The airport was taken over for use by the RAF during the Second World War before being returned to civilian use in 1946.

In 1950 the records show that Gatwick Airport had three operating runways. One was aligned South West – North East, 4,200 ft long and covered in steel mesh. The second was aligned East – West (3,600 ft) and also covered in steel mesh. The final one was aligned South East – North West (also 3,600 ft) and was grass covered. Unfortunately it is difficult to establish the layout of these three runways, but the most likely formations would be a letter A or a Greek Delta.

In 1956 the airport was closed completely and a custom built paved runway was built, the one that remains in use today. The new runway was 7,000 ft in length (2,100m) and was the first in the UK to feature high speed turnoffs onto the taxiways. Provision was made for a second 7,000 ft runway to the North of the new one. This was never built but the ground may have been surveyed and marked out. Most of the original runways have been subsumed into the new runway and taxiways, so even if they didn't intersect they couldn't now be resurrected. The revamped airport was officially opened by the Queen on 9th June 1958 as London Gatwick Airport (LGW).

The existing runway has been extended twice, once in 1964, adding 1,200 ft and again in 1970, adding a further 870 ft.

In 2004 Gatwick airport achieved a record of 906 flights in one day, equating to one landing or take-off every 63 seconds. This was the first time any airport with a single runway has ever handled more than 900 flights in one day. In 2015 Gatwick handled 40 million passengers.

A concrete runway suitable for use by modern aircraft could never be fully covered with grass, as can be seen on many disused World War II airfields, but its surface would become cracked which would allow grass to root in patches. If such a runway existed it would be cheaper to rip it up and start again than to repair it.

**Author's note:** At the time my answer was composed, the debate on putting in a third runway at Heathrow, or a second runway at Gatwick was underway. This is presumably what triggered the question. At the time of editing this book it is still in progress and if you are reading this in 2020 or later I suspect it will still be going on.

\* \* \*

**12th February 2016**

**In historical documentaries and dramas, medieval kings are addressed as "Your Grace". When did we start to address a monarch as "Your majesty"?**

The term "Your Majesty" was first adopted by Charles V (Charles I of Spain) after being elected Holy Roman Emperor in 1519. He believed he deserved a greater form of address than "Highness" which is what previous Kings and Emperors had used. He was soon mimicked by King Frances I of France and Henry VIII of England.

Prior to this both "Highness" and "Grace" had been used to address English monarchs and these remained in use in Scotland until the Act Of Union joined them to England.

Nowadays "Your Highness" is still used to address a Prince or Princess, while "Your Grace" is used to address a Duke or Duchess, a Bishop or an Archbishop.

**Author's note:** Films are not always known for their historical accuracy and in 2018 Netflix released "The Outlaw King", the (not so true) story of Robert The Bruce. In the film the cast continually refer to King Edward I and Edward II as "Your Majesty" and also use the tile for Robert The Bruce, while at the time it wasn't in use anywhere in the world. As if that wasn't bad enough, the film also has Robert and Edward II fighting each other at the battle of Loudoun Hill. Edward II wasn't present for that battle. He was present only at Bannockburn, 7 years later, never actually drew his sword and certainly didn't go head-to-head with The Bruce.

* * *

**16<sup>th</sup> February 2016**

**Do men and women see the colour red differently (making lipstick shade irrelevant)?**

Visible light is made up of seven different frequencies which, mixed together, appear as "white" light. The seven frequencies each form a distinct colour when seen individually: red, orange, yellow, green, blue, indigo and violet; remembered using the mnemonic "Richard of York gave battle in vain". These colours become visible when light is refracted through a prism and is shone onto a screen. Raindrops can have the same effect as a prism, which creates the optical illusion that we know as a rainbow.

The way we perceive colours is dependent on two main factors.

The first is the way that individual light frequencies are reflected, absorbed or scattered by the objects they strike. Something we see as red reflects more of the red light frequency towards the eye, while the other frequencies are either absorbed or scattered. Some surfaces absorb fewer light frequencies and reflect more, and these reflected frequencies mix to give us shades of colour. Something we see as white reflects all light frequencies equally, while black absorbs all the frequencies, leaving nothing for the eye to perceive.

The second factor is the way the rods and cones that make up our retinae receive the colour, which is subject to genetic variations. People who suffer from colour blindness have retinae that don't react to certain frequencies of light, so they have difficulty differentiating between certain colours. The most common form of colour blindness is the inability to differentiate between red and green.

Colour blindness is caused by abnormal photopigments in the cone cells of the retina. It is more predominant in males than females, with as many as 8% of men in Europe suffering from some form of it compared to 0.5% of women. Colour blindness is carried in a recessive gene, which means that it has to be passed on by both parents in order to be inherited. That doesn't mean that both parents are necessarily colour blind, only that they both carry the recessive gene.

Research by Professor Israel Abramov of the City University, New York, published in 2012, revealed that in some instances men and women with "normal" colour perception still perceived colour differently. It was already known that women were able to differentiate between shades of colour more efficiently than men. This is why women are able to appreciate pastel shades while men are not so sensitive to them. However, it has also been found that there are differences between the way men and women differentiate between primary colours, such as red.

Research carried out in 2010 revealed that women wearing red lipstick received "more prolonged glances" from men than women wearing other colours. This suggests men's eyes are drawn by the colour red, though this doesn't necessarily signify attraction. Red is also the colour most associated with danger. It also has to be borne in mind that up to 8% of men may not be able tell what colour lipstick a woman is wearing anyway.

Men, it was discovered, required a longer wave length of the colour red to identify it definitively than did women. This is caused by the way certain neurons in the brain behave when triggered.

This does not mean that things such as the colour of lipstick are irrelevant. While the differences in colour perception are measureable they are still only slight. Men respond better to a shade of red that has a longer wavelength than they will to shade with a shorter wavelength, but the important point is that they still respond, but they will respond more to a particular shade of red.

One also has to consider whether a woman is wearing lipstick in order to attract a male or merely as a form of self-decoration. Just because a woman wears lipstick it doesn't mean that she is trying to attract a man. Many women wear a shade of lipstick they personally find attractive and are unconcerned about how men perceive it.

\* \* \*

2nd March 2016

**During World War II, when a pilot or bomber crew didn't return from a mission, their friends in the mess turned down a glass on the top shelf of the bar. What is the origin of this custom?**

There appears to be no specific history to this tradition, but it is easy enough to see how it might have emerged.

A popular graduation present from initial training in the RAF was a tankard, usually made of pewter but sometimes silver. The airman would then carry this around from station to station and it was common for the owner to lodge their tankard behind the bar of the sergeants' or officers' mess when they reached the relevant rank to qualify for admission. Sometimes they were lodged behind the bar of a local pub and there are stories of many of these going unclaimed because the owners never returned from a mission. This tradition started well before WWII as the dates on antique tankards prove.

To take the tankard from its hook and turn it upside down would be to indicate that the owner had no more need of it. If the missing airman didn't have a tankard (or it was behind the bar of the local pub) then a pint glass would be substituted. In sergeants and officers messes the tankard would eventually be removed, to be returned to the owner's family with the rest of their personal possessions.

When I joined the RAF as an apprentice in 1968, one of the first things our 'entry' did was to set up a 'tankard fund' to save up to purchase our graduation tankards. We bought one when we celebrated a year and a day in the RAF and a second when we graduated at the end of our two years of training. I was also presented with other tankards along the way, as leaving gifts when I was posted, paid for out of the profits from the 'tea swindle'. I still have them all.

* * *

## 4th March 2016

On Friday, February 26th, I was on an aeroplane ready to leave Fuerteventura airport when a large U.S. military plane came into land. Why would the U.S. army/air force be landing on that island.

Following the demise of the Franco regime in Spain following the death of Franco in 1975, the new Spanish government applied to join NATO and became part of the alliance on 30th May 1982, becoming its 16th member and the first to join since 1955. In doing so it automatically made its infrastructure available to the forces of other NATO allies, within certain agreed boundaries. Some allied countries, for example, refuse to allow nuclear weapons on their soil.

Although the airport in Fuerteventura (opened in 1969) is civilian operated, in common with many such airfields in NATO countries it is also used for military flights when needed.

The simplest reason for a United States Air Force transport plane to be landing there would be because it was on route to somewhere else and needed to refuel. As a consequence of the Gulf War and other conflicts a number of airports, civilian and military, in the territories of NATO countries off the coast of Africa have been used as a staging post to and from the US mainland.

An alternative explanation would be that the aircraft was supporting American naval or military exercises in the area, either alone or in conjunction with the Spanish armed forces. The Spanish Army has a light infantry brigade based on Tenerife which commands the 9th Light Infantry Regiment based on Fuerteventura. There is a Spanish Air Force base on Grand Canaria and several naval patrol craft based in and around the Canary Islands.

A final explanation is that the aircraft was pre-positioning stores and/or personnel at the airport to be collected by an American fleet which was due to pass the Canary Islands. This is common practice amongst navies and the use of a large transport aircraft would suggest a fleet rather than a single ship. The location of Fuerteventura on the eastern side of the Canary Islands group makes it convenient for a fleet sailing between the islands and the coast of Africa and with its runway 4,000 ft longer than that of neighbouring Lanzarote it is more suitable for use by larger aircraft. The stores and/or personnel would be collected by relays of helicopters so that the ships wouldn't have to stop to pick them up.

* * *

10<sup>th</sup> March 2016

**Barnes Wallace had developed the 22,000 lb Grand Slam "Earthquake bomb" before his 9,000 lb bouncing bomb. Why wasn't it used against the Ruhr dams?**

There was a difference in physical properties between the two types of weapon that made the Grand Slam, or Earthquake Bomb, unsuitable for use against the Ruhr dams.

Most types of bomb exploded on contact with their target, which blew a hole in it or created a crater in the ground. However, the counter measure for this was to construct buildings with reinforced walls and roofs, or to bury them under a protecting layer of earth. Both methods would absorb the shock of the blast and leave the structure undamaged.

The Grand Slam, or Bomb, Medium Capacity, 22,000 lbs to give it its official RAF designation, was designed to penetrate the target, or the ground close to its target. It was a progression from the earlier, smaller 12,000 lb "Tallboy" bomb. The Grand Slam was specifically designed to penetrate concrete roofs, unlike the Tallboy.

The basic principle was that if a large enough bomb were to be exploded near or within the foundations of a target, the shockwaves created would resemble an earthquake and the structure could be made to shake itself apart.

The curved shape of the face of a dam and the thickness of its foundations meant that the explosive effect of the Earthquake Bomb would mainly be absorbed and would be further "damped" by the water on the inside of the dam wall, which meant that the dam wouldn't shake. If several bombs could be made to go off simultaneously then they might have had the desired effect, but the weight of the bombs limited them to one per aircraft and the targets were too narrow to allow more than one or two aircraft at a time to approach in safety.

In addition, trying to get the bomb to penetrate the thick wall of a dam would be like standing a £5 note on its edge and trying to pierce it by dropping a dart from above. If the bomb hit the sloping face of the dam on the way down it would be deflected away and probably fail to penetrate the ground. If it hit the water it's momentum would be slowed, meaning it couldn't penetrate the foundations and most of its blast would be absorbed by the water at the base of the dam where it was thickest and therefore strongest.

The Bouncing Bomb operated on a different principle. It was designed to bounce along the top of the water until it was close to the wall of the dam, but not in contact with it, sink to a pre-determined level (about a third of the way down) and then explode. The explosive force then set up a series of shock waves in the water that would batter the dam repeatedly at its thinnest and weakest point. The first bomb wasn't expected to destroy the dam, nor was the second, but it was expected that the dam would start to crack and after the third or fourth bomb went off the pressure of the water against the dam would do the rest of the work, which is what actually happened.

In the event the effect of the Dambusters Raid (Operations Chastise, 16-17 May 1943) was mainly psychological, caused by the loss of civilian life by the floodwaters. About 1,600 were killed, though around a thousand of those were Soviet forced labourers. The loss of electrical power from seven hydro-electric generators, designed to hit the armaments industry and the main objective of the raid, was replaced from other resources within a fortnight. Coal production also dropped by 400,000 tons, which was also attributed to the raid, but this also recovered.

**Author's note:** For some reason my carefully researched answer was ignored by the Daily Mail and an inaccurate and misleading answer was used instead. This caused me to do something I rarely do, which was to submit a second answer, reproduced below, rebutting the one that was published. That answer also wasn't published.

\* \* \*

## 30<sup>th</sup> March 2016

**Barnes Wallace had developed the 22,000 lb Grand Slam "Earthquake bomb" before his 9,000 lb bouncing bomb. Why wasn't it used against the Ruhr dams?**

The previous answer to this question was both historically and scientifically inaccurate.

The first Tallboy raids didn't take place until June 1944, more than a year after the Dambusters raid, and the first Grand Slam raid wasn't until March 1945. So the short answer to the question was that the bombs weren't ready in time for the raid.

The degree of penetration of the Grand Slam bomb, or its predecessor the Tallboy, is determined by the force with which it hits the ground. This is a combination of the weight of the weapon, its shape and its velocity on impact. The velocity, however, is limited by a physical property in the form of "terminal velocity".

As gravity acts on an object in free-fall it accelerates under the force of gravity at 32 ft per second squared. However, it doesn't continue to accelerate to an infinite speed. Drag and other factors act on the object to limit its maximum velocity, known as terminal velocity. Once terminal velocity has been reached it doesn't matter from what height the object is dropped, it will not increase its velocity any further.

The calculation of terminal velocity doesn't even include height as one of the variables, though height is important. If the object is dropped from too low an altitude, terminal velocity will not be reached before the object hits the ground. The variables used in calculating terminal velocity are: the mass of the object, its cross sectional area, its drag coefficient and the density of the medium through which the object is passing. Gravity is also used in the calculation, but that is a constant.

Both the Tallboy and Grand Slam bombs would reach terminal velocity well within a fall of 5,000 ft. This means that carrying a bomb in an aircraft flying at 10,000 ft , 20,000 ft or 40,000 ft is irrelevant in terms of the weapon's properties when it hits the ground. The only difference increased height makes is to improve the protection of the aircraft against anti-aircraft gunfire or fighter attack and to decrease the accuracy with which the bomb is aimed.

Instructing bomb aimers to "just miss" the target seems unlikely. The accuracy of bomb sights, combined with air speed, wind speed and wind direction, was such that the probability was that 70% of bombs would miss their targets anyway. If this wasn't the case then the RAF wouldn't have needed 32 Lancaster bombers to attack the Bielefeld and Arnsberg viaducts on 14th March 1945. Two aircraft, plus a couple of reserves, would have been sufficient. While the Bielefeld viaduct was destroyed the Arnsberg viaduct was undamaged. This was the very first Grand Slam bombing operation.

The answer to this question misses the point that the Grand Slam bomb wasn't suitable even if it had been available, because of the physical properties of the Ruhr dams. Had it been suitable the RAF and Barnes Wallis wouldn't have needed to develop the bouncing bomb approach. The bouncing bomb worked by setting up shock waves in the water immediately behind the dam, causing the dam to crack. Once these cracks had formed the pressure of water passing through the fissures forced them to widen and complete the destruction.

\* \* \*

## 17th March 2016

**Is there any connection between Liberia, a country in Africa, and Liberia, a city in Costa Rica?**

Other than the name there is no connection between the two places and their history is independent of each other. The name Liberia has its origins in the Latin word "liber' meaning free.

Liberia the city is the capital of present day Guanacaste Province of Costa Rica. It was founded as a hermitage, or place of rest for travellers, on 4th September 1769 as part of the general Spanish settlement of Central America that had been started with the invasion of Mexico by Hernan Cortes in 1518.

Originally Costa Rica was considered to be an insignificant part of the Spanish Empire and it wasn't until after the area broke away from Spanish rule in 1821 that any form of local or national identity started to develop from being part of the Federal Republic of Central America along with Guatemala, Nicaragua, Honduras and parts of southern Mexico.

Initially Guanacaste identified more with Nicaragua than Costa Rica, but when Costa Rica broke from the federation in 1838 the province became part of the new nation.

The nation of Liberia in Africa grew out of an idea in the USA that freed black slaves should have the opportunity to return to Africa if they wished. Societies sprang up to support this idea.

On 6<sup>th</sup> February 1820 the ship Mayflower of Liberia set sail from New York carrying 86 black settlers bound for West Africa. The ship landed at Sherbo Island of the coast of modern day Sierra Leone but the undertaking wasn't a success and many of the settlers died before the rest were rescued. Between 1821 and 1847 the American Colonisation Society helped to develop the first colony which became known as Liberia. It declared its independence on 27 July 1847. It is the only former colony to have gained independence without some form of armed struggle. Its first President was Joseph Jenkins Roberts, a wealthy, free born black American.

This was not the first area to be settled by people returning from other countries. In 1787 Britain had set up a colony in modern day Freetown, Sierra Leone, intended for the resettlement of poor black families from London.

Monrovia, the capital city of Liberia, is named after President James Monroe who was a prominent supporter of the black colonisation movement.

Overall the colonisation attempts weren't successful. Most of the migrants had lost any natural immunity they might once have had to African diseases which caused a high mortality rate. There was a peak in migration during the American Civil War when a number of slave owners freed their slaves and some of these chose to travel to Africa to start a new life. Many Southern slave owners saw Liberia as a way of getting rid of freed slaves. In all probably only 13,000 black Americans returned to Africa from 1820 onwards. Their influence can be seen in the architecture of Monrovia, which is reminiscent of the 19<sup>th</sup> century Southern states of America. The majority population of Liberia was always from the native Krus, Bassas and Grebos tribes.

\* \* \*

## 25<sup>th</sup> March 2015

**What is the significance of opus numbers in classical music? Who ascribes them? Does every piece of music have one?**

The word "opus" literally means "work" or "labour" in Latin and is used to catalogue a composer's output. The use of the term in relation to music dates from the 17<sup>th</sup> century.

Composers can be quite prolific and may produce a number of pieces that don't have a formal title. Instead a piece might be known as "Symphony in C". This can result in confusion over which work is to be selected for performance, as the composer might have produced more than one symphony in C. By adding the "opus" number it is clear which work is being referred to.

The opus number was originally assigned by the composer, in the chronological order of the work's composition. However, during the 18<sup>th</sup> century music publishers started to assign the opus numbers to collections of music that were being sold together, which meant that the chronological order of composition no longer applied to some collections. This also meant that unpublished work sometimes had no opus number and this was added later by music libraries, often after the composer's death. From around 1900 onwards it became the generally accepted practice for composers once again to assign their own opus numbers, which ended any confusion over who should assign the numbers.

Where the composer has written a number of pieces to form a series of works intended to be played together, the opus number may be followed by a second number. This is the case with Beethoven's Piano Sonata in E-flat Minor No 13, which is a companion piece to Piano Sonata in C-sharp Minor No 14, which was written later. Together they make up the Moonlight Sonatas, which bear the opus number 27 No 1 and 27 No 2, to indicate in which order they should be played.

* * *

25<sup>th</sup> March 2015

**Why was Romania's Iron Guard also known as The Legion of the Archangel Michael?**

According to the Book of Revelations the Archangel Michael led the armies of God against the forces of Satan to cast out Satan from Heaven. His name is often invoked by people who see themselves as fighting God's battles. However, this question might be posed more accurately as "Why was the Legion of the Archangel Michael also known as the Iron Guard?"

The founder of the Legion of the Archangel Michael inserted strong elements of Orthodox Christianity into fascist political views, combining religion with political ideology. The Legion's founder, Corneliu Zelea Codreanu, was a religious patriot who was aiming at attaining a spiritual rebirth for his nation.

In 1927 Codreanu gave up the Deputy leadership of the Romanian National Christian Defence League to found the Legion of the Archangel Michael, taking his inspiration from the ant-Semitic Russian group known as the Black Hundreds, who often invoked the name of the Archangel. The name was changed to The Iron Guard in 1930.

The group drew its support from the peasantry and students rather than from former military personnel, which is where other European fascist movements tended to recruit. It had a heavily male gender bias, with only 8 to 11% of its members being female, because at that time few Romanian women attended university where many members were recruited. As well as being anti-Semitic, the group also set out to combat the rise of communism which was seeping across the border from neighbouring Russia. The liberal government of Ion Duca banned the Iron Guard on 10<sup>th</sup> December 1933. After some brief fighting the Iron Guard retaliated by assassinating Duca on 29$^{th}$ December 1933.

The Iron Guard won its first Parliamentary seats in 1937, forming the third largest party, but they were kept out of power by King Carol II, acting as a dictator, until he was forced to abdicate in 1940. In 1938 Codreanu and several other Legion members were arrested and he was later strangled to death, supposedly while trying to escape from prison. Many of the Guard fled into exile in Germany where they found willing support from the Nazis.

While in exile the group fragmented into three factions, one of which focused around Horia Sima. With SS assistance Sima managed to take overall control of the party. After the outbreak of World War II the Iron Guard formed an alliance with the new leader of Romania, Ion Antonescu. Following the abdication of King Carol, Romania moved closer, in political terms, to Germany and formally joined the Axis alliance in 1941. Following this the Iron Guard became the country's only legal political party. After an attempted coup Sima was forced to flee to Germany where he was interned under fairly favourable conditions. He later escaped and fled to Italy, where he was again interned. Following the surrender of Italy he moved to Vienna to establish a pro-Nazi Romanian government in exile.

Following the invasion of Romania by Russian forces in 1944 the Iron Guard did an amazing about-turn to become hired thugs to terrorise ant-communist elements in Romania. They maintained this role until the communists completed their takeover of the Romanian government in 1947, when they were officially disbanded.

Sima was sentenced to death in-absentia in 1944 and never returned home. After living under the assumed name of Josef Weber in France and Italy he eventually ended up in Madrid under the protection of the Franco regime, where he died in 1993.

\* \* \*

## 28<sup>th</sup> March 2016

### When did the first recorded aerial dogfight occur?

The development of aerial combat followed changes to the design of aircraft, especially their armament, as World War I developed. However the first aerial combat actually took place during the Mexican Revolution (1910-1920). On 30<sup>th</sup> November 1913 two American pilots, fighting on opposite sides in the war, fired the first airborne shots. The two pilots were Dean Ivan Lamb and Phil Radar who fired pistols at each other until they were empty. Neither pilot was injured and no damage was done to either aircraft. This action is considered to be the first "dogfight", though it wouldn't have been considered as such by the standards of what was to follow.

The first aircraft to be downed in World War I was on 28<sup>th</sup> August 1914, when Lieutenant Norman Spratt of the Royal Flying Corps, flying an unarmed Sopwith Tabloid, forced down a German 2 seater aircraft, presumably by making it appear that he would ram the German if he didn't land.

Initially both sides in the First World War used aircraft mainly for observation purposes. Pilots and their observers carried hand guns and if they came close enough to the enemy they might take a pot shot. Things then escalated with the observer being issued first with a rifle and then with machine guns mounted on swivels. For the British this would usually be a Lewis Gun. However, the propeller of the aircraft always limited its fighting capability as it prevented the machine gun from firing forward. This meant that fighters flew alongside each other exchanging gun fire, or one aircraft might try get in front of and below the other so that the observer could fire at the aircraft above and behind them.

There were a number of ways this problem was overcome. The use of "pusher" aircraft, with the engine and propeller mounted behind the pilot, as in the French FE2, allowed the observer to sit at the front with a swivel mounted machine gun. This allowed the aircraft to approach from behind and beneath another and fire upwards at the undefended underside. The first aerial victory using firearms was scored when French Sgt Joseph Franz and his observer Louis Quenault, flying a "pusher" type Voisin biplane, shot down a German aircraft near Reims on 7th October 1914.

Other designs, such as the British SE5, had a fixed machine gun mounted on the upper wing so that it could fire over the propeller, but this wasn't particularly effective as the pilot couldn't take proper aim; he could only point the aircraft in the right direction.

The French were the first to come up with a machine gun mounted immediately in front of the pilot. Roland Garros, a pilot, and Raymond Saulnier, an aircraft designer, fitted metal deflector plates to the propeller of an aircraft, which allowed the gun to fire through the rotating arc without damaging the propeller itself. With this design Garros scored three victories in April 1915. In recognition of Roland Garros's bravery the arena that is the home of French tennis was named after him. He was a dedicated tennis player and fan.

It was the Germans who came up with the game changing invention of synchronising the firing mechanism of the machine gun to the turning of the propeller so that the gun would only fire when the propeller was clear of the gun. Dutch designer Anthony Fokker, who also designed several aircraft types for the Germans, came up with the idea. On 1st July 1915 Lieutenant Kurt Wintgens, flying a Fokker M5 "Eindecker" aircraft, shot down a Morane-Saulniere two seater-aircraft using the new gun. This innovation allowed aircraft to fly patrols at maximum altitude and then swoop down on the enemy to take them by surprise and gave birth to the dogfight as we know it.

The British soon developed their own synchronisation gear which allowed them to fit forward firing machine guns and the Bristol Scout and Sopwith 1½ Strutter were the first aircraft to be fitted with the Challenger design (named after designer George Challenger) in December 1915. However, mechanical problems made the guns unreliable and they were unpopular with RFC pilots until late 1917, when improved designs became available.

The German Ace Oswald Boelke developed the Dicta Boelke, the 8 essential rules for dog fighting: Attack from above, preferably with the sun behind you; Always press home the attack once you have begun; Fire only at close range; Don't let yourself be tricked by clever ruses; Always attack from behind; If attacked, turn to meet your opponent; When over enemy lines keep your own line of retreat clear; Attack in groups of 4 to 6 but if the fight breaks up into single combat multiple aircraft should not take on the same target.

These rules remained the doctrine of air to air combat right up until the arrival of the jet age, when the development of guided and heat seeking missiles meant that fighter aircraft could engage their targets from a distance.

Boelke died on 28th October 1916 flying an Albatross D2 and it appears that he was ignoring the 8th rule of his own dicta at the time. He and other aircraft from his own Jagstaffel (Squadron) were chasing the same British DH2 single seat fighter when a collision with the undercarriage of one of his comrade's aircraft damaged Beolke's upper wing. He managed to make a relatively soft crash landing which should have been survivable. However, in his rush to get airborne at the start of the mission Boelke had neglected to fasten his seat belt and he died in the crash. Boelke had claimed 40 "kills" before his death, exactly half the number claimed by the famous Baron Manfred Von Richtoffen, who also participated in the dogfight in which Boelke died and was still in the early days of his career at the time.

**Author's note:** I was raised on the stories of Biggles, by Capt W E Johns, which start off in World War I. It never occurred to me that aerial combat was known as anything other than dog fighting. Johns was a genuine pilot, serving first with the Royal Flying Corps and later with the RAF, before becoming a successful author of children's books.

* * *

### 30<sup>th</sup> March 2016

**A tombstone at Kirby Cemetery in Essex is said to be inscribed with a prophecy predicting the end of the world. What does it say?**

The prophecy reads "When pictures look alive, with movement free, When ships like fish swim beneath the sea, When man outstripping birds can soar the sky, Then half the world deep drenched in blood shall die."

This was originally thought to be an extract from the sayings of Mother Ursula Shipton (1488-1561), a visionary from Yorkshire. She was well known for various sayings which were mainly related to events in the area where she lived. She is only thought to have made two actual predictions, one of which appears to have been the Great Fire of London (1666). Her best known prophecy, however, was: "The world to an end shall come, In eighteen hundred and eighty one." A good rhyme but one that history can demonstrate to be inaccurate. The most memorable events to happen that year would seem to be the introduction of the Postal Order and Scotland's football team beating England 6-1. For the English, at least, that may have seemed like the end of the world.

Many of Mother Shipton's sayings were published in 1641 and then updated by astrologer and alchemist Sir William Lily in his book "Collections of Prophecies" published in 1646. The quote is taken from a far longer visionary poem which was attributed to Mother Shipton, but which turned out to be a hoax.

In 1862 editor Charles Hindley admitted writing this particular prophecy and inserting it into a book containing Mother Shipton's sayings. This, of course, throws into doubt the date of the tombstone on which the extract is engraved. It is supposed to date from the 17th century, but Hindley's admission means that it could date from no earlier than 1862, unless he had seen the poem on the tombstone and incorporated it into his hoax.

Even as a hoax it seems to be remarkably prescient, as the extract appears to predict the cinema, submarines, aircraft and, of course, three world wars of which we have only had two. Other parts of the poem predict cars and women wearing trousers, and references to Britain's good relations with France and Germany could be interpreted as referring to the European Union.

What would have made the predictions seem credible, however, is a reference in later lines to the building of a great glass house. This would have been the Crystal Palace which housed the Great Exhibition held in Hyde Park, which opened in 1856, seven years before Hindley's admission. Reading a reference to something that had happened quite recently would seem incredible and could account for the lasting belief in this hoax as being real prophecy.

However, many of the things predicted in the poem are of the sort that scientists and engineers would have been discussing at the time of the Great Exhibition, even if they did not actually exist at that time, so it would be no surprise for Hindley to have heard of the ideas. In fact the first submarine was demonstrated in 1620 and the USS Alligator had been used during the American Civil War, becoming operational on 13th July 1862, the year of Hindley's hoax (it sank in 1863).

There have been many claims of prophecies being made, the common factor in most of them being the prediction of war as a forerunner to the end of days. Given the frequency with which wars are fought this would seem to be safe ground for prophecies.

The existence of Mother Shipton herself also seems to be in doubt. Her 1684 biographer appears to have made up most of the details of her life and most of her sayings are now accepted as having been made up by others.

* * *

### 14<sup>th</sup> April 2016

**How did the Romans know where to build Hadrian's Wall? How could they know it was the narrowest point in England?**

Among their many skills the Romans were good map makers and soldiers with map making skills were attached to each Roman legion to map the terrain over which the legions marched. With the legion advancing at marching pace it was quite easy for map makers to explore the countryside on either side of the line of march on horseback, so that legionary commanders always knew what was on their flanks. When the legion settled into a garrison, usually for the winter, this work of map making continued in order to fill in any gaps.

At the same time the Roman navy was carrying out similar work, trying to identify safe harbours in the coastal areas of newly conquered territories. Very often the legions would deliberately follow coastal routes so that they could be resupplied by sea, which was usually safer than using road routes that might be subject to ambush. This meant that land maps and sea charts could be combined to form a more complete picture of the conquered territory.

The conquest of Britannia (as the Roman's called it, named after the Emperor Claudius's son) wasn't a short process. It started in AD 43 but Hadrian's Wall wasn't built until much later. The defeat of

Boudicca in AD 61 is often seen as the date for the pacification of Britannia, but that would be very inaccurate. Cornwall, Wales and all the territory to the North of the Mersey/Trent rivers were still under the control of the Celts and there were frequent outbreaks of fighting with the Romans.

Britannia was unique in the Roman empire in requiring so many soldiers to be permanently stationed here, with four legions at any time (about 32,000 men) plus several thousand more non-Roman soldiers serving in auxiliary cohorts. In AD 71 Emperor Vespasian, a veteran of the AD 43 invasion when he commanded the II Legion, ordered the conquest of Northern Britannia. The Romans gradually moved northwards and established two new fortresses at Deva (Chester) and Eboracum (York). In conquering the north the Romans took two routes, one advancing from Deva in AD 78 and the other from Eboracum in AD 79, but the two armies would have stayed in contact through couriers and so would have known how close they were to each other as they crossed the River Tyne and the Solway Firth, drawing maps and comparing notes as they went. They both arrived at what is now the Scottish border in late in AD 79.

A common mistake nowadays is to assume that the Romans never conquered Scotland, which was untrue. South and south west Scotland were pacified by AD 82 and in AD 84 the Romans were deep inside the country, defeating the Caledonii tribe at Mons Graupius. The precise location is unknown but was probably somewhere in the Highlands.

There was pressure elsewhere in the Roman empire and troops had to be withdrawn from Britannia, resulting in a withdrawal from northern Scotland. There is evidence that in AD 87 a large Roman settlement at Inchtuthill (in Tayside, Scotland) was completely dismantled and taken away. In AD 100 Emperor Trajan declared that the northern frontier of Britannia should be along a line from the Solway Firth to the River Tyne, a conveniently narrow point in the

British Isles. By that time, of course, the Romans would have had a very good grasp of the geography. This allowed Trajan to remove more troops to deal with unrest in Dacia (modern day Moldova). This was the line that Emperor Hadrian chose for his wall, with construction commencing in AD 122, 80 years after the original invasion of Britannia.

However, this wasn't the only wall to be constructed. In AD 142, not long after the completion of Hadrian's Wall, a new emperor, Antoninus Pius, ordered the construction of the Antonine Wall to form a new northern border, running 37 miles from the Firth of Clyde to the Firth of Forth. This was an attempt to once again subdue the Scottish tribes in the lower portion of the country. However, two decades later Roman policy changed again and in AD 163 the Antonine Wall was abandoned and Hadrian's Wall once again became the northern frontier of the Empire, marking the end of any significant attempts to conquer Scotland.

In AD 367 an alliance of Celtic tribes from Scotland and Ireland, and Franks and Saxons from Northern Germany, crossed Hadrian's Wall in an attempt to seize Northern Britannia. It took two years of fighting for the Romans to evict the invaders.

Roman military occupation of Britannia effectively came to an end in AD 400 when Roman troops were withdrawn to Italy to defend against invaders from North of the Danube. In AD 410 Emperor Honorius told the Romans in Britain that they "had to look to their own defences", which signalled the end of Roman rule. The Anglo-Saxon invasion of Britannia started in earnest soon afterwards.

* * *

**21<sup>st</sup> April 2016**

**On holiday in Singapore, visiting Kranji War Cemetery, I came across the graves of ten men of Z Force executed for attempting to blow up Japanese ships in Keppel harbour in 1945. What is their story?**

Z Force, or Z Special Unit to give it its proper name, was the name used by Special Operations Australia for a reconnaissance and sabotage unit during World War II. While predominantly Australian it also had British, Indian, Dutch, New Zealand and Timorese members.

The force mainly operated in Borneo, but it carried out two operations against Japanese shipping in Singapore Harbour.

Special Operations Australia was established at the suggestion of the commander of Allied Land Forces South West Pacific Area, General Thomas Blamey, and was modelled on the already established Special Operations Executive based in the UK. In June 1942 an Inter-Allied Service Department (ISD) raiding/commando unit was established under the name of Z Special Unit.

The first assault against Singapore was named Operation Jaywick. It was the brainchild of Captain Ivan Lyon of the Gordon Highlanders and an Australian civilian by the name of Bill Reynolds.

On 2$^{nd}$ September 1943 the MV Krait left Australia carrying a crew of 11 Australians and 4 British personnel. By dying their skin brown and wearing sarongs they hoped to pass themselves off as Malay fishermen. The raid was led by Ivan Lyon. A party of 6 paddled ashore in folboats (collapsible canoes), waited until nightfall and placed limpet mines on several ships, before returning to the Krait. The mines sank several Japanese ships, while the Krait returned safely to Australia. No allied casualties were sustained.

Operation Rimau was less successful. On 11$^{th}$ September 1944 Lyon (now a Lieutenant Colonel) took a much larger team, 24 men, and left Australia on the submarine HMS Porpoise.

On 28th September the Porpoise captured the junk Mustika, which Lyon planned to use in the raid on Singapore, again by disguising themselves as Malay fishermen. On 10th October, while approaching Singapore, disaster struck when the Mustika was challenged by a Malay Police patrol boat, the Hei Ho. After an exchange of shots the Hei Ho fled, but Lyon knew it would summon help. Lyon decided to scuttle the Mustika. He divided his force into 4 groups and continued the attack using folboats.

Lyon led a force of 6 men into Singapore harbour, The 6 were Lieutenant Commander Donald "Davo" Davidson, Lieutenant Bobby Ross, Able Seaman Andrew "Happy" Huston, Corporal Clair Stewart, Corporal Archie Campbell and Private Douglas Warne. It is thought that they sank 3 ships using limpet mines, but this was never confirmed. The Japanese launched a punitive search for the raiders using approximately 100 troops.

Lyon and his men mounted a fighting retreat across three local islands, Soreh, Tapeh and Merapas, where they linked up with the others in the party. Lt Robert Ross and Cpl Archie Campbell were killed on Tapeh and the bodies of Sub Lt Gregor Riggs and Sgt Colin Cameron were found on Merapas.

Although a rescue attempt was mounted by the Australian navy, the submarine HMAS Tantalus failed to rendezvous with the survivors on several occasions. By early December all the remaining commandoes had either been killed or captured.

On 3rd July 1945 eleven of the force were put on trial by the Japanese in Singapore, on charges of espionage and sabotage. They were sentenced to death and ten were beheaded. These were: Maj Reginald Ingleton, Capt Robert Page, Lt Albert Sargeant, Lt Walter Carey, WO Alfred Warren, Sgt David Gooley, Cpl Clair Stewart, Cpl Roland Fletcher, Able Seaman Walter Falls and LCpl John

Hardy. It is probable that the eleventh man either died from his wounds or of natural causes before he could be executed.

As well as those ten, another seven members of the raiding force, including Lt Col Lyon who died on 16th October 1944, are buried at Kranji War Cemetery.

*  *  *

## 22nd April 2016

**In 1966 a Morris Minor Traveller was sent to RAF Gan, an island in the Maldives a mile and quarter long and a quarter of a mile wide, with a single road running the length of it. Have other vehicles operated in such restricted conditions?**

RAF Gan may have had the highest density of motor vehicles per square foot anywhere in the world at that time. In order to function as an airfield prior to the arrival of the Morris Minor it needed a fire tender and an ambulance as a minimum and the communications staff needed transport in order to maintain the radio and radar installations at the extremes of the island. Typically that would have been a Landrover. Bowsers were required to transport fuel to visiting aircraft. Civil maintenance staff used lorries to carry tools and equipment around. There were other vehicles in use for other purposes.

The significance of the arrival of the Morris Minor would have been that it was such an unusual location for such a car to be seen. They were a common enough sight at other RAF airfields, where they were used as a utility vehicle to transport staff and small items of equipment.

The military use of Gan in the Addu Atoll of the Maldives started in August 1941 when Royal Navy engineers arrived to construct the first airstrip for use by the Fleet Air Arm. In 1942 the RAF created a base on the neighbouring island of Hithadoo, in support of Sunderland and Catalina flying boats. Hithadoo remained in use as a radio transmitter station until RAF Gan closed.

The RAF took over Gan in 1957 to act as a staging post for aircraft flying between the UK and the Far East. This allowed for air travel to replace the lengthy sea voyage by troop ship that had been the normal method of travel for military personnel up until then. The runway length of 8,694 ft (1.23 miles), almost the entire length of the island, was just long enough to accommodate the VC10 when the RAF introduced it in 1965.

VC10s flew from Cyprus to Gan and then on to either Singapore or Hong Kong. Shorter range aircraft, such as the Britannia and Hercules, had an additional staging point at RAF Masirah, in the Indian Ocean just off the coast of Oman.

RAF personnel served 9 months on Gan, with no break for annual leave. They weren't accompanied by their families and no women were allowed to serve there. The island was kept re-supplied by regular visits from Royal Fleet Auxiliary ships, with more urgently needed items being flown in on scheduled aircraft.

As the 1970s progressed the number of British bases in the Far East declined until the arrival of an aircraft at Gan became a rarity.

The base was closed on 1st April 1976. After a period of disuse the airfield was refurbished by the government of the Maldives and is now known as Gan International Airport, which serves the tourist industry in Addu Atoll, particularly the Equator Village resort on the island. The former military buildings have been converted to other uses. For example, the hospital is now a diving centre.

**Author's note:** I never served on RAF Gan. I did my "unaccompanied" posting on RAF Masirah, so I was determined to shoe horn that location into my answer. It didn't make any difference. This was one of my answers that wasn't published.

* * *

## 18<sup>th</sup> May 2016

### In broadcasting, why does radio have stations, but TV has channel?

The reason for this difference is in the misuse of language rather than in technology. In fact radio has channels as well as stations. Technically speaking either a radio or a TV broadcaster transmitting from a fixed point on a unique frequency is a "station". However, if a radio or TV station broadcasts different content on different frequencies to different audiences then it is using different "channels" for each set of content.

The term "channel" has its origins in telegraphy, the method by which written messages were sent along wires. Each character of the alphabet, and the numbers 0-9, were produced by a machine as a mixture of positive and negative voltages in a five bit code, similar to that used by computers today. However, this meant that only one machine could send its message along a pair of wires at any time.

If those voltages were used to trigger an alternating current, however, several machines could send their message over the same pair of wires at the same time using a different pair of frequencies for each machine. The frequencies simply mixed together in a similar manner to those used by the human voice; in fact it as known as voice frequency (VF) telegraphy. The frequencies were separated at the receiving station by using filters, so that they could be converted back to positive and negative voltages again.

Each pair of frequencies was known as a "channel". This same principle was later applied to radio signals, with up to 16 VF channels being applied to a single radio frequency. This was the mainstay of long range radio communications from the 1930s until the arrival of the communications satellite in the 1970s and remained in use with the military and maritime agencies into the 80s.

The BBC is both a radio station and a TV station. However, it uses different channels to send different content to different audiences. On the radio these channels are Radio 1, Radio 2, Radio 3 etc, while on the TV they are BBC1, BBC2, BBC News etc.

With the arrival of digital broadcasting there is now plethora of TV and radio channels offering different products targeted at different audiences, so we have specialist sports channels, news channels, music channels, comedy channels etc.

\* \* \*

## 24th May 2016

**The old Irish song Derby Kelly relates to the exploits of a dynasty of British military drummers, the grandfather of whom was at Blenheim and Ramillies, the father at Quebec and the son in the Peninsular War. Might this have been possible?**

This is theoretically possible as drummers were usually recruited as boys, hence the term "drummer boy", sometimes as young as 9 or 10 years of age.

At the same time there was no fixed term of engagement for soldiers. A child would graduate from being a drummer to becoming a fully-fledged soldier. They signed on pretty much for life and their discharge only came when they were injured too badly to resume their service, or were considered too old for further service, assuming they survived at all.

In the song there is no inference that the first Derby Kelly was still serving at the time his son became a drummer, similarly for the son still being in the army when the grandson enlists. The only clear reference is that all three generations followed a similar path.

Drummers were used to relay orders across noisy battlefields, using different drum beats to signal changes of formation, the advance or the retreat.

The Battle of Blenheim, the earliest of those named, was fought in 1704. Assuming that Derby Kelly joined the army at age 10, in time to serve at Blenheim, he might have been discharged after 40 years, making him 50 years old. If he then settled down and married (a much younger woman of course) he might easily have had a 10 year old son who joined the army in time to serve at Quebec in 1759. The first battles of the Peninsular War were fought in 1807, only 48 years later, so the arithmetic works even more in favour of a grandson of Derby Kelly serving there. The song refers to beating "the Mounseers out of Spain", which suggests that the last Derby Kelly was still a drummer in 1814, when that war was concluded.

Taking the story further, a great grandson might have fought in the Crimea (1853-1856) and the Indian Mutiny (1857), a great great grandson at Isandlwana (1879) and so on through to the Boer War (1899-1902). It wasn't until the First World War that a lower age limit was introduced into the British Army, set at 18. Fixed terms of service in the army had been introduced as part of the Cardwell reforms of 1870.

Even during the First World War the rules were widely ignored and teenagers as young as 14 are known to have fought in the trenches.

In the song Derby Kelly it is the grandson who tells the story and in the third line of the song actually refers to his grandfather being a "lad".

\* \* \*

## 26th May 2016

**During the Battle Of The Atlantic, the cargo ship Nerrisa was sunk by U-552. She was loaded with war material and 175 members of the Royal Canadian Mountain Police – with their horses. Why was this?**

This would seem to be a story that has no origin in fact other than it includes Canadians who died when the SS Nerissa was torpedoed. The Nerissa was carrying a number of Canadian servicemen and a few of these may have been former members of the Royal Canadian Mounted Police (RCMP) but there are no contemporary accounts of any horses having been on board.

At the outbreak of World War II the Canadian Army was without a military police unit, so on 13th September 1939 the RCMP were granted permission to form the Canadian Provost Company (RCMP). Initially it was made up of 120 volunteers, most of whom were serving in the UK by 1940. On 15th June 1940 the Canadian Provost Corps was founded, assuming full responsibility for policing within the Canadian Army, meaning that its members were no longer a part of the RCMP and many of its newer members had never been police officers before enlisting.

The SS Nerissa was a 5,583 ton passenger ship built by C T Bowring & Co Ltd of Liverpool for the Red Cross Line. She entered service on 5th June 1926 working mainly on the busy transatlantic route. The three ships of the Red Cross Line were later sold to the Furness Withy Group who owned the Bermuda & West Indies Steamship Co. Ltd. At the outbreak of war the Nerissa was pressed into service for war work, and refitted to carry 250 troops and armed with a 4 inch gun and a Bofors Gun.

By April 1941 the Nerissa had made 39 crossings of the Atlantic in wartime service. On 21st April she began her 40th crossing from Halifax, Nova Scotia, to Liverpool with 306 passengers and crew, 145 of which were Canadians. On 23rd April, on Admiralty orders, she separated from her convoy to make the crossing alone, her speed being considered to give her some protection against attack by submarines. At nightfall on 30th April a Liberator bomber of RAF

Coastal Command signalled the Nerissa that the way ahead of her was clear of submarines.

At 11.30 pm the Nerissa was struck amidships by a torpedo fired from U-552, commanded by Erich Topp, which had been patrolling the waters north west of Ireland looking for targets. The ship was 200 miles from its destination and 100 miles off the coast of Donegal in the Republic of Ireland. The responsibility for the sinking wasn't formally attributed to U-552 until examination of Kriegsmarine records after the war. She was mainly known for the sinking of the American destroyer USS Reuben James in October 1941, more than a month before the USA entered the war.

Contemporary accounts by survivors state that an orderly evacuation was in progress when a second torpedo hit the ship, fired 3 minutes after the first. This spilt the ship in two. In between the two explosions the ship's radio officer had been able to get off a distress signal. At first light a Blenheim aircraft located the lifeboats carrying 84 survivors and circled them until the arrival, an hour later, of the destroyer HMS Veteran. The survivors were later transferred to the corvette HMS Kingcup and taken to Londonderry, the nearest British port.

Listed as passengers on the Nerissa are 145 Canadians, none of whom were serving members of the RCMP but some may formerly have been so. A few were civilians but the majority were drawn from all branches of the Canadian Army; mainly medical, signals and clerical. Seven were from the Canadian Provost Company. Of those 145, 83 lost their lives in the sinking, along with most of the graduates of an R.A.F. British Commonwealth Air Training Program class, 3 Norwegian pilots and 11 American ferry pilots, along with other members of the military and ship's crew. The Nerissa has the dubious distinction of being the only troopship carrying Canadian soldiers to be lost at sea as a result of enemy action.

The U-552 was responsible for the sinking or damaging of 193,684 tons of allied shipping before being scuttled by her crew at Williamshaven on 2$^{nd}$ May 1945. Erich Topp survived the war and was the third most successful U Boat commander in terms of shipping sunk.

The story of the RCMP and their horses first appears in a book called, "The Fourth Service - Merchantmen at War 1939-45," by John Slader (published 1988) and also in "Atlantic Star," by David A. Thomas (published 1990). The claim is that 175 North West Mounted Police (sic) officers and their horses died on the Nerissa. However, there is no evidence to substantiate these claims and they are not borne out by the ship's passenger list or contemporary accounts, so the real origin of the story is unknown.

The graves of nine of those killed on the Nerissa may be found in Ireland and a further three in Scotland, where their bodies were washed ashore. A poem, the Merchant Seamen, was written by James J. Brown AIIE and Brian G. Redding AB, in memory of the casualties of the Nerissa and the names and units of the Canadians who died are recorded on the Halifax Memorial, Nova Scotia.

* * *

## 17$^{th}$ June 2016

**Is it true that the Waddington's toy company made an Ouija board for children?**

The Ouija board has its origins in China around the year 1,100, where it was known as planchette writing. People believed it was a way of talking to the dead. It found its way into the west in the 19$^{th}$ century, when spiritualism was popular and a better way of "talking to the dead" was desired.

American businessman Elijah Bond patented a method of planchette writing that was combined with a board, on which was inscribed the letters of the alphabet and the words "yes" and "no". His patent was filed on 28th May 1890, thus crediting him as the inventor of the Ouija board, though it wasn't called that at the time. That name wasn't used until an employee of Bond, William Fuld, took over production and created the name.

Fuld claimed to have come up with the name by using the board to talk to a dead Egyptian, but it is in fact a combination of the French and German words for "yes". Fuld changed his story several times and even claimed to be the board's inventor.

Ouija boards enjoyed their heyday between the 1920s and 1960s. Fuld's estate then sold the patent to Parker Brothers, makers of board games. Parker Brothers in turn sold the company to toy makers Hasbro in 1991.

In the 1960s toy and board game manufacturer Waddingtons did produce an Ouija board as a child's toy, but Fuld and Parker Brothers had already been marketing the board for children in the USA.

Science regards the phenomenon of the Ouija board as an ideomotor response (IMR). This is an involuntary muscular response created by the subconscious mind. Whatever words are spelt out are therefore the common denominator of what is going through the minds of the group of users.

The belief that Ouija boards actually work may stem from the condemnation of its use by Christian groups early in its history, though no evidence is offered to support that any spirits had ever been summoned. The idea that Ouija boards are capable of channelling evils spirits is mainly the work of popular film and fiction.

**Note:** This question reappeared in a slightly different guise on New Year's Eve 2019, so I submitted the same answer once again.

\* \* \*

## 17th June 2016
### Was Trooping The Colour held during the World Wars?

The concept of the Queen having an "official" birthday arises from the habit of monarchs to grant a public holiday to celebrate the day of their birth. Naturally a public holiday was more popular if it was granted during the summer months, so if a monarch was inconveniently born during the winter they moved the celebration of their "official" birthday to a warmer season. It was Edward VII who moved the Trooping the Colour ceremony to its present June date. To this day Civil Servants get an extra day's holiday for the Queen's birthday.

Regimental colours owe their origin to medieval times when knights were preceded by a standard (a small rectangular banner) that bore their coat of arms or personal symbol. Men at arms serving a knight wore the same symbol embroidered onto their jacket or on a surcoat.

The Trooping the Colour ceremony itself originated on the battlefield. The Regimental colours were the rallying point for troops who became separated in the heat of battle. To ensure that the soldiers went to the correct colour it was paraded through the ranks ahead of a battle so that all the soldiers could recognise it.

Each regiment traditionally has two colours. The Queens's (or King's) Colour is presented by the monarch and is treated as being the personification of the monarch herself. The Regimental Colour usually incorporates the regiment's cap badge and lists the regiment's battle honours. It is treated with equal respect. In the Royal Artillery the guns are considered to represent the colours as artillery was, historically, the property of the monarch.

The origin of the present day ceremony go back to 17th June 1768 when the King George III ordered the Grenadier Company of the Coldstream Guards to "mount guard" on the day of His Majesty's birthday was to be kept.

Since 1807 this guard mounting has taken place every year on the sovereign's official birthday. Exclusions were in place between 1811 and 1830 due to the illness of George III, but were held in 1813 in honour of his Queen. From the reign of George IV they became an annual event, except for the period of the two World Wars. The only other times that the ceremony wasn't held was during periods of official mourning.

* * *

## 27th June 2016

**There is an internet story doing the rounds that claims Michelle Obama has a personal staff of 24 people. Is this true?**

The First Lady Of The United States (FLOTUS) carries out numerous official and semi-official duties each year and is far more involved in the public and political life of the President than we would expect from the wife of our Prime Minister. To help her manage these duties the resident FLOTUS has, for many decades, had a personal staff. Duties include secretarial, research, a chauffeur, stylists, press and public relations as well as political staff. They do not include her Secret Service protection detail.

An entry on the White House official blog of 1st July 2009 listed the duties of many of the White House staff. The number shown as working for Michelle Obama created something of a stir on the internet and prompted questions about how many staff were working for her and what they earned.

It was revealed that there were 16 staff whose job titles linked them directly to FLOTUS, plus a further 6 whose duties were mainly in relation to FLOTUS. Katie McCormick Lelyveld, Michelle Obama's press secretary, later corrected this to a total of 24.

A chain e-mail circulating in 2009 claimed that the number Michelle Obama's staff was extreme, given the figures for Laura Bush

(1) and Hillary Clinton (3), but this has since been shown to be incorrect and way off target. Laura Bush, wife of George W Bush, had a staff of 18 and Hilary Clinton 19. Jackie Kennedy, initially reported as having a staff of only 1, was revealed to have had a staff of 9. This was because, at the time Kennedy was in office, only the most senior was listed as working for her.

Of Michelle Obama's 22 staff that can be positively identified, their total salary is $1.6 million, compared to $1.4 million for the 18 positively identified staff of Laura Bush.

**Author's note:** Since June 2016 it has come to light that the British Prime Minister's wife also has a personal staff, some of whom received honours in David Cameron's resignation honours list. How many staff there are and how they are funded is not clear.

* * *

## 30<sup>th</sup> June 2016

**Was nose art on some World War II planes commissioned from well-known artists or did the aircrew paint it?**

The original purpose of painting aircraft was to provide an additional layer of weather protection. With early aircraft skins being made of canvas stretched over a wood or metal frame they were vulnerable to rotting if the canvass became soaked. Oil based paint was a simple remedy. It was also noted that aircraft painted in certain colours were harder to spot and so it became the practice to camouflage military aircraft, using browns and greens on the upper surfaces and blues and greys on the lower. As metal skins were introduced this became an essential, as shiny metal was much easier to see, especially when it reflected the sun.

The leaders of many German Jagstaffelen (squadrons) thought that camouflaging aircraft was ungentlemanly and deliberately flouted the regulations by painting their aircraft in garish colours.

The best known example was the bright red Fokker DrI triplane flown by Baron Manfred Von Richtoffen, earning him the nickname of the Red Baron.

The Germans and Italians were the first to use distinctive art on their aircraft. The first was seen on an Italian flying boat in 1913, a depiction of a sea monster. At the start of World War I it was common for the Germans to paint a "mouth" on the sides of the air intakes at the front of the aircraft. The first allied example is the "hat in the ring" symbol adopted by the American 95$^{th}$ Squadron, as in to throw one's hat in the ring when accepting a challenge to fight. A shark face was adopted for the Sopwith Dolphin by the American Volunteer Group. Depictions of sharks were a recurring theme on many aircraft types throughout both world wars.

The Flying Tigers, American volunteers flying in the Chinese war against Japan, used a motif of a leaping tiger jumping through a V for victory, which was designed by artists working for the Disney corporation, but this still followed the tradition of aircraft all carrying the same artwork as a squadron insignia.

True nose art of the type referred to in the question made its appearance with the entry of the United States Air Force into World War II. A mixture of professional civilian artists and talented service personnel was used to produce the work. Scantily clad females were the most popular theme. The US Navy, however, forbade nose art and allowed only small lettering to depict names.

The 91$^{st}$ Bomber Group, part of the US 8$^{th}$ Air Force based in England, had its own resident artist, Tony Starcer, who created over 100 works of nose art, including that of the "Memphis Belle" which was recreated for the 1990 film of the same name. Many artists copied the art of Alberto Vargas, whose work was used to illustrate Esquire magazine

Skilled artists were in high demand and were well paid for their work. It is not clear how service personnel were recompensed.

The largest ever piece of nose art was "The Dragon And His Tail", depicted on the nose of a B24 Liberator in 1944, which was created by Staff Sergeant Starkis Bartigan of 64th Bomb Squadron, 43rd Bomb Group. This artwork extended from just below and in front of the cockpit, along the sides of the aircraft with the tail of the dragon just below the tail of the aircraft. In common with a lot of the artwork, a nude woman was incorporated, held in the mouth of the dragon.

Changing attitudes, especially towards women, led to a decline in artwork on American aircraft after the Korean War. Where it endured it mainly represented animals or mythical beings and creatures.

The RAF never allowed much in the way of nose art. Perhaps the most distinctive ever used was the representation of a shark's mouth on the sides of the air intakes beneath the propellers of the Curtiss Tomahawks flown by 112 Sqn in North Africa.

During the Gulf Wars of 1990 and 2003, restrictions were lifted (or perhaps ignored) and nose art made its first real appearance on RAF aircraft with its use on Tornado squadrons. The art work was all done by enthusiastic amateur service personnel.

**Author's note:** I was quite surprised when this answer, which was published, sparked a flurry of responses from other correspondents. Most claimed that "nose art" was more common in the RAF than I had suggested. However, in relation to the number of aircraft in service during WW2 nose art was still comparatively rare on RAF aircraft.

* * *

# 4th July 2016

**Nick Clegg helped to push through the Fixed Term Parliaments Act, but now wants an early general election. In what**

**circumstances can a general election be held before the end of the five-year term?**

The Fixed Term Parliaments Act 2011 allows for early General Elections under certain circumstances and Section 2 of the Act lays out those circumstances.

A motion must be put before the House "That there shall be an early parliamentary general election." This motion must then be passed by a two thirds majority of MPs. The need for the two thirds majority prevents a government from calling a general election just because the timing is favourable to them as it would be impossible to achieve the majority without the support of opposition parties.

There can also be an early general election if there is a successful motion of no confidence in the government. However, there is a period of 14 days grace in which a counter proposal of confidence in the government can be made, in which case the earlier vote of no confidence is nullified. If a confidence vote isn't successful within those 14 days then an early general election is triggered automatically.

It is rare for a government to lose a motion of no confidence if they have a working majority, unless several of their own MPs rebel, so this protects the government from political manoeuvring by the opposition. There would have to be a real crisis in progress for a motion of no confidence to be carried, or the government would have to slip into a minority position.

In the wake of the Panama Papers scandal earlier this year a petition, on the Parliamentary Petitions website, calling for an early general election gained the 100,000 signatures necessary for it to be discussed in Parliament. The official Government response was that because of the 2011 Act an early General Election couldn't be called. Technically this was correct, because none of the motions described above had been put before Parliament. Had the person who raised the petition worded it in accordance with Section 2 of the Act they might have been more successful.

Historically the monarch triggered a general election by dissolving Parliament. This could be for any number of reasons, but was usually because the Government wasn't delivering what the monarch wanted. As Britain became more democratic the monarch tended to act more on the "advice" of the Prime Minister, who has to visit the monarch to request the dissolution of Parliament. This led to Prime Ministers acting more for reasons of political expediency, calling general elections at times when they felt they had the best chance of winning.

When he introduced the Act, Nick Clegg said "By setting the date that Parliament will dissolve, our Prime Minister is giving up the right to pick and choose the date of the next general election—that's a true first in British politics." It is unlikely that Nick Clegg's call for an early general election would now be successful because of the requirements of the Act.

**Author's note:** Boris Johnson called a general election in December 2019 and was accused of political manoeuvring to choose the timing to suit himself. Given that he had to adhere to the terms of the Fixed Term Parliament, this is clearly a false accusation. At the time he was leading a minority government and the election couldn't have gone ahead without the Labour Party voting with the government to achieve the requisite two thirds majority. Labour had previously opposed motions to hold as general election, proving that it was Parliament's choice when the election should be held, not Boris Johnson's. The election, when it did finally take place, did result in a landslide victory for Johnson, so the accusations would appear to have been more sour grapes than anything else.

* * *

## 4<sup>th</sup> July 2016

**Further to the answer about magicians on the radio, didn't a ventriloquist once have his own radio show?**

Peter Brough (born 26<sup>th</sup> February 1916) was a well-known radio ventriloquist. His best known puppet character was Archie Andrews, who took the form of a cheeky little boy.

Brough started his radio career in 1944, using ventriloquism to create a variety of different voices. The radio shows on which he appeared were performed in front of a live audience, so the idea of a ventriloquist on the radio wasn't as absurd as it sounds. The character of Archie Andrews had his debut in 1950.

Archie was so successful as a character that he was given his own show, "Educating Archie", supported by such notable performers as Dick Emery, Harry Secombe, Benny Hill and Bruce Forsyth. Archie even had a girlfriend for a short time, played by the future star of Mary Poppins, Julie Andrews. One of the main writers for the show was Eric Sykes.

Peter Brough and Archie Andrews made the transition to TV in 1956 in the TV sitcom "Here's Archie". They moved to ITV two years later, reprising Educating Archie, with Marty Feldman joining the writing team.

However, Archie was never as successful on TV as he was on radio, because of a major flaw in the ventriloquism. Peter Brough's lips could be seen moving while Archie was talking! Following the death of his father, also a ventriloquist, Peter Brough retired from show business in 1961 to take over the family textile firm. He died in 1999.

* * *

## 6<sup>th</sup> July 2016

**Why do some aircraft have propellers with only two blades while others have up to eight blades?**

The ability of an aircraft to fly is dependent on the amount of lift that is generated. The shape of the wing creates a reduction in air pressure above it and an increase in air pressure below, causing the wing to rise. However, the air must be moving in order for that lift to be created and the greater the speed at which the air moves the greater the lift that is generated.

Wind alone, in certain circumstances, can create sufficient lift for the aircraft to raise itself off the ground, but it would then be blown backwards. So, to create forward motion the aircraft must also have thrust. In order to create forward movement the aircraft requires a force to get it moving, in accordance with Newton's first law of motion. In propeller driven aircraft this force is provided by the combined effects of the engine and the propeller that it is powering.

The aerofoil shape of the turning propeller creates a decrease in air pressure in front of it and a pressure increase behind, dragging the aircraft forward. This is the force we call thrust. This is the same principle that allows helicopters to fly without wings, as the aerofoil shape of the helicopter's propeller blades act as a rotating wing.

The more power that the engine generates the greater the amount of torque that is applied to the propeller, so the faster it turns and the greater the thrust it creates. However, the number of blades that the propeller has also increases the amount of thrust. A more powerful engine will produce more torque than a less powerful one, while a three bladed propeller will produce more thrust than a two bladed one. Aircraft designers are always looking to save money on powerful, but expensive, engines by using more blades on the relatively cheaper propellers.

A two seater aircraft with a small engine can function quite well with only a two bladed propeller, but maximum speed will be limited, usually to around 150 mph. But as the weight of the aircraft increases more thrust is required to get it airborne, so the engine power is increased, as is the number of propeller blades. Larger commercial aircraft require a higher operating speed than pleasure craft, so again more thrust is required.

Modern turbo-prop engines can rotate at very high speeds and by the use of gears can develop high levels of torque, which means that larger aircraft need fewer engines, but to compensate they will usually power more propeller blades.

The Bombardier Dash 8 aircraft, operated by many short haul airlines, has two engines, each powering a 6 bladed propeller, which gives it a typical airspeed of 310 mph with a range of up to 1,174 miles, while carrying up to 40 passengers.

There have also been aircraft that used contra-rotating propellers (CRP) where each engine powers 2 x 4 bladed propellers (8 blades in all) on the same axis, but with each set of four blades rotating in opposite directions. This design cuts down on the amount of energy being wasted by air being deflected at angles that don't provide thrust, by catching the wasted air with the rear set of propellers and redirecting it backwards.

**Author's note:** This is another question that prompted a flurry of "Further to" answers from other correspondents. It made me wonder why they hadn't written in reply to the original question if they knew the answer already.

\* \* \*

## 13th July 2016

**Apart from making individuals rich, do hedge finds perform any useful function in the economy of a country?**

A "Hedge Fund" derives its name from the gambling practice of "hedging one's bets", by which the gambler protects themselves against large losses by placing bets that are guaranteed to pay if their primary bet is a losing one.

For example, if a gambler has £10 he may place a £1 bet that a particular horse will win a race, at odds of 10/1. He may also, however, place a £9 bet that the same horse won't win. Because this is more likely (under most circumstances) the gambler might only get odds of 1/10. If the horse wins he wins £10, plus the return of their stake, which leaves them £1 in profit. However, if the horse loses, he wins 90p, plus the return of his £9 stake, leaving him with a loss of only 10p, rather than the loss of £1 if he had only backed the horse to win.

Over the long term the gambler is guaranteed to break even providing he places a winning bet for every 10 losing ones, which is not the case if they only bet on each horse to win. In practice and experienced gambler is more likely to win 4 or 5 times out of every 10, so they generally make a profit.

Hedge fund managers place their "bets" on the financial markets on the basis of considerable research and knowledge of companies and financial markets, so the likelihood of a bet not being a winning one is already reduced. However, because they hedge their bets they never lose in the long term. The only question is how much the fund makes. The more money that is placed on a single bet the higher the rate of return if it wins.

The most successful hedge fund managers are able to charge the highest fees so funds limit themselves to the most lucrative clients; those that can afford to pay those fees even if a bet loses.

The profits of hedge funds are taxable so, providing there is no aggressive tax avoidance involved, the most direct benefit to the economy is through taxation, both of the fund manager's income and the investors' profits. Hedge funds generally only make short term bets, so there is usually no benefit to any company in which an "investment" is made.

Conversely, if a leading hedge fund manager is known to have placed certain bets it can influence the markets. If, for example, a hedge fund manager is known to have placed heavy bets on the value of the pound falling, it may influence the foreign exchange markets in the belief the hedge fund manager knows something that the foreign exchange dealers don't, thereby causing the value of the pound to fall for no reason, or to fall further than it would under normal circumstances..

In principle investing in hedge funds is morally no different than gambling or any other form of investment. Where the real question of morality comes in is the fact that it makes already rich people even richer, while poor people are effectively excluded from participation.

\* \* \*

## 13<sup>th</sup> July 2015

**Is a "shyster" specifically a crooked or disreputable lawyer. Rather than a cheat from any other trade or profession?**

The origin of the term "Shyster" appears to stem from the mid 19<sup>th</sup> century and a lawyer by the name of Sheuster, who was considered to have used some unsavoury practices. His name seems to have been transferred to others whose behaviour is less than ethical and was therefore not exclusively applied to lawyers. Its use may have been conflated with the vulgar German word s*heisse,* meaning excrement.

There have been accusations that the word is anti-Semitic and this may be because of its similarity to Shylock, the Jewish money lender from Shakespeare's play The Merchant Of Venice. However, there is no evidence that its use was ever purely associated with Jewish lawyers or business people. However, there are commentators that suggest that the word is more commonly applied to Jewish people than to non-Jewish.

Sheuster was a lawyer in New York City, or possibly Philadelphia, and the term shyster seems to have been first used in a Manhatten newspaper dating around 1843-44. Sheuster or Shuster is a common Germanic name from the Bohemia region, part of the Chez Republic. It dates back to medieval times, relates to the craft of shoe making and has no intrinsic Jewish connection.

\* \* \*

## 21<sup>st</sup> July 2015

**It was recently claimed that Melania Trump had plagiarised Michelle Obama by using the phrase 'my word is my bond'. Surely this is an old saying? What are its origins?**

The origins of this phrase go back at least as far as 1801 and probably earlier.

It was the practice of brokers in insurance, shipping, company stocks and other commodities to seal deals on a hand shake, with little or no paper work to back up the transaction. Therefore the word of the two parties had to be taken on trust.

In this context a bond is a financial security, usually lodged with a trusted third party, that would ensure that neither party defaulted on a contract. If such a thing were to happen the plaintiff would be able to claim some or all of the defaulter's share of the bond in compensation.

Bonds of this sort still form part of normal business practice. For example, very large transport operators, such as Royal Mail, don't insure their vehicles. Instead they lodge a cash bond with the Accountant General of the Supreme Court as surety that they will pay legitimate claims made against them. Section 143 of the Road Traffic Act permits this and it saves a considerable amount on the cost of annual fleet insurance.

The term "my word is my bond" therefore means that the parties agreeing a contract need no other form of surety, because they are trustworthy people. In 1801 this became the motto of the London Stock Exchange, rendered into Latin as "dictum meum pactum". It was probably in use prior to this amongst maritime brokers, who negotiated the rental of ships and insured cargoes.

In the context of the Melania Trump/Michelle Obama speeches, it was not the use of this term alone that caused controversy, but the use of other extracts from the Michelle Obama speech. The "my word is my bond" portion was only a small part of the whole.

\* \* \*

## 22nd July 2016

### What was Captain William Mudge's contribution to map making?

Captain William Mudge was a military officer who was largely responsible for the first Ordnance Survey maps that are used by so many people for their leisure time. But their origins were purely military.

Born in 1762 Mudge attended the Royal Military Academy, Woolwich. On graduation he was sent to the Carolinas to serve under the command of General Cornwallis. Following the defeat of the British, resulting from the American War of Independence, he returned to Britain and was stationed at the Tower of London.

Around 1800 Dunnose on the Isle of Wight was taken as the base point for triangulation for Great Britain, the point from which all other geographic points would be measured and the basis on which British maps would, in future, be drawn. During 1801 and 1802 William Mudge was responsible for the measurement of 23 points along a line that ran from Dunnose to Beacon Hill near

Doncaster, along the meridional arc 1° 11' 28" W. A meridional arc is the measurement of points along the same line of longitude.

In 1813 it was decided to extend the measurement of the meridional arc into Scotland and Mudge was charged with that work. With the assistance of a Frenchman, Jean Baptiste Biot, and Mudge's own son Zacharia, the work was eventually extended to the Shetland Islands. It even inspired Wordsworth to pen the words *"Written with a Slate Pencil on a Stone, on the Side of the Mountain of Black Comb"* in the poem Black Combe.

Mudge rose to the rank of Colonel and as well as his work on surveying, he was also appointed commander of the Royal Military Academy, Woolwich, and as a supervisor of exams at Addiscombe Military Academy, where the officers of the Army of the East India Company were trained.

William Mudge died in April 1820, shortly after being promoted to the rank of Major General. While Mudge's contribution to the mapping of Great Britain is significant, it must be recognised that this was a military project and if he hadn't been tasked with it, someone else would have been. His fame, therefore, wasn't so much won as ordered.

\* \* \*

## 1st August 2016
### Who invented the idea of distance learning?

Distance learning goes back at least as far as 1728. It was in that year that an advertisement in the Boston Examiner offered correspondence courses from "Professor" Caleb Phillips, in short hand. This was followed in 1840 by Sir Isaac Pitman, another inventor of short hand writing techniques.

Pitman's teaching method was innovative because it provided a method of feedback between pupil and tutor. Pitman sent out shorthand texts on postcards and students corrected the deliberate errors before returning them, allowing Pitman to award performance related grades.

Pitman's course proved so popular that it led, 3 years later, to the Phonographic Correspondence Society being founded to provide three courses of distance learning using the Pitman model as its basis. These are the origins of the non-degree level correspondence courses that are offered by many providers and which now cover subjects from accountancy to zoology.

In terms of higher education, the University of London (later renamed University College London) started offering external programmes in 1828. These were courses of study offered at local educational institutes, but overseen by the university and didn't involve any "correspondence" element. The programme was controversial because London University was the only higher educational establishment that didn't ground its teachings in religion, consequently it was given the nick-name of "the Godless university".

Other correspondence courses were offered over time, but the big breakthrough in distance learning at degree level was the establishment of the Open University. This was an educational establishment that offered full degree level education to the masses via a mix of correspondence courses, radio and TV programmes, tutorials held in local facilities and summer schools. Planning for the Open University started in 1965 with the first students enrolling in 1971.

I studied for a BA (Hons) and an MBA with the Open University. As I was serving overseas in the RAF it wouldn't have been possible to gain my BA (Hons) if the OU hadn't existed.

Since its inception The Open University has had over 1.5 million students and has granted over 800,000 qualifications. It also enrols foreign students in many of its programmes. It is rated in the top

5 universities in the country for student satisfaction. Many students study with the aid of bursaries or other financial assistance. Today much of the university's delivery is provided "on-line" though it still uses more traditional delivery methods.

Perhaps the greatest exponents of distance learning were the Australians, who established the Schools Of The Air (SOA) for children living in remote rural areas where attendance at a primary school was impractical.

The SOA emerged from the Flying Doctor Service (FDS), when the Vice President of the South Australia FDS, Adelaide Miethke, noticed that the children in rural areas had all been taught by their parents to use short wave radio to summon the FDS. She then developed the idea for the radios to be used for educational purposes. The first school was established in 1948, covering the Alice Springs area, and the SOA was formally established in 1950. It gained international recognition when it was featured in an episode of Skippy The Bush Kangaroo.

In 2005 there were 15 SOAs in operation covering more than 1.5 million square kilometres of the "outback". Only the Australian Capital Territory (Canberra) and Tasmania don't offer an SOA for children living in the outback. Again, modern technology has enhanced the way that the schools operate.

**Author's note:** When this answer was published it omitted all the information regarding the SOA, which is surprising as it was one of the great educational innovations of the 20$^{\text{th}}$ century.

\* \* \*

## 2$^{\text{nd}}$ August 2016
**Is a universal vegan diet environmentally sustainable?**
There are many factors involved in this question that suggest the answer is "no". The three main problems with a switch to a universal

vegan diet are (1) the size of the global population, (2) what to do with the animals that we currently farm, and (3) the need for animals to provide fertilizers.

A vegan diet also suggests an organic diet. It isn't a stated essential for veganism, but the two seem to go hand in hand.

Therefore the idea of using chemical fertilisers in farming would be opposed if we were to become true vegans.

Compost produced from domestic and gardening waste can be used as a fertiliser but it would probably cost more in terms of calorific input to collect, process and deliver than it would provide in calorific output for the soil, making it highly inefficient for farming purposes. The alternative would be to grow crops just to provide compost, which again is extremely inefficient. This means that we would be highly dependent on animal fertiliser (manure) in order to keep the soil viable for crop growing.

However, to grow enough crops to feed entire populations without also using animal based foods (meat, eggs, milk) requires many times more land than is needed to rear animals. The ratio is approximately 3 to 1 in terms of the calorific value of the food produced. With the need to also maintain land for animal rearing this means that we would need to cultivate 4 times as much land than is currently cultivated.

There are, of course, massive areas of land that are currently uncultivated. But the reason they are uncultivated is because they are either forested, arid, or they are under permanent layers of ice and snow. Deforestation or the removal of ice cover in arctic areas increases the levels of climate change, so those are non-starters. To irrigate the deserts, on the other hand, would require massive levels of investment in irrigation technology. Even then it would require years of soil management to increase levels of soil fertility to a point where it would sustain crop growth, which would require huge amounts of animal based fertilisers and therefore huge numbers of animals, all of which have to be fed.

Each animal needed to produce manure would consume far more calories in terms of its food than it would be capable of producing in terms of its fertiliser output, meaning that it is an extremely inefficient model for agriculture. The model would be likely to end up rearing well fed animals while people went hungry.

The only way to make the system sustainable would be to radically reduce human population levels. The level of reduction is open to question, but with a current global population of 7 billion people it is likely that this would have to be reduced to 3 billion or less. How to achieve that reduction is a question no one wishes to try to answer.

If we accept the need for chemical fertilisers to replace or supplement compost there is then the issue of what we do with the animals if we no longer eat meat. We have a choice of destroying them all or releasing them into the wild. If we destroy them we lose their input into the agricultural process, and that is without having to deal with the question of whether or not we have the ethical right to destroy them in the first place.

If released into the wild the animals will still require food, which would limit our ability to expand the amount of land under cultivation in order to grow vegetables. They would also breed in an uncontrolled manner, increasing their demand for land in competition with humanity. In many parts of the world there are no longer any natural predators (wolves, large cats, bears) that can assist in controlling animal population levels. If you thought the badger cull was contentious, imagine the controversy that might be caused by having to cull cows, pigs and sheep.

We would almost certainly end up pushing the animals onto uncultivable land where they would be forced to live on such a restricted diet that they would suffer more than they do on even the most badly run farm. This is already happening in Africa, Asia and South America where human incursion into wild habitat is pushing many species of animal to the edge of extinction and in some cases pushing them over the edge. Pushing previously domesticated farm animals into this same territory would only accelerate the process.

If vegans wish us all to adopt their diet, they must first come up with the means of resolving these issues, which they don't seem inclined to do.

**Author's note:** There has been a notable rise in militant veganism over recent years, with restaurants being invaded by vegans in an effort to shame meat eaters into changing their ways. While these acts are still a rarity they are probably a sign of things to come. In the meantime, vegans have still to provide a solution for the conundrums mentioned in my original reply - which wasn't published.

\* \* \*

### 4<sup>th</sup> August 2016

#### Why is a police informer a 'grass'?

The earliest written use of "grass" to mean an informant is in Arthur Gardner's book "Tinker's Kitchen", published in 1932. However, the expression is older than that.

One possible origin is from the Roman author and philosopher Virgil, who used the term "snake in the grass" ('latet anguis in herba) to describe an untrustworthy person. It was used as early as the 17<sup>th</sup> century in England to mean a traitor.

An alternative origin is from cockney rhyming slang. Farmer and Henry's 1893 book "The Dictionary of Slang" defines grass as deriving from grasshopper, to rhyme with copper, slang for a police officer. So to "grass someone up" would be to inform on them to a grasshopper or copper.

This origin was repeated in the 1950s by Paul Tempest when he wrote "The Lags Lexicon: a comprehensive dictionary and encyclopaedia of the English prison today."

In 2005 a burglar stole a parrot along with other property from a house in Hungerford, Berkshire. When asked by the police why he had stolen the parrot he replied that it was an African Grey, which are well known for their speaking ability, and he didn't want the parrot to grass him up. Presumably if it had been a Norwegian Blue it would have been left to pine for the fjords.

* * *

## 8<sup>th</sup> August 2016

### Did Nostradamus predict the rise of ISIS/Daesh?

A four line verse, or quatrain, written by Nostradamus has been interpreted to predict the rise of ISIS/Daesh. It reads:

"He will enter wicked, unpleasant, infamous,
Tyrannising over Mesopotamia.
All friends made by the adulterous lady,
Land dreadful and black of aspect."

Mesopotamia is modern day Iraq, which ISIS have held considerable sway over with their tyrannical regime in the territory they control. The adulterous lady is interpreted as meaning money or a consumer-oriented society and, of course, the ISIS flag is "black of aspect."

Whether or not this is a prediction of the rise of ISIS or is an interpretation of events with the benefit of hindsight, is a matter of opinion. Before the rise of ISIS the quatrain wouldn't have meant much, but afterwards it can be interpreted to fit events. This is true of much of Nostradamus's writings. As the prediction refers to the singular "he" it could equally refer to Saddam Hussain.

Further quatrains are said to point to the start of World War III as a consequence of the rise of ISIS. The verse "Finally the third (anti-Christ) will cause an inundation of human blood and one will not find Mars (the God of war) fasting for a long time."

The first two anti-Christs are interpreted as referring to Napoleon and Hitler. The verse goes on to predict the war will last for 25 years. 2016 has featured strongly in several predictions of the end of the world that aren't related to Nostradamus and if these are coupled to the Nostradamus prediction it could mean WW3 starting this year. However, the most recent prediction of the end of the world was for it to happen on 29th July, which it most clearly didn't.

Michel de Nostradame (Latinised as Nostradamus) was born in 1503 in St Remy de Provence, France. He studied at the University of Avignon before qualifying as an apothecary (pharmacist). After the death of his wife and two children, possibly from the plague, Nostradamus became interested in the occult. From that interest he started to produce an annual almanac, the first being published in 1550. Taken together these almanacs contain at least 6,338 predictions for their years of publication.

It was as a result of these predictions that the wealthy and influential started to consult Nostradamus and ask him to cast their horoscopes. He wasn't a good astrologer and made frequent errors in the star charts he created for his clients, so he encouraged them to provide their own. Catherine de Medici, wife of Henry II of France, was a fan.

Nostradamus set about writing a complete set of prophesies but, fearing religious persecution, he deliberately disguised his writings, which is why they are so difficult to interpret. Due to a dispute with his publisher the last 58 quatrains that he wrote were never published and have been lost.

The majority of Nostradamus's prophesies deal with war and disaster but their interpretation has been mainly done with the benefit of hindsight. It is not thought that anyone has successfully interpreted any of the quatrains in advance of an actual event. A lack of dates in the prophesies mean they can be reinterpreted time and again in response to the latest events.

There has been much scholarly study of Nostradamus's writings, but it is rare for any two experts to agree on the interpretation of any of the quatrains. However, it does fuel a lucrative market in books about the man and his predictions. The first written in English was by Henry C Roberts and was published in 1947, entitled "The Complete Prophecies of Nostradamus". It was so popular that it was reprinted 7 times. Many other authors have since followed this path.

Nostradamus died in 1566.

* * *

### 19th August 2016

**In July 1954, the first flight of the Boeing 367-80 jet took place. Only one of this type was built. Why, and what happened to this aircraft?**

The main reason for this aircraft not being brought into commercial service was that it was never intended to. Just as many car manufacturers now produce "concept cars", so Boeing produced a "concept aircraft".

Following De Havilland's successful maiden flight of the Comet 4C, in 1949, the first true jet airliner, Boeing realised that the future lay in jet travel. In 1950 Boeing produced the first specification for a jet airliner, bearing the designation 473-60C. However, American customers were unconvinced, as they were enjoying success with modern piston engine aircraft such as the DC4 and DC6, produced by rivals Douglas, the Lockheed Constellation and Boeing's own

Stratocruiser. Boeing was better known as a producer of military aircraft and there was a degree of sales resistance because of this. To overcome this bias Boeing decided to show the customers a completed aircraft. They invested a massive (for the time) $16 million dollars in the project, making it a high risk gamble.

They developed the 367-80, or Dash 80 as it was commonly known. However, for public consumption the model was always referred to as the 707, to differentiate it from other Boeing products. The 700 series of numbers hadn't been used by Boeing before and was intended to indicate a new era in aircraft design. While the Dash 80 wasn't identical to the finished 707, there were many similarities and they used some of the same tooling. The Dash 80 could be viewed as a prototype and was used to develop many of the features that would make the 707 such a successful aircraft, such as the swept wings and podded engines mounted beneath the wings for easy maintenance. From project launch in 1952 to finished aircraft took only two years and the Dash 80 made its maiden flight on 15$^{th}$ July 1954.

The Dash 80 began a programme of demonstration flights, entertaining airline executives and demonstrating features that would later appear on the 707. It made regular appearances at air shows around the world. One pilot, Alvin "Tex" Johnston, was disciplined for performing barrels rolls in the Dash 80, which had never been done before with such a large aircraft.

After the roll-out of the Boeing 707 in 1959, the Dash 80 became a general experimental aircraft and many innovations were tried out on it, such as changes to aerofoil design and the installation of a fifth engine to the rear of the cabin area. After 2,350 flying hours the aircraft was removed from service and put into storage in 1969. Following a refurbishment, in 2003 it made its final flight, from the desert storage 'boneyard' in Arizona to Washington's Dulles International Airport. It was put on display at the Steven F

Udvar-Hazy Centre, an annex to the Smithsonian Institute located adjacent to the airport. The Smithsonian rates the Dash 80 as one of the 12 most influential aircraft of all time.

From the 707 a whole family of aircraft emerged, from the short-haul 737 to the latest model, the 787 Dreamliner. The different models have many components in common, which made them much cheaper to maintain in comparison to competitors, so operators loved them. This brought about the demise of Douglas and Lockheed as serious competitors in the commercial airline market and Boeing was unrivalled until the arrival of the Airbus range, produced through a series of international partnerships between European aircraft manufacturers.

\* \* \*

## 19<sup>th</sup> August 2016

**When I told my nine-year-old daughter no one in the world had the same DNA, she asked: 'What about Siamese twins?'**

One very specific group of people do have identical DNA. These are monozygotic (identical) twins. Identical twins come from a single egg which is fertilised by a single sperm but which then splits into two separate embryos. This produces two foetuses with identical DNA, each eventually developing into a child. Identical twins are always boy/boy or girl/girl.

Siamese, or to give them their correct name, conjoined twins, are identical twins whose single embryo didn't separate correctly, resulting in them growing up as a single physical entity, although they can still develop individual personalities. Because they are identical twins they, too, have identical DNA. Separating conjoined twins after birth is notoriously difficult and dangerous because they often share vital organs.

A subset of identical twins is 'mirror twins' These twins have identical features but they are mirrored. For example, if one twin's left eye is green but their right eye is blue, this will be reversed in their twin. They too have identical DNA. The mirroring is created during the growth process in the womb.

Fraternal (non-identical or dizygotic) twins come about because two eggs are fertilised in the womb at the same time, forming separate embryos from the very start of their life. Boy/girl twins are always non-identical. Each twin has unique DNA, if they didn't then one of them couldn't be a girl. However, boy/boy and girl/girl fraternal twins also have unique DNA. They can have different eye or hair colouring or one can be taller than the other. Physically one could favour the features of the mother while the other favours the father, all of which show that they have different DNA.

Triplets generally follow the rules for fraternal twins, with 3 eggs being fertilised at the same time to produce three embryos, each with their own unique DNA. However, in some rare cases they can be monozygotic, all coming from the same egg and therefore having the same DNA. They can also be a mixture, with two embryos coming from a single egg, giving a pair of siblings with identical DNA and the third being fraternal, with different DNA. The same can apply with other multiple births, such as quads or quins.

\* \* \*

## 22nd August 2016

**Does anyone recall a cartoon strip in which a working-class boy routinely thrashed posh boys in athletics races?**

Alf Tupper, a.k.a "The tough of the track" appeared in comic strips from 1949 until 1992, but made a 2014 reappearance in the magazine Athletics Weekly.

In an era when athletes were mainly amateur, it required a generous income to be to able afford to train. The premise of the Alf Tupper comic strip was that, with grit and determination, it was possible for someone from a poor background not just to compete, but to be the best. Throughout his career Alf was always the underdog, having always to overcome adversity to live his dream.

Alf's story lines often involved him falling asleep on his way to an athletics meeting after a hard shift, then missing his bus or train stop. Needless to say the rich, snobby athletes were always looking down their noses at Alf and set out to beat him by foul means if fair couldn't be achieved. It was a feature of the strip that they always got their comeuppance. Alf was routinely snubbed by the posh people who ran the Amateur Athletics Association.

Alf first appeared in The Rover comic in 1949 where he worked as a millwright at the Graystone Aviation Factory or as a plumber for Charlie Chipping of Gas St, Graystone. Alf later moved to The Victor comic, where he became a self-employed welder, but still in Graystone.

Graystone was a drab fictional town of cobbled streets where employment was mainly manual, in heavy manufacturing industries. In 1973 The Victor started a prequel storyline with Alf growing up as an orphan in Graystone.

Alf's last regular appearance was in the Scottish newspaper The Sunday Post, in 1992, where he was seen training for the Barcelona Olympics.

Alf's first writer was Gilbert Lawford Dalton, born in 1904 and died in 1963. He was born in Kidderminster but lived in Royal Leamington Spa from 1945 before moving to Bournemouth in 1958, where he died and is buried. He started work as a journalist for the Coventry Evening Telegraph, before taking up fictional writing, mainly for comics produced by the D.C Thompson group. During World War II he served in the Royal Observer Corps.

Other Dalton creations were "Wilson The Wonder Athlete" who appeared in The Wizard, and "Matt Braddock" a fictional World War II bomber pilot who appeared in 1952, again in The Rover. Matt Braddock was also given a less posh background by starting his career as a Sergeant in the RAF, rather than as an officer.

* * *

25<sup>th</sup> August 2016

### Did the British army invent an invisible tank?

This story emanates from around 2014, when it was announced that British armoured vehicles were going to be fitted with the sort of electronic counter measures used by military aircraft, which would make them "invisible" to certain threats. It didn't mean that they would be invisible to the naked eye.

This story spawned a flurry of fake videos on internet channels such as YouTube, which purported to show tanks becoming literally invisible.

The countermeasures used include "chaff", strips of metal foil which are thrown into the air around a target vehicle in order to confuse radar. They would also use flares which act as a distraction to heat seeking missiles and, ultimately, would launch "killer missiles" which would destroy incoming munitions before they could strike. The systems would be operated by radar, to detect the missiles, which feeds command signals to computers which not only deploy the counter measures, but which also automatically target the missile launch vehicles, using the tank's gun.

Some of these innovations are thought to be already installed on Russia's new main battle tank, the T-14, which is currently being introduced into service. Their use is described in the opening chapters of the Tom Clancy novel "Command Authority".

Another innovation that is being developed is adaptive "ecamouflage". This uses cameras mounted on the outside the vehicle to view the local terrain and then projectors replicate this on light reactive paint to make the tank blend in with its back ground more effectively than conventional painted camouflage would permit.

Anyone who saw the James Bond film "Die Another Day" will be familiar with the idea, as it was simulated on the Aston Martin V12 Vanquish that Bond drove in the film. However, the concept is some years away from becoming a reality, and even then the tank will still be clearly visible to anyone standing within tens of yards of it.

* * *

## 27<sup>th</sup> September 2016

**In his version of The Battle Of New Orleans, Lonnie Donegan sings about American troops 'taking a little trip – along with Colonel Packenham down the mighty Mississip' to fight the British...' but Packenham was commander of the British forces. Did the songwriter get this wrong?**

It would appear that Lonnie Donegan made an error when he recorded his version of the song The Battle Of New Orleans, rather than the songwriter. His lyrics differ markedly from the original.

The American forces at the battle were led by Colonel Andrew Jackson, later to become known as Stonewall Jackson, of American Civil War fame. The British forces were led by Major General Sir Edward Packenham, the brother in law of the Duke of Wellington.

The song The Battle of New Orleans, was written by Jimmy Driftwood and he included it on the album "Newly Discovered Early American Folk Songs" in 1957. A version more suited for the radio (fewer "cuss words") was released in 1959 by American Johnny Horton, who made the Billboard Top 100 with it. It is through this version the Donegan will probably have first heard it, either on the radio or on an imported record. He released his own version the same year.

In 1960 Jimmy Driftwood was awarded a Grammy for the song in the category of Song Of The Year and subsequently won 4 more Grammys.

Jimmy Driftwood penned the opening line as "In 1814 we took a little trip,

Along with Colonel Jackson down the mighty Mississippi" It was this line that Donegan changed to refer to Packenham. Whether Donegan knew that he had forced Packenham to switch allegiance isn't clear.

Later in the song is the line "Old Hickory said we could take 'em by surprise,

If we didn't fire our muskets 'till we looked 'em in the eyes." Old Hickory is the nickname ascribed to Jackson at that time, but Donegan changes the words to "Packenham said".

Rather than making an error it is possible that Donegan changed the lyrics so that they might scan better when sung to a skiffle rhythm, historical accuracy taking second place to the needs of a good song. While there are similarities between the tunes used for the two versions of the songs their rhythms are very different.

The battle itself was the final battle of what is now known as the War of 1812, fought between the British and the newly independent U.S.A. Upset by trade restrictions imposed by the British as part of their war against Napoleon, in 1812 the U.S.A declared war, but because of the Peninsula War there was very little direct combat between the two nations until 1814, following the French surrender and Napoleon's exile to Elba. Instead the British concentrated on mounting a naval blockade of America's Atlantic ports.

In 1814 three British armies were dispatched with different objectives. After the Battle of Bladensberg the British captured and burnt Washington, including the half built White House, but things turned out badly after that, with all three armies being defeated at New York, Baltimore and New Orleans.

With a force of 11,000 soldiers the British far outnumbered the Americans with only 4,000. The British marched North from their landing point on the Mississippi, but instead of attacking New Orleans at once they decided to rest for the night at a plantation. Andrew Jackson launched a surprise night attack and inflicted heavy casualties, forcing the British to retreat. This allowed the Americans time to build artillery batteries, which proved crucial in the second battle.

The British had to cross a canal to make their assault, but had failed to bring the necessary equipment they needed to help them do this. In their efforts to wade across the canal they were exposed to withering artillery fire from the American side. Deaths among the senior British officers left the troops without leadership and they withdrew. On 9th January the British laid siege to Fort St Philip, at the mouth of the Mississippi, but finally withdrew after a week.

Between 23rd December 1814 and 16th January the British lost a total of 386 killed and 1,521 wounded. It may be assumed that some of the wounded died later from their injuries. The Americans lost a total of 55 killed and 185 wounded. It was the last war fought that had Britain and the USA on opposing sides.

* * *

## 10th October 2016

In an article on the proposed memorial to Polish World War II airmen, Norman Tebbit was quoted as saying that Britain had plenty of planes but not enough pilots. I have read that at the start of the Battle Of Britain we had 9,000 pilots, but only 5,000 planes, most of which were bombers. Which is correct?

The answer to this lies within the question. The RAF always had more pilots than planes, but bombers usually had a crew of both a pilot and a co-pilot. So if the majority of the RAF's aircraft were bombers, then it meant that the majority of pilots would be employed on flying bombers. If 4,000 of the RAF's aircraft required two pilots, that accounts for 8,000 of the pilots, leaving the remaining 1,000 to fly aircraft that required only a single pilot, such as the Spitfire or Hurricane.

In fact, in 1939 the RAF had over 10,000 aircraft, of which just over 3,000 were combat aircraft (bombers, fighters, maritime etc). The remainder were transports, training aircraft, or army co-operation aircraft – spotting for the artillery. A significant number of these aircraft, about a third, were deployed overseas, protecting Britain's empire and trade routes.

By mid-1940 the new Spitfire factory at Castle Bromwich was producing 320 aircraft per month, or about ten per day, and more were being built in factories around Southampton and Reading. This meant that the re-supply of aircraft was able, by and large, to keep up with combat losses. By comparison it took the RAF about 9 weeks to train a pilot, which meant that replacing combat losses was a slow process. Many pilots were trained in Canada, away from the European combat theatre, adding extensive travel time to the equation.

At the time of the Battle Of Britain there were no conversion courses for fighter pilots. This meant that newly qualified pilots who had learnt to fly in biplanes had very little flying time recorded on either monoplanes or the type of aircraft they were to fly, the Spitfire or Hurricane, and virtually no knowledge of aerial combat techniques. This made new pilots very vulnerable and the attrition rate amongst them was high. New Zealander Allan Deere, a hero of the Battle of Britain, recalled two inexperienced pilots who joined his squadron, both of whom were shot down on their second sortie.

The effects of combat on pilots was heavy. A pilot could not be expected to fly multiple sorties per day, 7 days a week, and not suffer from mental and physical exhaustion. That meant that pilots had to be rested, which meant that each squadron had to have more pilots on its strength than it had aircraft. Longer periods of "rest" were provided by posting pilots to areas where there was less risk of combat, such as the north of England and Scotland, replacing them with pilots from those areas.

A pilot that had to bail out of a stricken aircraft wasn't able to return to combat straight away. They had to be medically assessed and even minor injuries could keep them away from operations for a week or so, though some might be back in the air the next day. Any injury that affected vision, hearing, balance or mobility was enough to ground a pilot.

It only required a minor ailment for a pilot to be grounded. A cold, for example, can upset a pilot's sense of balance, which was dangerous given the aerial acrobatics the pilot was expected to perform in combat. Toothache is aggravated by cold air and high altitude, so a pilot suffering from toothache might be more of a danger to himself than to the enemy. Such human frailties placed a further burden on already over stretched squadrons. Never had the bible quote "the spirit is willing, but the flesh is weak" been more true.

**Author's note:** Once again the editor used his knife on my answer, removing all references to the medical restrictions suffered by pilots.

\* \* \*

## 13<sup>th</sup> October 2016

**Why do different Guards Regiments have different button patterns on their dress uniforms?**

The grouping of the buttons on guards' uniforms is used to distinguish their seniority within the Household Division. The most senior regiment, the Grenadier Guards, has their buttons spaced as singles, while the most junior, The Welsh Guards, has their buttons grouped in fives. The regiments are also distinguished by the plumes worn on the side of the bearskin. White for the Grenadiers, worn on the left and white over green for the Welsh, also worn on the left.

The others are: Coldstream Guards, pairs, red plume on the right; Scotts Guards, threes, no plume; and Irish Guards, fours, blue plume on the right.

The plume indicated where in the line of battle the regiments stood, the Grenadier Guards on the left and the Coldstream Guards on the right, with the Scotts Guards in the middle. The Welsh and Irish Guards didn't form until after the army stopped forming lines to fight battles, but their plumes indicate where they now stand when the regiments are on parade together.

Why the practice of grouping buttons came into being is unclear, however, it can be noted that the coloured plumes are worn on the side of the bearskin and can easily become hidden in the depths of the fur. Therefore the system of button groupings provides a more reliable form of regimental recognition when a soldier is seen from the front. Regimental cap badges, the standard form of recognition for all British soldiers, are not worn on the bearskin.

Seniority should not be confused with the age of the regiment. The oldest of the Guards regiments is the Scotts Guards, who can trace their history back to 1642 with the raising of the Duke Of Argyll's Royal Regiment in support of Charles I. Next oldest is the Coldstream Guards who were raised in 1650 as General George Monk's Regiment, part of Cromwell's New Model Army. Their first action was at the Battle of Dunbar, where one of the regiments that opposed them was Argyll's Regiment, now renamed the Lyfe Guards of Foot on the orders of the exiled Charles II. Following the defeat of Charles at the battle of Worcester the Lyfe Guards of Foot ceased to exist, along with the rest of the Scottish army that supported the monarchy, which makes the Coldstream Guards the oldest continuingly serving regiment in the British army.

In 1656 the Grenadier Guards were formed as Lord Wentworth's Regiment, in Brugge. They claim their seniority because they were formally adopted as the bodyguard of King Charles II, making them the only Guards regiment actually in existence at the time to hold that accolade. Monk's Regiment didn't become foot guards until 1661 when they formally renounced their membership of the New Model Army and were immediately recreated as The Lord General's Regiment of Foot Guards in King Charles' new army.

The connection of Monk's Regiment to the small town of Coldstream in the Scottish borders is a tenuous one, having stayed there for only a short period in 1659 prior to moving to London to help quell riots in opposition to the pending return of Charles to the throne. The Scotts Guards were re-created shortly after the restoration, based on the remnants of Argyll's Regiment, but didn't become a full regiment until 1666. They were initially used to garrison the royal castles in Scotland and to combat the Covenanters, Scottish Presbyterians opposed to the restoration of the monarchy.

The Irish Guards were formed in 1900 on the insistence of Queen Victoria, who wished to honour the contribution made by Irish soldiers during the Boer War. The Welsh Guards were created in 1915 by a Royal Warrant issued by George V, who wished to include the Welsh in the foot guards. This may have been aimed at encouraging enlistment into the army from Wales during the First World War.

* * *

## 18<sup>th</sup> October 2016

**There is a huge acreage of solar panels sited on reclaimed land just south of the M4 between junctions 11 and 12. On average, how much electricity do these panels generate?**

Solar panels work by converting sunlight into electrical energy. However, the electricity is in direct current (d/c) form, so to be useable by most domestic and industrial equipment, and to be fed into the National Grid, it has to be converted to alternating current (a/c), which is achieved by applying the d/c output from the panel to a device called an inverter. However, this conversion comes at a cost in efficiency terms. 1 kw of d/c power fed into the inverter does not equal 1 kw of a/c power fed out.

The output of a solar array (a collection of solar panels) will then be applied to a transformer and fed into the National Grid. In domestic solar power systems any excess energy can be sold to the National Grid in what is referred to as a "feed in". Privately owned businesses generating their own solar power can also benefit in this way.

Solar panels vary in size and the larger they are the more power they produce. Typical roof mounted solar arrays will produce between 1kw and 4 kw of power. With an average power consumption of about 3.9 kw the largest systems are enough to power a typical house with a little bit left over to feed into the National grid to earn the householder a small amount of cash. Typical repayment periods to recover the cost of installation are in the order of 20 years.

There is no difference in power output for a panel used for domestic purposes and those used for commercial power generation. Each panel has an output of about 1kw, so count the number of panels and you can calculate how much power is generated.

The largest commercial installation in the UK is in Leamington Spa and covers an area about the size of two football pitches. Its power output is around 2 Megawatts (2 million watts) after conversion to a/c. If applied to houses it could power just over 500 average family homes. Typical commercial installations can repay their cost of installation in 5 to 10 years, depending on how much power is sold to the National Grid. Landowners who allow the building of solar installations on their land make their money from the rent they charge, rather than from the installation, which is usually owned by a third party.

The downside of solar power is that when the sun stops shining the solar panels stop producing electricity. This can be overcome by storing excess electricity in batteries and using them to keep the inverters operating at night. However, there are efficiency costs to that. 1kw of electricity fed in would only provide about 0.9 kw out, which is then further reduced by the efficiency losses of the inverter. There is also the additional cost of the batteries and the space they consume to be taken into account.

The largest solar power installation in the world is in China at Longyangxia Dam Solar Park. It produces 850MW of power and covers about 9 sq km, or 3.5 sq miles. It generates enough power to run approximately 218,000 homes, at least during daylight hours.

The hidden and rarely mentioned cost of both solar and wind power is the need to keep conventional power stations running in order to fill the gap created when the sun isn't shining and the wind isn't blowing. Power stations can't be started up from scratch at a moment's notice, they have to be kept ticking over, with all the attendant running costs but without the income generated by energy sales. It's like keeping your car engine running when it's parked outside your house just in case you need to go somewhere at short notice. As an island nation our most promising form of renewable energy is from wave power, as the sea is almost always in motion, but we are still some years away from a commercial wave powered generating system.

\* \* \*

**27<sup>th</sup> October 2016**

**Was Margaret Thatcher's "There's no such things as society" speech misconstrued?**

This famous quote comes not from a speech, but from an interview that was published in Woman's Own magazine, on 23<sup>rd</sup> September 1987. The interviewer was Douglas Keye, a journalist working for the magazine.

It is probably the most wilfully misconstrued quote in political history. As with many quotes, it is easy for them to lose their meaning when taken out of context. This is the relevant extract of the article as it appears in the magazine:

"I think we've been through a period where too many people have been given to understand that if they have a problem, it's the government's job to cope with it. [...] They're casting their problem on society. And, you know, **there is no such thing as society**. There are individual men and women, and there are families. And no government can do anything except through people, and people must look to themselves first. It's our duty to look after ourselves and then, also to look after our neighbour. People have got the entitlements too much in mind, without the obligations. There's no such thing as entitlement, unless someone has first met an obligation."

Taken in full it becomes clear that Mrs Thatcher is talking about the need for individuals to take responsibility for themselves first, then for us as a whole to help those who still need helping. Whether one agrees with that sentiment or not is then a matter of opinion. However, by removing that context it makes it appear that Mrs Thatcher was somehow saying that society doesn't exist or has no role in the lives of people, when her actual argument is very different.

The transcript of the actual interview shows that Margaret Thatcher went further in her description of what she thought society was, but No 10 chose not to correct the Woman's Own article. However they did issue a statement to correct a Sunday Times misrepresentation of the article, which may have been the first newspaper to do so and therefore may have been the source of the misquote.

There are numerous examples of this quote being used to portray the remarks as something that they weren't, by leaving out the surrounding context.

Is what Margaret Thatcher saying so much different from this?

"We, the People, recognize that we have responsibilities as well as rights; that our destinies are bound together; that a freedom which only asks what's in it for me, a freedom without a commitment to others, a freedom without love or charity or duty or patriotism, is unworthy of our founding ideals, and those who died in their defence." – Barak Obama.

**Author's note:** When this letter was published it was without the final paragraph, quoting Barak Obama.

* * *

## 1st November 2016

**In World War II, did the German, Japanese and Italian governments close their embassies in the Republic of Ireland?**

Ireland was a province of the United Kingdom until 1921 and so didn't conduct any diplomatic relations of its own with other nations until after that date. As with most small countries it didn't maintain embassies or other diplomatic missions with every nation, instead using other nation's embassies in some countries to look after its interests and the interests of its citizens.

Despite contacts that date back 130 years, Japan didn't establish an embassy in Dublin until 1964 and the Irish Embassy in Tokyo didn't open until 1973.

Formal diplomatic relations between Ireland and both Germany and Italy began in 1922. Both countries maintained their embassies in Dublin throughout the war years and Ireland maintained its Embassies in Berlin and Rome during the same period.

In April 1945, on the death of Adolf Hitler, the German embassy in Dublin opened a book of condolence which was signed by both the President of Ireland, Eamon De Valera and the Secretary for Foreign Affairs, Joseph Walshe. Irish envoys elsewhere in Europe also visited German embassies to sign books of condolence. The only other heads of state of neutral countries to sign these books were General Francisco Franco of Spain and Oliveira Salazar of Portugal, both fascist dictators in their own countries. Understandably, De Valera's act was widely condemned, particularly in the USA.

Throughout the Second World war military personnel from the combatant nations who found themselves on Irish shores were interned at The Curragh, a former British military barracks in County Kildare which was still being used to imprison members of the IRA who had fought against the Irish government during and after the Irish Civil War. Reports of life inside the camp show it as being quite relaxed and comfortable, though the food wasn't great. Internees were allowed to phone or visit their embassies whenever they wished. Internees were even allowed out on parole to visit local towns and, under supervision, to visit Dublin. There were some marriages between Irish women and internees.

The Curragh camp was divided into 3 sections. One section housed the IRA prisoners, one the Germans and one the British. Americans captured in Ireland were repatriated under a bi-lateral agreement between the two nations. Only one American, Roland 'Bud' Wolfe of 133 "Eagle" Sqn, was interned at The Curragh. He was a pilot who had joined the RAF and whose American citizenship was stripped from him because of that. His aircraft crashed in Donegal in 1941, having suffered engine failure.

On 13th December 1941 Wolfe walked out of The Curragh, made his way to Northern Ireland and returned to his base at RAF Eglinton (now City of Derry Airport) from where he had taken off in his Spitfire just two weeks earlier. Expecting a hero's welcome he was very surprised when he was placed under arrest and promptly returned to the Curragh by the British, who didn't want to upset the Irish or give them an excuse to impose a harsher regime on the British internees.

In October 1943 the allied internees were transferred to a camp at Gormanston, Co Meath, and then secretly freed, although the official version is that they escaped. German internees remained at The Curragh until the end of the war.

\* \* \*

### 3rd November 2016

**Did Marie Antoinette actually say 'Let them each brioche'?**

The accepted story is that when Marie Antoinette heard that the French people were protesting at not being able to afford to buy bread, she said "Qu'ils mangent de la brioche", or "let them eat brioche". The brioche made at that time would have been more akin to a cake, so "let them eat cake" would have been the closest English translation of the time. However, it is doubtful if she ever said anything of the sort, referring to either cake or brioche.

The story coincides with other sayings attributed to aristocrats or royalty being out of touch with the living conditions of the general population, especially in relation to the price of staple foods, such as bread. For example, a 16th century tale from Germany tells of an aristocrat wondering why the poor didn't simply eat krosen, a type of sweet bread.

The first appearance of the story in French comes from Jean-Jacques Rousseau, who uses it in Book VI of his "Confessions" and attributes it "to a great princess", without naming her. While Marie Antoinette was doubtless a great princess at the time of writing, around 1767, she was still a child aged about 12, living in her native Austria.

It has been suggested that as the revolutionaries were inspired, in part, by Rousseau's writings, they picked it up from them and wrongly attributed the saying to Marie Antoinette. However, there is no supporting evidence in the form of its inclusion in revolutionary papers or pamphlets of the period. Given its value as a piece of propaganda this lack of any trace of its contemporary use is notable by its absence.

The first report linking the quote directly to the late Queen didn't appear until 50 years after the revolution. In an 1834 edition of a magazine called Les Cuêpes the writer, Jean-Baptiste Alphonse Karr, reports finding the phrase in a 1760 book, which would have been written when Marie Antoinette was only 5 years old. Karr concluded that the quote was falsely attributed to Marie Antoinette, but given that he seems to have been the one to have raised the subject in writing he may have, inadvertently, been the one to have made it popular.

\* \* \*

14<sup>th</sup> November 2016

**Did a former US Vice-President write the popular song It's All In The game?**

An American Vice President didn't write the words to "It's All In The Game", but one did write the tune. However, the tune pre-dated the song by about 40 years. He also wasn't a "former" Vice President, because at the time of writing the tune his candidacy was still in the future.

Charles G Dawes was born on 27<sup>th</sup> August 1865. He became a lawyer, a banker, a politician and a military figure, as well as being a part time composer. He attended Marietta College and Cincinnati Law School and practiced law in Lincoln, Nebraska, where he also became a businessman, investing in gas plants.

He was a noted amateur musician and composer and in 1912 wrote "Melody in A Major", which would one day be used for the song "It's All In The Game". Although never formally published it became a popular tune for both violin and piano and Dawes used it as his "signature tune" at many business and political functions, which is how it became known to a wider audience.

As a prominent businessman Dawes was asked to manage the Illinois portion of William McKinley's bid to become President in 1896, which brought him into the circle of Republican politics. He took up public office and ran for the Senate in 1901, but the assassination of William McKinley saw the seat go to the candidate favoured by Theodore Roosevelt. During the First World War Dawes held a commission in the US Army, rising to the rank of Brigadier General in the Corps of Engineers, serving in France from 1917 to 1918. In 1925 Dawes shared the Nobel Peace Prize for his work on helping to stabilise the German economy in the post war era.

Returning to America after the war Dawes continued to pursue a political career, becoming Vice President to Calvin Coolidge between 1925 and 1929. He then became the American Ambassador to London from 1929 to 1931. President Herbert Hoover recalled him so that he could run the Reconstruction Finance Corporation, which was aimed at relieving the ravages of the Great Depression. He later returned to commercial banking. He died in 1951.

In 1951 Carl Sigman wrote the words to "It's All In The Game" and put them to Dawes's 1912 tune. It became a hit in 1958 for singer Tommy Edwards and has been covered many times since. It is the only popular song to have been composed (in part) both by an American Vice President and a Nobel Peace Prize winner.

Carl Sigman (1909-2000) was a prolific songwriter and was also responsible for songs such as "What Now My Love" and "Pennsylvania 6-5000". He did a lot of work with band leaders such as Glenn Miller and Guy Lombardo.

Tommy Edwards had a recording career that ran from 1951 to 1966. In total he had 21 songs that entered the Billboard Hot 100, but "It's all in the Game" was the only one to make the Top 10, ultimately reaching No1 in both the US and UK. His only other UK chart success was "Melancholy Baby" which reached No 29 in 1959. He died in 1969 from a brain aneurysm.

\* \* \*

## 18<sup>th</sup> November 2016

### When was "Mentioned In Dispatches" formalised into a specific accolade?

All commanders in the field were required to send reports of their activities to higher authority, a practice that is as old as warfare itself. In Britain the dispatches sent back to Parliament were published in the London Gazette, the official newspaper of the British Government, a practice dating back to the Gazette's first publication, in 1665.

As part of the dispatch it was the practice of the commander to mention the names of those soldiers who had acted with particular valour or performed with merit, which is the origin of the phrase. A reward for such action was commonly a promotion, sometimes even a commission in the field. Sir Charles Napier was the first British commander to mention those below commissioned rank, on 2nd March 1843, during the conquest of Sindh province in what is now Pakistan. The list of names was usually attached to the main dispatch.

The publication in the London Gazette of the names of soldiers mentioned in dispatches was started during the Boer War. However, until 1919 there was no emblem to signify that a soldier had been mentioned in dispatches. The granting of an award for bravery or meritorious service was still subject to the writing of a specific citation for the event that earned the award.

In 1919 the War Office decided to grant a certificate to denote a mention in dispatches, plus an emblem to be worn on the uniform. This was granted retrospectively to all soldiers who had served in the First World War and who had received an MID. The emblem was a spray of bronze oak leaves, slightly shorter in length than the width of a medal ribbon. The emblem was usually sewn onto the campaign medal to which the award relates. In the case of First World War awards this was the Victory Medal. For the Second World War it was the War Medal 1939-1945 and for many other campaigns it was the General Service Medal. In 1920 the emblem was changed to a single bronze oak leaf.

A Mention In Dispatches is one of only 3 awards that can be granted posthumously, the other two being the Victoria Cross and The George Cross.

**Author's note:** This was the second time I had answered the same question at different times. The awarding of an oak leaf symbol had originally been for taking part in a "Forlorn Hope", which was an assault by volunteer soldiers on a breach in a fortification such as a fortress wall. It was called a Forlorn Hope because the enemy knew where the attack would be and therefore increased their defences around the area of the breach. Officer volunteers who survived the assault could expect a promotion while the soldiers would get the first opportunity to loot, which was a strong motivation to volunteer. The final outcome, however, was nearly always a bloody death.

\* \* \*

## 22$^{nd}$ November 2016

**When did delivery companies first start describing their activities as 'logistics'?**

The origin of the word logistics is probably Greek, having the same root as the word logic, meaning reason. However, in relation to the logistics industry it stems from late 19$^{th}$ century France. Its use is first attributed to Baron de Jomini. It was originally logistique, stemming from the French verb loger, meaning to lodge. In this sense you would be lodging materials in a warehouse.

The Oxford English dictionary describes the modern use as the military science relating to procuring, maintaining and transporting material, personnel and facilities. It is critical to note the multi-functional nature of this description. A company that focuses purely on doorstep delivery, for example, would not be regarded as a true logistics business, regardless of how they describe themselves.

The modern usage came about during the Second World War from the American military use of the term. However, great military leaders of the past such as Hannibal, Alexander The Great and the Duke of Wellington were considered to be geniuses in the art of logistics – or at least they appointed people who were geniuses in those fields.

There is a quote from the ancient Chinese military leader Sun Tzu that says "The line between disorder and order lies in logistics", and from Alexander the Great "My logisticians are a humourless lot ... they know if my campaign fails, they are the first ones I will slay." However, the use of the word "logistics" in both quotes must be seen as a modern interpretation of whatever the original words were. Had the logistics of arrow re-supply at the Battle of Agincourt failed, the battle might well have had a different outcome.

In military logistics the science involved includes not just the procurement, storage and distribution of materiel, but also the repair and maintenance of equipment, which is an area in which few commercial logistics businesses get involved. It also includes the safe and environmentally friendly disposal of materiel once it is no longer fit for use or is surplus to requirements.

The primary aim of modern commercial logistics is to integrate the various components of the system so they work in the most efficient manner possible, reducing both cost and waste. When done properly it is almost invisible, but when done badly it is noticed all too easily, for example, in empty spaces on the shelves of supermarkets. Key to this is the integration of information technology. The ideal integration of the food supply chain, for example, would extend from the consumer's larder and refrigerator all the way back to the farms where the food is produced. However, that degree of integration is still just a gleam in the logistician's eye.

**Author's note:** Given the importance of logistics and its ability to save businesses and public bodies money, it is astonishing how inefficient some organisations are. While a serving member of the RAF and also, much later, working for the Ministry of Defence at one of their two major logistics depots, I was amazed at how archaic their systems were and how little investment military logistics attracted. A million pound spare part for an aircraft could be housed in a leaking old World War II vintage warehouse on a rusting old bit of racking and there was a high probability that its location wasn't properly recorded, so it might never be found again. I thought it was just a military thing until I joined Royal Mail until I saw how they moved mail around the country in thousands of small vans rather than in a few big lorries. At least Royal Mail did eventually modernise its practices, though it was in the face of stiff opposition from many of its own "managers".

\* \* \*

## 30<sup>th</sup> November 2016

**What is the origin of the term 'shooting yourself in the foot'?**

This term is now used to denote an act of reckless behaviour, in that the perpetrator commits an act with one intention, which then rebounds on the perpetrator with adverse consequences. For example, a politician might leak damaging information about a rival to a newspaper, only for that newspaper to print something even more damaging about the politician himself.

The origin of the saying goes back to the First World War. Soldiers desperate to escape the trenches might inflict a non-life threatening injury on themselves in order to be withdrawn from the front line for medical treatment. The "accidental" discharging of their rifle to inflict a foot injury was one such act.

So prevalent did the number of self-inflicted injuries become that the military authorities court martialled any soldier who was believed to have self-inflicted an injury, which could lead to imprisonment in the British army and death sentences in some other armies. This was the unwanted consequence that led to the later usage of the phrase. The number of self-inflicted injuries dropped rapidly, though were never fully eradicated.

An older saying with the same meaning was "to be hoist by one's own petard". A petard was a slow burning fuse used by military engineers to set off demolition charges. However, because the fuse was slow burning, using too long a fuse could allow defenders time to remove it and prevent the explosion. If, on the other hand, the engineer cut a fuse that was too short to allow time for them to retreat, it could trigger the explosives prematurely, killing the engineer himself.

There is also a school of thought that the phrase originated with the cowboys of the old west. When drawing their gun in a gunfight a cowboy might accidentally pull the trigger too early, injuring themselves in the foot in the process. However, most types of revolver used in the old west were single action, which required the user to cock the weapon before it could be fired. This minimised the risk of this type of injury unless the gun's user was adept in drawing the weapon, cocking it and pulling the trigger in a single fluid movement. While there may have been cowboys who were "quick on the draw" this would have been more a matter of showmanship than combat. The act of drawing a revolver from a holster would actually angle it so that it was unlikely to injure the foot if discharged prematurely.

The first true double action revolver, which only required the user to pull the trigger to fire it, wasn't introduced until 1889, with the Colt Model 1889. By that time the days of gun-fighting were already on the wane as better law enforcement spread through the western territories. While one-on-one duals are a staple of western films and TV shows, they were more myth than fact. The majority of gun duals were caused when one party drew their weapon, causing the other party to draw theirs, which quickly disintegrated into both parties shooting from cover until they ran out of ammunition, one was injured or a law enforcement officer broke up the fight. The pistols of the era were notoriously difficult to fire accurately, which made dualling a fruitless occupation that was more likely to injure bystanders than the intended target.

\* \* \*

# 8<sup>th</sup> December 2016

**In BBC's Who Do You Think You Are, Danny Dyer discovered that his 22x great grandfather was Edward III. How surprising is this?**

In its simplest terms this can be seen as a mathematical progression. If Edward III had two children and each of those children had two children and so on, it is possible to make a rough calculation of how many descendants Edward III might have by the time the 23rd generation is reached (22 'greats' plus the grandfather).

The mathematical expression is $2^{23}$, or 2 to the power of 23. It works out at about 8 million people who could trace their ancestry back to Edward III, or approximately 13% of the British population.

However, this calculation can be varied by a number of factors. Firstly there are descendants who didn't have any children or children that survived to parenting age, as well as descendants who had more than two offspring of their own. The tendency of Royal families to intermarry also skews the figures. At least two of Edward's great grandchildren (second cousins) married each other. They would have had to have 4 children to maintain the mathematical progression. It is clear that making any sort of accurate calculation would be an arduous, if not impossible, task.

Royal descendants were often married into the royal families of other nations, which means that some of the descendants of that line wouldn't now be British. Others might simply have emigrated.

In fact Edward III had 14 legitimate children, of whom six had children of their own. This immediately gives a possibility of the number of descendants increasing to about 25 million, or roughly 38% of the population, based on each subsequent generation having only two children each. That, of course, assumes that all of those descendants remained in Britain, which is unlikely.

There is also lineage through illegitimate children. One mistress. Alice Perrers, is thought to have had three children fathered by

Edward. This, and the children of other mistresses, sets up a whole new mathematical progression to arrive at an even larger total.

It would require only 2 more generations (about 40 years) for the progression from the legitimate line to reach a possible 1 billion descendants of Edward III. That's more people than are currently living in the UK and would mean that every British family had some distant connection to Edward III.

Edward the III's lineage is not the only one that can be used to calculate the likelihood of being related to someone famous. Based on his profligacy and the number of generations since his death, it is theoretically possible that everyone on the planet is related to Genghis Khan.

**Author's note:** I may be being cynical (who, me?) but I suspect that when the BBC made this edition of "Who Do You Think You Are" they found so little of interest in Danny Dyer's ancestry, or so little that Dyer would wish to be made public, that they fell back on this distant relationship in order to end up with something that could be broadcast. Since that broadcast Danny Dyer has traded on this "ancestry" to increase his TV income.

\* \* \*

## 8<sup>th</sup> December 2016

### When did the British Army start wearing 'bearskin' headwear - and why?

The origin of the bearskin hat is in Europe. It appears to have been used to enhance the height of soldiers in order to make them look more fearsome. As well as Guards regiments, units in the armies of Belgium, Denmark, Italy, Netherlands and Sweden still wear the bearskin for ceremonial duties. It is also worn by 4 Canadian regiments and the drum major of United States Marine Band.

The introduction of the bearskin into the British army stems from the Battle of Waterloo. For defeating the French grenadiers of Napoleon's personal guard, the First Regiment of Footguards were awarded the bearskin as a battle honour, along with the title of Grenadier Guards. In order to maintain the uniformity of the Guards regiments, in 1831 the privilege was extended to the other two guards regiments in existence at the time, the Coldstream Guards and Scots Guards.

Other British regiments that are entitled to wear the bearskin as part of their dress uniform include the Honourable Artillery Company and The Royal Scots Dragoon Guards. The officers of Royal Fusiliers also wear it, but not the other ranks, who wear a seal skin cap instead.

The expense of maintaining bearskins was so high that they were soon removed from everyday use. However, it was still being worn in combat at the time of the Crimean War.

The standard bearskin cap used by the Guards regiments is 18 inches high, weighs 1.5 lbs and is made from the fur of Canadian black bears. Their original cost was about £7 and 5 shillings, the equivalent of about £600 today.

Recent calls for the banning of bearskins on the grounds of animal cruelty have failed to produce an end to the practice. In 2005 a 2 year trial using artificial fur was started, but was deemed to be unsuccessful. To meet the army's needs about 100 bearskins are taken from an annual cull carried out by the Canadian wildlife authorities and is only a fraction of the number of bears actually killed. It can therefore be argued that the army's demand for fur does not, in itself, promote animal cruelty as the cull is done out of necessity to control the numbers of bears.

* * *

## 14<sup>th</sup> December

### Has any TV writer thought of a title first, then written the drama around it?

Further to your previous answer, as a novelist I frequently come up with a title of a book before knowing what sort of story I am going to write to fit it.

The title of my first novel, The Inconvenience Store, was originally submitted to Sir Terry Pratchett as a plot device for one of his books, but his agent declined my offer. I loved the title so much, however, that it inspired me to write the book myself.

The title of a later book, The Girl I Left Behind Me, was inspired by the background music from a John Ford western, but it wasn't until I saw British soldiers on the TV news, returning from Afghanistan to be reunited with their families, that I came up with the idea for a plot.

I came up with Please Keep Phoning In as the title for a novel set against the background of a charity telethon without knowing what I would do with that. This was later re-titled as The Charity Thieves on the suggestion of my publisher.

Within my 9 volume Magi series, I have come up with 5 of the 6 titles of the books so far written without knowing until later how I would convert them into stories, except that they would somehow involve my protagonist, An Kohli.

**Author's note:** This supplement to an answer supplied by another correspondent was a naked attempt to plug my books. Unsurprisingly it wasn't published. However, its inclusion here is also another naked attempt to plug my books. Sorry, but this is how I make my living. All nine books in the Magi series have now been written and eight have been published at the time of going to press.

\* \* \*

## 15<sup>th</sup> December 2016

**Was the Ethiopian famine made famous by Live Aid deliberately perpetrated by the Ethiopian government?**

While it might be inaccurate to say that the Ethiopian government caused the famine that raged from 1983 to 1985, there can be no doubt that the actions of the government exacerbated the problems caused by the famine.

Internal strife in the two decades before the famine had already killed 150,000 people. With agriculture making up 60% of the Ethiopian economy, anything that disrupted that would have a considerable impact. In 1973 a famine in the Wollo region had killed 40,000.

The government of Emperor Haile Selassie was overthrown in 1974, to be replaced by a military regime made up largely of junior officers and soldiers. However, the famine in the Wollo region resulted in the creation of a new Marxist movement, the Derg, led from 1977 by Mengistu Haile Mariam, who had previously been a low-ranking member of the military government. He became President in 1977 after the Derg seized power in the country. This was opposed by the Ethiopian People's Revolutionary Party, resulting in further conflict and large scale politically motivated bloodshed. Estimates of deaths during this period, known as "the red terror", are as high as 500,000.

As with Stalin's agricultural policies of the 1920s, regional governors were charged with extracting food from the rural population to feed the urban masses, a policy that led to food shortages in the countryside, just as it had in Ukraine and the Caucusus in the 1920s and 30s. Drought in the Wollo region not-withstanding, the citizens were required to pay "famine relief tax" until 1984. This tax was payable largely in food.

Part of the problem was that the famine that started in 1983 was unpredicted. Rainfall from the late 1970s to 1982 was rated as "normal" or "near normal". The harvest in 1982 was one of the largest on record, with the exception of central Tigray province. While the people at risk of famine rose from 2.8 million in 1982 to 3.9 million in 1983, it was still below the 4.5 million level of 1981, when there had been no famine.

During the mid 1980s there were record low rainfalls in four Ethiopian provinces: Gojjam, Hararghe, Tigray, and Wollo. This was the natural cause of the famine. At the same time, in the South of the country, the government was facing a fresh insurgency from the Oromo Liberation Front. President Mengistu announced that 40% of the country's GDP would be allocated to military spending, the largest proportion of any nation in sub-Saharan Africa. Health spending was halved to 3%. The combined effect of that meant that there was little money available for spending on famine relief.

During the period from 1981 to 1985 the price of grain quadrupled, which meant that what grain there was available wasn't affordable for a large proportion of the population and the government was reserving most of it for the army and the urban populations. There was a heavy reliance on foreign food aid to fill the gap, which was the trigger for Live Aid.

Estimates of deaths caused by the famine were quoted by the UN as being as high as 1 million, but noted famine expert Alex de Waal challenges that and gives a lower estimate of 4 to 5 hundred thousand.

In 1991, facing defeat by the Ethiopian People's Revolutionary Democratic Front and having lost his Russian backing, Mengistu fled to Zimbabwe with 50 family and Derg followers. In his absence Mengistu was charged with genocide for the deaths of 2,000 political opponents, but has never been held to account for his mismanagement during the famine. He is under sentence of death in absentia and still lives in exile in Zimbabwe.

\* \* \*

## 22<sup>nd</sup> December 2016

**Concrete acoustics discs were developed by the British as an early warning system. Did they work? Do any survive?**

As we all have ears, we all have the ability to use acoustics to detect the source of sound. This ability was applied a little more scientifically in Victorian times when they developed the simple ear trumpet and used it to locate artillery.

A person wearing what amounted to a pair of ear trumpets, would rotate their head until they perceived the volume of the artillery fire to be the loudest, then take a compass bearing on the source of the noise. The process would be repeated from a second location and the two bearings would be "triangulated" to provide an approximate position for the artillery, so that counter-battery fire could be engaged. Similar systems could be used at sea to locate enemy ships that were hidden by fog.

World War I saw the development of more sophisticated acoustic systems, some resembling giant tubas mounted on wheels.

When aircraft were introduced into warfare it was soon realised that similar systems could be used to detect the sound of their engines and therefore locate the aircraft, even if they were hidden by cloud or fog.

Between the wars acoustic listening posts were built in various locations along the south east and north east coasts of England. One that survives is Denge, near Dungeness in Kent.

The development of stereo microphones allowed fixed acoustic positions to be used to detect noise from within a fixed arc. One of the installations at Denge is a concave wall, at the focal point of which would sit a stereo microphone. The varying volume of engine noise being reflected from different angles of the wall would then provide a bearing for the location of the aircraft. The concave concrete dishes, called sound mirrors, similar in appearance to modern satellite dishes, performed the same function but allowed altitude to be calculated at the same time as the horizontal bearing.

The problem with the system is that sound travels in straight lines, so an aircraft would already have to be above the horizon before the detector would sense it. By the time the relevant calculations had been completed an approaching aircraft would have travelled some distance and would be visible to an observer on the ground. This was the basis for the establishment of the Royal Observer Corps. This meant that the system was really only of use at night or in times of poor visibility. The invention of radar rendered acoustic systems completely obsolete.

The structures at Denge are located in a wildlife reserve operated by the Royal Society for the Protection of Birds (RSPB) and so can't be accessed by the general public. The only time they can be visited is during an RSPB open day. Two experimental sound mirrors may be found in an area known as The Roughs, near Hythe. There is another near Kilnsea Grange, East Yorkshire. A sound mirror at Selsey, in Sussex, has been converted into a dwelling.

* * *

Deborah Ross, who used to write a column in the Daily Mail on a Saturday, once used her column to pose a set of rather silly questions. Being in a rather frivolous mood I decided to submit answers to them. This is a transcript of what she used in her column a few weeks later. At the time of writing Jason Donovan and Kerry Catona were the faces of the Iceland food chain.

### At last, the trivial truth about Commandos

Questions, questions, questions, and no more so than a couple of weeks ago when the Club launched its own book of puzzling queries - Do Commandos Truly Not Wear Pants? - in the hope that readers would answer them and thus give us a best-selling Christmas book.

Happily, Mr Bob Cubitt of Yahoo - which we believe to be near Bournemouth - has done just that.

**Do Commandos truly not wear pants?**

No.

The risk of accidents involving zippers which might affect their combat readiness is too great. Female commandos have been known to go without pants, but only if planning a night out at Yates's Wine Lodge.

**Are men genetically programmed to open their dressing gown on the way to the bathroom, do a 'whoo-hoo!', and always find it funny?**

Yes.

**Do Kerry and Jason ever look at that spread from Iceland and think: 'This is partying at its most chav. I'm off to Nobu.'?**

Dur! For Kerry and Jason, Iceland IS Nobu.

**What is the point of forking out on the family holiday to discover that the Acropolis is 'really, really boring' and: 'I would have been all right at home on my own?**

The alternative is to leave the stroppy teenager at home and return to find the house reduced to pile of rubble, and the excuse that 'I put an ad on Facebook for a few friends to come over'.

**If, as is well-known, North is uphill, why am I always getting lost?**

The trouble with women's navigation is that they only ever remember half the story. North is only uphill when travelling away from home. When returning home, North is downhill.

**Why can't women be from Mars and men from Venus for a change?**

Men were actually going to be from Venus, but got lost, refused to ask directions and ended up on Mars instead. Women were going to be from Mars but forgot that North was uphill and ended up on Venus.

**Is this the very best book of this type?**

No. The very best book of this type is Can Crocodiles Cry? published in association with The Daily Mail's Answers to Correspondents' Questions.

Naturally, Mr Cubitt wonders if there might be any money in this for him. Well, after a great deal of thought, that took no time at all, the following was unanimously decided upon: No.

*Reproduced with the kind permission of Deborah Ross. Deborah now writes a regular column for The Times.*

\* \* \*

The last letter of 2016 brings to an end this volume of my answers, however I doubt if I'll stop answering the questions that are posed in the Daily Mail, so be on the lookout for Volume 3 in about 3 years' time.

# And Now

Both the author Robert Cubitt and Selfishgenie Publishing hope that you have enjoyed reading this book and that you have found it useful.

Find Robert Cubitt on Facebook at https://www.facebook.com/robertocubitt and 'like' his page; follow him on Twitter @robert_cubitt[1]. You can also e-mail Robert Cubitt at robert.cubitt@selfgenie.com

Please tell people about this book, write a review or mention it on your favourite social networking sites.

For further titles that may be of interest to you please visit the Selfishgenie Publishing website at selfisgenie.com[2] where you can join our mailing list so that we can keep you up to date with all our latest releases (or maybe that should be 'escapes').

---

1. https://twitter.com/robert_cubitt
2. http://www.ex-l-ence.com/

9 798215 375662